Jessica

Enjoy!

Jeffrey

Jessica

◆

The autobiography of an infant

Jeffrey Von Glahn, Ph.D.

iUniverse, Inc.
New York Lincoln Shanghai

Jessica
The autobiography of an infant

Copyright © 2006 by Jeffrey Von Glahn

iUniverse books may be ordered through booksellers or by contacting:

iUniverse
2021 Pine Lake Road, Suite 100
Lincoln, NE 68512
www.iuniverse.com
1-800-Authors (1-800-288-4677)

ISBN-13: 978-0-595-36429-9 (pbk)
ISBN-13: 978-0-595-80861-8 (ebk)
ISBN-10: 0-595-36429-2 (pbk)
ISBN-10: 0-595-80861-1 (ebk)

Printed in the United States of America

For Jessica, for her daring proposal
to radically alter the course of her therapy
and her unwavering commitment
to the recovery of her "lost" humanness.

To Harvey Jackins, for his pioneering insights
into the process of recovery from traumatic experiences.

Contents

Prologue

The psychological dimension of human life speaks to the very essence of human life itself. It gives us our uniqueness and makes us human beings. We may never know when the psychological dimension begins. However, when it does, it signals the start of the most vulnerable period of our development when the foundation supporting all later development is being pieced together, that is, when our basic sense of who we are is being created.

In watching Jessica recover from psychologically damaging experiences that interfered with the earliest stages of her development as a human being, I felt I had been granted a privileged window into an unexplored dimension of human life. It was a dimension my training and twelve years of experience as a therapist had not prepared me for and had not even given me the tiniest hint of how to handle.

Listening to Jessica vividly describe her experiences was the same as listening to an infant who could talk describe every psychologically dramatic moment of its life as it was happening. As a result, my perception of infants was radically altered. I will never again think of infants as simple, little beings primarily interested in eating and sleeping. They are far more complex than I had ever imagined. When I am now in an infant's presence, I am acutely conscious that an active force in the world is before me. What I say and how I act will be watched with great interest by a mind that, though not as developed as mine, is probably more curious about the world and definitely more sensitive to it.

Infants, especially newborns, pull me toward them with what seems like an invisible force. Whenever I see one, I must fight my urge to drop whatever I am doing and immediately rush to this brand-new human being. In my fantasy (I only approach on the sly in public), I slow down as I approach my goal and unhurriedly cover the last bit of distance. I lead in with the most incredibly joyous smile anyone has ever seen. My eyes bulge in unabashed delight while my smile and eyes speak for me. They speak the language of infancy, a life rich in feelings, hopes, dreams, potential, and an insatiable curiosity about the world. It is a life as exciting and as intriguing as one can imagine. My eyes and smile express the words I would like to say:

1

Yes, I know how powerful your mind is. I know what new information about yourself and the world you are trying to figure out. I know what fundamental psychological processes are happening inside of you. If you could talk, I know what wonderfully exciting details you would tell us about your life.

My journey with Jessica seems—even now after it is over—more a flight of fancy, an excursion into science fiction, than a real-life story. Had I not been a fellow traveler who saw and heard everything with my own eyes and ears, I would certainly exclaim, "How interesting! I wish I could think of a clever story like that!"

Like the seagoing explorers of old, we also ventured beyond land's end into the unknown sea, the psychological unknown, with only the equivalent of a navigational system to guide our way. We did not know where our travels would take us or what dangers or surprises awaited us. Like the pioneering, seagoing explorers, we also started on our journey to a New World with only faith to sustain us that our goal, the land of psychological riches, was in the realm of the possible and to reassure us we would not plunge into an unknown abyss guarded by some psychological "demon" and never find our way out.

From my unique position as an observer, I watched transfixed as new realms of the human psyche—the human infant psyche—paraded before my eyes. Watching Jessica as an adult relive her infant experiences and listening to her translate into words her psychological reactions at the time was a totally mesmerizing experience. My eyes and ears were glued to every word she said.

When Jessica first became aware of the process that creates the human side of human beings taking place within herself, her feeling—perhaps her very first feeling about herself—was that something was interfering with how she was being "made up." When this most terrifying of all psychological experiences arose during her therapy, all of the unthinkable questions flashed before me in my mind's eye. When did the actual "piecing together" of our humanness begin? Early childhood? Infancy? Birth? Before birth? If so, how much before birth? Regardless of when psychological development actually begins, what happens if this natural process is interfered with, especially in its earliest stages—when the newly emerging psychological embryo is most vulnerable? If the interference is severe enough, could the basic structure of our humanness be altered, as can happen to the human body? If you tried repairing the cracks in the basic foundation of our humanness, was there a limit to how deeply you could delve into a person's psyche? Would you meet primordial forces that should not be tampered with? Was there a chance of creating further damage? Would we be treading in forbidden territory, a land guarded by a huge sign with the intimidating prohibition of

"No humans allowed!" Finally, should I, as Jessica's therapist, dare hold out the prospect for a full recovery just because I believed it could happen?

My belief that recovery was possible was not based on knowing that anyone had recovered from such very early assaults to their basic humanness. Instead, my belief (that is, my faith) in recovery came from my not knowing of any reason why it could not happen. When Jessica and I first realized she had suffered traumas in the earliest days of her life (more than two years into her therapy), I had been a therapist for approximately twelve years and had quite an excellent understanding of catharsis. My understanding of catharsis was as a complex healing process. The mainstream version was that it was just "emotional release." At best, all it did was make someone feel better. In fact, some thought it might even be dangerous, not only a waste of time and energy for both the client and the therapist. By this time in my career, I had numerous dramatic successes with it with both adults and children. I had never applied it to events from infancy. However, that was not enough of a reason for me to think it could not be done. Although I did not burden Jessica with my musings about what might—or might not—be possible, I did readily share any interesting piece of news that was related to our adventure, which she was eager to hear about. Whatever factual information I knew, she knew. While I was scouring books and academic journals and consulting with friends and colleagues for the latest tidbits of reassuring information, I probably should have asked Jessica for her thoughts on the matter instead. One day, when we were discussing an article I had read, she suddenly expressed a very reassuring insight, "If the hurt went in, there must be a way for it to come out." "Now that," I thought to myself then, "was the true voice of experience."

Overall, Jessica's determination and courage to persist week after week (and month after month) produced this previously unknown window into an infant's inner life. Particularly, her daring proposal to radically alter the way we had been working—a way that was only piling one unproductive session on top of another—ultimately led to our pioneering journey.

When Jessica made her spirited proposal, to which I immediately and enthusiastically agreed, neither one of us knew the tremendous obstacles we would face. We did not know the strength of the personal commitments we would have to make. We did not know the hundreds of hours of mentally, emotionally draining effort that was ahead for both of us. We did not know what others would think of our spending so much time together. We did not know what thrilling (even awe-inspiring) discoveries we would make about an infant's rich inner life.

Many unavoidable practical necessities that demanded her time—time away from regaining her humanness—severely tested Jessica's commitment to her therapy and drained her energy. This included having the emotional turmoil and financial worry of a marital separation and divorce; being a single parent for a young child; cleaning people's homes to support herself and her daughter; squeezing in as much work as possible in a few days to make free time for her therapy; and starting college in her late twenties while simultaneously working part-time to supplement her grants and loans.

Jessica's ability to undertake so much work, handle it all so responsibly, and somehow find time for her therapy amazed me. Her resolute decision to disallow any obstacle to interfere with the recovery of her full humanness was evident.

What thrilled me even more was Jessica's appreciation of the pioneering nature of our work. After she remembered what had happened to her as an infant and could see how her humanness was twisted from its natural course of development, she no longer thought of her therapy as just for her own personal benefit. She now saw herself as engaged in a process that was revealing the most important information that human beings could have, that is, how to help someone begin life with a rock-solid psychological foundation and how to help someone recover from very early assaults to this foundation, if the unfortunate happens.

Watching Jessica struggle with the fundamental psychological forces of the human psyche was an unforgettable lesson in the human spirit's strength. The series of life-threatening experiences she had to relive from her infancy in order to recover her full humanness was like battling with a line of demons guarding a secret treasure. Each one was seemingly cleverer at hiding its presence than the last one. Each one was even more tenacious about not yielding its grip. Every time Jessica won back another part of her humanness and felt more like the real Jessica, another experience from her infancy, more threatening to her life than any she had yet faced, reared up from the depths of her psyche and dared her to try for more…and more of what was rightfully hers!

At times, I was convinced she had won her last battle, that is, she had won back all of the lost parts of her humanness that had been snatched away so early in life. However, one last demon always seemed to be there, one last symptom that resisted our best efforts and stubbornly hung on.

Every time I saw one last problem surface, seemingly mocking us, I felt my heart rip in two. I did not know how far the human spirit could be stretched. I did not know if Jessica's mind would shatter or if her spirit would be completely destroyed if she had to face one more obstacle. I sometimes wondered if fate was against us. At times, I desperately longed to jump into the battle myself and slay the dragons that robbed her of parts of her humanness.

The singular experience Jessica and I shared together is unique in many ways. Most importantly, it is a window into heretofore unexplored psychological territory, that is, to put it most succinctly if somewhat figuratively, the inner workings of an infant's mind. That information, so vital to understanding the beginnings of human development, is inestimable. What can possibly be more important?

The path to obtaining that information required a radical change in how psychotherapy is usually conducted. Undoubtedly, the most important change was Jessica's daring proposal to dramatically increase both the frequency and the length of her sessions. Not once, but twice! Without that, this journey, most assuredly, would not have happened. (Sessions at once a week and lasting an "hour"—usually 50 minutes or less—are primarily for economic reasons for both the therapist and the client. That format is not necessarily in the best therapeutic interest of the client, particularly when traumatic events are the focus.)

Another change was in the therapist's role. Here, it was as a midwife, someone whose primary responsibility is to establish facilitative conditions for healing, work at his or her creative best in those conditions, and wait for nature to take its course. Here, "nature taking its course" means strict reliance to a belief that a healing process for assaults to our basic humanness exists and operates under its own mechanisms when facilitating conditions are present. An understanding of the most important features of this healing process was formulated by a few, independent-thinking therapists and researchers over many years, primarily during the 1950s to the 1970s. My two primary sources were not aware of each other's writings. Therefore, my task was to synthesize those separate sources of information into a whole and discover how to apply those ideas to the challenge that Jessica's therapy presented in the best way. That required an unfailing belief on my part in the intrinsic healing powers of the human psyche as well as communicating that to Jessica with a calm, but persistent and reassuring, confidence.

An important feature of this concept of healing involves the remembering of forgotten events, that is, a recovered memory. In the context of this concept, such a remembrance is, despite its inherent fascination, nothing more than a by-product of a more fundamental, comprehensive process. My primary aim as a therapist is to see that healing occurs. It is never to hunt for buried memories; however, I do very actively hunt for buried emotional hurt, which may, quite naturally in my view, lead to the remembering of forgotten events. That is, one must activate the unresolved hurt to reach the buried details of the traumatic event.

In presenting this truly unique story, I wanted to be as accurate as possible, especially about what happened to Jessica as an infant. Fortunately, I could interview her mother, Dorothy, before she passed away a few years later. Jessica had already told her about her birth some months before our meeting. Dorothy was initially astounded, but she confirmed every detail. She also knew I was gathering information for this book. Without any of my prompting, she extensively detailed Jessica's birth. She also described her struggle with her extended family about spoiling her firstborn, Ellen, who was one-and-a-half years older than Jessica, and how that affected her attitude toward having another child so soon. That information completely convinced me on Jessica's remembrance of the most traumatic event of her infancy, the one I dubbed the battle of wills, which no one else witnessed. I did not ask Dorothy about it. Because she had serious physical health problems, I did not have the heart to add to her anguish. Whatever she could remember—or was willing to tell me—was fine with me.

There were a few other events in Jessica's life that I could not rely on anyone else's firsthand observations, aside from her own. For those events, I found her recall as convincing as the ones that I did have another person's observations as corroboration. In those cases, I felt quite confident in using her memory as the basis for describing the scene.

I did not make up any scene or any details for dramatic effect. I didn't have to! The initial and eagerly anticipated therapeutic breakthrough occurred exactly as described, down to the minutest detail. The intuitive urge that made me start taping sessions occurred exactly as described. Dorothy was in an auto accident about a month before Jessica's final exams. Its consequent effect on Jessica is as described. The revelation of her haunting secret happened exactly as described. Two cardinals and a Baltimore oriole were perched in the trees in front of her house for many weeks, and they definitely made their presence known. Even with all of the trials and tribulations that Jessica and I faced, I never even wondered why I was engaged in this quest. To put my motivation in its simplest terms, this was far too fascinating to refuse to do.

Years later, as I write, I remain in awe. Every time I read one of the few heartrending scenes, I am thrown right back to that particular session. Tears are in my eyes, even if I am reading it for what seems like the umpteenth time. Ultimately, the tears are ones of great joy and elation. This is a story about the most basic of human values: one person helping another in time of need and the eventual triumph of two human spirits working in harmony.

The dream had always been with her.

The courtroom was packed. Outside, in the hallway, down the steps, and out onto the sidewalk, everyone was jammed together. All traffic had stopped for the emergency news bulletin. The verdict to "The Trial of the Ages," as it had been dubbed from the start, was about to be read.

The judge stared down at her. She knew what was coming. It was the moment she had always dreaded. She had been convinced of it for as far back as she could remember. She had offered no defense.

"I have no idea how you came to be here or even who you are," the judge began and then hesitated before declaring for all to hear, "but you have been found guilty of impersonating a human being."

While heads nodded, the words echoed throughout the room. A deadening silence followed. There was no cheering, just a collective sigh that it was over and the impostor, the alien, had been weeded out. There was nothing else to say. There could be no punishment because no known law had been broken.

The judge was the first to stand. With a last glance at the defendant, the black-robed figure scurried from the room. The others quickly followed. No one looked back at the lone figure standing in place. When the room emptied, the one pronounced guilty remained rooted in place. All she could see was tomorrow's headlines: "Scientists Gather to Examine Alien Impostor."

1

"I'm Here!"

What I had witnessed in the past forty-five minutes had been more electrifying than anything I had encountered in my ten years as a dedicated, hardworking psychotherapist. Neither my training nor all I had learned since had prepared me for it. If someone, even another therapist, had excitedly said, "You'll never believe this!" and described the same exact scene, I would have summarily dismissed that person with, "Oh, really! What have you been smoking?"

I was sitting with Jessica Page on her living room floor. We were in her house because of her daring proposal to radically alter the way we had been working. To be perfectly honest, it was a way that piled one unproductive session on top of another for more months than I cared to remember. Our mutual frustration about the lack of progress certainly was not from laziness or lack of motivation in either of us. For nearly three years, Jessica had never missed, canceled, or even been late for a session. I tried everything I could think of to jump-start her therapy. There had been plenty of promising beginnings (I was full of new ideas), but they had all flamed out. I had no way of knowing then that I was laboring under an illusion about who was sitting across from me and I had been ever since Jessica first stepped into my office. If someone tried convincing me of the error in my thinking, I would not have given the attempt even a second's thought because I would not have conceived of the explanation as a psychological problem. I would not have even understood it as a human problem.

Jessica was sitting in a yoga position. She had been sitting like that for the past forty-five minutes. Her upper body was thrust slightly forward. One hand cradled the other in her lap. Waves of brown hair lay on her shoulders. I was leaning with my back against the couch. My legs were stretched out in front of me, nearly touching hers. Her eyes remained focused on the wall behind the couch. Her line of sight passed just over my shoulder. She had not looked me in the eye the entire time. All of her attention had been focused inward, that is, on what she had been experiencing.

Her last words still rang in my ears. Tentative and reflective, she initially said, "Do you remember all this stuff? Do you think I'm cuckoo?" Assertively and quickly, she then said, "I know all this happened."

"All this stuff" was nothing less than Jessica's birth experience in all of its phenomenal detail. From her first words of "I was floating in water and hearing it flutter in my ear" to her last, I had no doubt she believed every word of what she was reporting.

All the while, she remained in a trancelike state. One part of her was seemingly aware of me staring at her. My eyes and every other part of my body silently urged her to continue while the rest of her waited to discover what new and exciting thoughts about her birth experience were going to emerge next. Most of her words came out in bits and pieces. Sometimes, there were whole sentences. A few times, she hurried back to a previous point and filled in more detail. Her voice rang with the excitement of unexpected surprises. Awe and, at times, disbelief tinged it. There were also short bursts of tears, sharp indignation over how she had been treated, and laughter over the medical team having a bad day. All the while, she seemed as mesmerized as I was. She was finally giving voice to mind-altering experiences from before she was even aware she had a mind. I, the silent, but privileged, listener, sat back. I simply watched and did not say a word, even though I savored this completely unexpected and, as I quickly perceived, truly once-in-a-lifetime experience. I only watched and waited, fully trusting the genuineness of what Jessica was revealing. Out of fear I might break the magic spell, I was not about to do anything, including say a word, move a muscle, or change my facial expression. I saw what was happening as all perfectly natural. All movement driven by internal healing mechanisms, which only operated if certain conditions existed. Establishing those conditions was my job. There was not anything mysterious about them. They included creating a safe atmosphere, expressing patient (but persistent) interest, and not doing anything that might interfere with what a small number of like-minded colleagues and I considered the natural healing process. Like a midwife at an imminent birth, I had to wait. If Jessica's psyche decided the time was right, healing would occur. In this instance, it had.

"I was floating in water and hearing it flutter in my ear. I heard a steady heartbeat. I was stretching and yawning, calm and peaceful. My only concern was growing. All that was happening seemed to be in preparation for a different dimension in my life.

"I remember 'thinking' before I was born all that was going to happen. I was going to be born so somebody could love and touch me, so I could be enough, so

I could be a part of a big, working thing and I could have an effect upon the world.

"All of it was going to be so neat. I was going to be a part of a whole big world. The world was a good place, and I was going to be a part of it! Me! The world was going to be better because I was here, because there was nothing like me. Nowhere could the world get what it was going to get from me. I was important, as important as anything. Even the tiniest speck!

"During labor, I felt squeezed. I wasn't frightened. I was going along with the process of being born. I was starting to get out when somebody pushed me back in. Gosh darn it! I was not in charge of my birth anymore. They were pushing my head in, and I couldn't breathe. I was very frightened and confused. I thought I was going to die before I could get out.

"Somebody was jerking me and scaring me. Everything was just jerking and pulling and turning. It hurt everywhere on my body. I didn't know what to do. I was dizzy. I wanted to go back to where it was quiet. Make them stop! Leave me alone! Everyone leave me alone, and I'll be just fine. Let me do it!

"The doctor simply plucked me out of my mother and said, 'Here's the little troublemaker. I can tell she's going to be a stubborn one.' My mom hurt, and she hurt physically because of me. There was a lot of confusion. The lights were bright, and the room was noisy. The medical team was in a panic, and everyone was yelling.

"It seemed like the whole world was a mess. Things weren't going right, and it was all because of me—because I was ready to be born and I wasn't doing it right! Everyone was frightened and scared, and they didn't understand.

"Two nurses took me and washed me roughly. They were talking and laughing with each other and were unaware of how they were treating me or how I felt. I remember one of them saying, 'Who do you think you are? You're just another person to take care of.'

"I was hungry and screaming and scared. It didn't matter. Nobody wanted to touch me and hold me and smile at me. There was a whole room full of people. I just had to wait! I wasn't any more important than anybody else! Everyone was doing what had to be done, and I had to just behave and stop crying.

"And I'd learn…I'd learn I was a nobody, that I was just like everybody else. It didn't matter what I wanted or expected. I was in the real world, and I'd just have to wait. I was nobody special, and I didn't deserve anything anymore than anybody else did. It didn't make any difference who I was. I was just one more person to take care of. It all made me feel like I wasn't what they were looking for, like I was a nobody. Who the hell was I?

"They weren't concerned about me. They were just concerned with what I had done and how hard I had made it for everybody. Like I had any control over it! All I had done was be born. And it was no big deal! I came out 'thinking,' 'Ta, ta, I'm here!' And everybody goes, 'Big deal!'

"Everybody felt like I had to prove myself. It was like everybody thought it was a tough, mean, crummy world. Welcome to it, kid! You're no different than the rest of us. It's all crummy and rotten and look what you're a part of. They must have had a lot of bad attitudes.

"I felt like going and hiding. What did I do good? I was just born! It didn't matter what I had to offer. Nobody saw any good in me. I was waiting for someone to be so delighted and happy I was here, that I was out and now the world was a better place because there was one more good thing. Nobody felt I had contributed something only I could. I thought something unique had just happened and never in the space of time would anything like that happen again because I was different. I was one of a kind, and I could contribute things nobody else could.

"I do feel like I've committed a grave transgression because I was born. Because of me, I added more hurt to this world. I didn't add good things. I wasn't good, and special, and one of a kind. I felt so awful, like I didn't have a right to live.

"Everybody thought the world was crummy and a mess and that I added to the awfulness and the crumminess. I felt so disappointed. Yuck. This was what I had waited for?

"After being cleaned up, I went to sleep. When I woke up, I decided to give the world another chance. It was tough being born. It was.

"Do you remember all this stuff? Do you think I'm cuckoo? I know all this happened."

I certainly did not think she was cuckoo and immediately reassured her. Although I had never witnessed anyone remembering his or her birth or even read about it, I had been hearing from several people, all friends of mine (not fellow professionals), that it was possible. All were interested in psychology solely for their own personal growth. Alternative therapies also intrigued them, and I found myself intrigued by them as well. That is where some of the most creative work was being done, as well as some of the craziest. One had to be careful in assessing any of it. All I had heard about birth memories were verbal reports, and no one went into any extensive detail. No one produced a videotape or even an audio recording. Whenever I heard someone making such a claim, I just smiled and appeared interested. I believed the person must have had quite an unusual recall and their best explanation was to describe it as a birth memory. None of it had been enough to convince me. From the way it all naturally flowed out of Jessica, I now had no doubt that such a recall was possible. In addition, it was confirmation of Jessica's perceptiveness in making her spirited proposal to drastically change how we had been meeting. It showed, as well, her faith in her committed but bumbling therapist who could not figure out how to energize her therapy.

As fascinating and unexpected as this was, it was only a tantalizing tidbit compared to what I would eventually learn about how the earliest stages of Jessica's developing humanness had been twisted from its natural course of development.

2

If Newborns Could Speak

Dorothy Thomas hesitated at the top of the stairs to secure her grip on the banister before following her husband, who was a few steps ahead, down from their second-floor apartment. Perhaps it was nothing more than fate or, as she preferred to think, her silent prayers that had brought on her contractions before Henry left for work. As the head electrician for a construction firm, he would be hard-pressed to say what—if anything—was more important than being on time. All the others living in the spacious house, Dorothy's father, her three sisters, her uncle, and her mother-in-law, were in various stages of preparing for their day and took a quick minute to wish her their best.

During the ten-minute drive to the hospital, Henry was his usual silent self. Dorothy was certain, if she asked, she would hear his eager anticipation for a son, sentiments he expressed even before they married. He ignored Ellen, their first-born, now one-and-a-half. He turned down all invitations from Dorothy to do something with her. He declared, "That's women's work." Dorothy would freely admit she prayed for a son from the moment she knew she was pregnant again. She did not know what else might turn her husband into a family man.

At the hospital, Henry waited until someone came with a wheelchair before pecking his wife on the cheek. Before hurrying off for work, he only said, "I'll call when I can." Dorothy did not expect to see anyone else until the end of the workday, and she did not know if he would come or not. She never knew how late he might work or how much he would have to drink before showing up. In the late afternoon, two of Dorothy's sisters stopped in, but they did not stay very long. Dorothy guessed she was not interesting company. By now, she was close to physical exhaustion. Some hours ago, she felt excruciating pains in her back, as if someone was maliciously driving a red-hot poker up her spine and twisting it. Her brief cries of pain prompted a doctor to suggest a painkilling shot. However, she wanted a drug-free birth very much and decided against it. She did not have any illusions about childbirth. With Ellen's birth a year-and-a-half ago, she had been in labor a short time. The same red-hot poker pains had come suddenly and, just as quickly, went. She now stoically accepted them as a natural part of childbirth. In her view of the fundamental order of things, women were women so they could have children.

This birth, however, was taking much longer. The pushing down pains had not started yet, and she was not dilating. She reluctantly agreed to the doctor's suggestion of a shot to help her sleep. Maybe nature would take its course. A nurse in a starchy white uniform led her from the labor room to a small, sparsely furnished room just down the hall. She pulled back the sheet on the lone bed and helped her patient lie as comfortably as possible. Then a doctor entered and quickly administered the shot.

"This will help you sleep, Mrs. Thomas," he said.

The nurse covered the expectant body with a sheet and a light blanket before turning off the light. "We'll be ready when you wake up," she reassured her patient.

With a few smart steps, each accompanied by a squeak from her rubber-soled shoes, she opened the door and closed it gently behind her. Light from the hallway squeezed in from under the door. The person left in the semidarkness lay as comfortably as she could. She closed her eyes and waited for sleep to come. The air in the room was quiet. The hospital was settling down for the night. An occasional muffled sound drifted in under the door.

Sleep did not come to Dorothy Thomas. She was alone and frightened. Medical practice in the mid-1950s did not encourage family members to be in the labor and delivery rooms. The doctor she had asked to do the delivery, the one who delivered Ellen, a doctor she liked and trusted, had been called away on an emergency a few hours ago. His replacement, an olive-skinned man with brown hair, seemed visibly annoyed he had to fill in at the last minute. When Dorothy finally agreed to be put to sleep, his manner spoke for the rest of the team.

"Go to sleep, and don't wake up until after the night shift has arrived."

Before the medication could take effect, the pushing down pains began. In spite of the shot, Dorothy was wide-awake and fully alert. This was what she had waited for. What she had to go through to get here was not important anymore. She was ready to deliver, but she feared the staff thought she was asleep. From the darkness she called, "Nurse!"

She peered at the light under the door and strained her ears. A few moments went by. Nothing.

"Nurse!"

She waited, her head aimed at the door. No voices. No squeaky shoes. The pushing down pains pulsed through her.

"Nurse!"

No one came.

Throwing back the blanket and the sheet, Dorothy struggled to a sitting position. She reached over and turned on the lamp. Slowly, she leaned forward as far as she could and looked down. She saw what looked like the top of the baby's head. Frightened, she was about to lower herself to the floor and crawl to the door on her hands and knees in search of help. She was afraid to stand because she did not know if the baby would fall out.

Before she was off the bed, the door opened. The nurse, the same one who had tucked her in a short time ago, rushed in. A quick look was enough.

"You're going to have to walk to the delivery room!" she commanded. "And you must keep your legs crossed."

Stunned, Dorothy did not understand why she could not be wheeled in. Before she could say anything, the nurse grabbed an arm and tugged forward. This was the last straw. Being alone, frightened, and in an already long, painful labor with an impatient medical team was bad enough. She now believed there was danger to the baby and decided she had been a good patient long enough.

"I can't!" she cried out. "What if I can't hold the baby in? What if it starts coming out?"

"Just keep your legs crossed and your muscles tight," said an insistent voice.

Dorothy raised her body off the bed, stood in place for a few moments, and cautiously pushed one leg forward. Very slowly and carefully, she crossed it in front of her. She felt the slimy wetness between her legs. She was torn between fearing she would hurt the baby if she squeezed her legs too close together and worrying it would fall out if she did not.

"Good! Now take another one."

She managed a few slower, painful steps. She then said, "I can't do anymore! This is too painful! I'm afraid I'll drop the baby!"

"But you're doing it. Take some more!" The nurse was holding Dorothy's arm and stepping forward.

"What if I hurt the baby?" Dorothy did not care if she was shouting. Maybe someone would come and stop this nonsense.

"You won't if you keep your legs crossed. Come on!" The nurse tugged on the arm she was holding.

The fear of squeezing or dropping her baby and the pain from keeping her muscles tight became too great. Dorothy let loose with another, "I can't!"

Shouts flew back and forth between the two women. The nurse constantly encouraged Dorothy to take another step forward. They eventually reached the delivery room across the hall. When Dorothy stepped in, no one on the medical team even acknowledged her presence. All were busy with their preparations. The air was thick with resentment.

Dorothy continued plodding toward the delivery table. The nurse helped her up. When she had her feet in the stirrups, she felt she had done her part—more than her part. She was ready to relax and let the baby come.

"Can you hold a few minutes?" asked the anxious voice of the olive-complexioned, substitute doctor. His face was buried in his instruments, and he did not see the burning eyes scorching the back of his neck.

All of the actors rushed to prepare for the imminent birth. The glaring, overhead light came on. The instruments sparkled. The air was antiseptic.

"Okay, you can relax now. Just let the baby come." The doctor stepped between Dorothy's legs. A big sigh filled the room. Painfully tight muscles finally relaxed.

The doctor moved in for a closer look. The newborn was coming out with its face down. Hands found the top of her head and pushed her back in. Fingers found a shoulder and spun her around. The baby's head came back out. This time, its face was up. A sharp cry came from the table. A split-second later, there was another. White knuckles squeezed the edges of the delivery table. There were more gasps of pain as the baby struggled to get out.

"Damn! She's tearing! Get the baby out!"

Rich, dark, red blood flowed from Dorothy. Barked instructions from the medical team mingled with cries of pain. Minds and bodies rushed to prepare for this unexpected—and unplanned—emergency. A needle was jabbed into Dorothy. Stitching would begin as soon as the anesthetic took effect.

The baby was still struggling to get out. The doctor reached for an arm that had just emerged and tugged on it. A high-pitched wail came from the baby. More gasps of pain came from the mother. More blood flowed. The baby's shoulders came out. The doctor found the other arm and pulled on it. Another high-pitched wail followed. The doctor grabbed a leg and yanked the baby clear.

"Here's the little troublemaker," he announced. "I can tell she's going to be a stubborn one!"

The instant the baby was out, green-robed figures rushed toward Dorothy. Anxious voices filled the air. Rubber-covered hands held the new arrival in the air. An anxious face scrutinized her body. While the visual examination continued, the intruding face never smiled to greet her. She had been crying ever since the doctor had first pulled on an arm.

Finished with his exam, the doctor held the robust-looking infant aloft for Dorothy to see. The compressed face, tightened fists, and piercing high-pitched wails made her think, "She came out fighting."

Neither Dorothy nor anyone else said a word. No one had spoken to the new arrival or smiled at her yet.

As if being forced to handle an unwelcome burden, the doctor quickly handed the infant to a woman in green. She carried the wailing newborn away from the tense atmosphere around the delivery table to the other side of the room. She laid her down on a cloth-covered table, where another green-robed woman waited. Each woman took a towel and began rubbing the tender skin. While they scrubbed, as piercing cries continued filling the room, the two women chatted and laughed with each other. Every so often, they peeked down at their job. One of the women suddenly stopped rubbing, fixed one hand on the edge of her hip, and glared at the wailing infant.

"Who do you think you are?" she scolded. "You're just another person to take care of."

The baby kept screaming while the two women finished their job. A few minutes later, one of the women carried the freshly diapered new arrival out of the delivery room to the nursery. Dorothy was not in any emergency, but her torn body required many stitches. The first intimate meeting between mother and daughter would have to wait.

By the time they reached the nursery, the baby's crying had stopped. Her arms and legs, which had been jerking spastically in tempo with her crying, slowed down as well. The woman swaddled the newborn in a blanket and tucked her into her crib. Finally finished, she left.

Quiet descended over the dimly lit room. The lone occupant was lying perfectly still and absolutely quiet. However, all was not peaceful behind the seemingly placid façade. If the woman had stayed to watch and peer into the infant's eyes, which no one had done yet, except to scold her, she would have seen a depth of distress flashing from the tiny eyes whose full complexity would not be revealed for many years.

The newborn slept a long time as her body and psyche took the time needed to recuperate from her ordeal. When she awoke in the morning, her eyes spoke of renewed hope and tolerance. When she was taken to her mother in the morning, the first words she heard from the person reaching up for her were, "You're a girl, but you'll do."

3

Battle of Wills

Events that would have a fateful effect on the newborn during the first weeks of her infancy had been set in motion with the birth of Ellen. From the moment Dorothy realized she was pregnant again, she fervently prayed for a "good" baby, a baby who was the exact opposite of Ellen, a baby who never cried. Dorothy knew such babies did not really exist. However, just imagining one helped soothe her fear of a repeat of Ellen's infancy.

When Ellen was born, Dorothy and Henry were living in the same upstairs apartment of the house her father had built years ago in his spare time. He finally finished his labor of love just after his wife, the mother of his four daughters, had died from spinal meningitis. With the death of their mother, Dorothy, at six years old and the second oldest, started her training under her paternal grand-mother's tutoring as the woman of the house and mother's helper to her three sisters. Dorothy's older sister, who was one year older, was considered too nervous and timid to take on such a responsibility. Their grandmother firmly believed a sharp tongue was the best motivation. Dorothy acted so responsibly that, when-ever expressions of pity were voiced for the girls being motherless at so young an age, the comments never included her. She often wanted to cry out, "Don't I need a mother, too?"

When Dorothy was fifteen, her grandmother died. Her father made her quit school in the ninth grade to be the woman of the house and mother to her sisters.

When Dorothy and Henry married and moved into the upstairs apartment, Dorothy's new responsibilities as wife and mother-to-be were added to her already existing ones. Although she had to be only an occasional mother to her sisters, she was expected to maintain all the rooms downstairs and do everyone's laundry. Even though she cooked only for herself and Henry, she did everyone else's breakfast dishes.

When Ellen arrived less than a year after getting married, the only extra help Dorothy received was from her mother-in-law. That only happened whenever the spirit moved her, which was not very often. Two of Dorothy's sisters were engaged and busy planning their weddings. The youngest was used to being waited on. Henry did not help ease his wife's burden. From the beginning, he let everyone know who was responsible for housework and childcare.

All Dorothy ever heard from him about having their child was, "You had her. You take care of her!" Moreover, he expected spotless perfection in their part of the house. When it became fashionable some years later, Dorothy called him Mr. Macho Man.

Henry used the spacious grounds surrounding the house to raise some horses and goats. He often came home from work too late or too drunk (or both) to attend to the animals. When that happened, Dorothy fed them. If she didn't, no one else would.

When Dorothy came home from the hospital with Ellen, the rest of the adults could not wait to hold the new arrival. However, it was only after she had been fed and cleaned. When they did have her, they held her so much and gave her so much attention that she cried constantly when she was not being held.

In the morning, after the others had left, Ellen started crying as soon as Dorothy started her chores. She could tolerate the piercing screams only for so long. She then dropped whatever she was doing to comfort her baby. Then there was peace. As much as Dorothy enjoyed the silence, broken only by the sounds of birds in the trees, she knew the unchanged beds, bathrooms, piles of laundry, dusty tabletops, dishes in the sink, and dirty floors and carpets waited their turn. Although she knew what would happen as soon as she put Ellen down, she did not have a choice. She tried shutting out the wailing infant who sounded as if her heart was being ripped apart. She also tried ignoring the thoughts that assailed her about not being a good mother.

After a few months of keeping quiet, Dorothy's patience ran out. She pleaded with the others to stop spoiling Ellen. She would just have to learn that she could not be held all the time. The others agreed to try, but Dorothy's mother-in-law insisted, "I only pick her up when she's crying!"

Over the next week, Dorothy's pleas had obviously been ignored. She decided to take a drastic step. One day, after everyone had left for work, Dorothy finished feeding Ellen and put her in a stroller. She positioned the stroller so it was facing the sink. She then started the breakfast dishes. Ellen immediately started crying. She cried while Dorothy did the dishes and ironed clothes. Dorothy then went downstairs with Ellen and the stroller and worked there. Ellen cried for the whole day. She only stopped when she was fed, changed, or asleep.

When Dorothy was finished, she fled to her apartment. After awhile, in between Ellen's crying, she heard the others coming home from work. As usual, Henry was late. Dorothy later heard his unsteady footsteps on the stairs. He let himself in and found his wife in the living room ironing clothes while watching television, her only entertainment for the day. Ellen was in her playpen, also in the living room. She was crying. Henry's eyes jumped from Dorothy…to Ellen…and then back to Dorothy.

"You're just going to let her cry?" he yelled above the sounds of crying and the television.

Dorothy attended to her ironing and gave a little nod of her head.

"You're just going to iron and listen to the television and let that child cry?"

Dorothy kept ironing without looking at Henry.

"You're not going to pick her up?"

A firm shake of the head came from the woman holding the iron.

Henry threw his hands in the air and glared at his wife. "I don't understand you women. You want children. Now you've got one, you're just going to watch television while she cries!"

Dorothy finally turned in his direction and gave him an icy stare. She thought of many things she wanted to say to her husband, but she held back. She did not make any move in Ellen's direction, who was now crying louder.

"I'm not staying around no screaming kid!" Henry was not aware he was also screaming.

Dorothy kept staring.

Henry whirled around, stomped out of the apartment, and went downstairs. Dorothy locked the door.

This next day was a repeat of the day before. By evening, Dorothy was locked in her apartment with a crying baby. She heard Henry come into the house, but he did not come upstairs.

In the middle of the evening, Dorothy heard a knock on her door. Dorothy's mother-in-law announced herself.

From behind the locked door, Dorothy asked, "What do you want?"

"Are you going to let the baby cry like that?" the voice demanded.

Dorothy did not answer.

"Will you please let me in?"

Dorothy knew what would happen if she did. She did not like the crying either, but it had to stop.

"If you don't let me in," the pleading voice vibrated through the door, "I won't spend another night in this house. You're breaking my heart!"

Dorothy did not say anything. Some moments later, she heard footsteps going down the stairs. A minute later, the front door opened. Then a car went away.

Ellen cried through the next day, the third. Henry slept downstairs again. Sometime during the next day, the fourth, Ellen stopped crying when she was not being held.

A little more than a year later, when Dorothy came home from the hospital with her second baby, who was named Jessica, everyone was eager to greet the new arrival. They were just as eager as they had been with Ellen. However, an unspoken command—"Don't spoil Jessica!"—was in the air this time.

On the first day home, everyone moved in close for a quick look. All complimented Dorothy on an adorable, healthy looking baby. However, they, even her mother-in-law, kept their distance and their hands off.

Dorothy had not wanted another child so soon, but Henry had not stopped complaining about not having a son. Dorothy took her husband's grumbling to heart and hoped his behavior would improve if their next child was a boy. It didn't. He remained firm in his old-fashioned beliefs.

For the first week of Jessica's life, Dorothy had not decided if her prayer for a perfect baby had been answered or not. So far, her new daughter seemed like most other newborns. Having to get up during the night to attend to an infant was expected. Dorothy just hoped Jessica would get through that stage quicker than other babies did.

One morning, perhaps a week later, Dorothy's first sensation upon awakening in an empty bed (Henry had left at dawn) was of having had a restful night's sleep. She felt her body give a long, relaxed sigh. The tension and worry of being a mother again began draining away. A hopeful smile hesitantly broke out on her face when she thought Jessica had not cried during the night. An uninterrupted night's sleep was unexpected, especially after the previous night when Jessica's insistent crying had awakened her once more, as it had every night since she had brought her home from the hospital.

The night before, she stayed in bed while listening for a few minutes, hoping the crying would stop. Perhaps it was only a minor upset. However, when the crying did not stop, she knew she had to get up. She found a hungry, wet baby. After a hurried feeding and changing, Dorothy laid Jessica back in her crib. The moment she slid her hands out from underneath the tiny body, the crying started again. Then, the battle of wills started.

A fully grown woman was on one side. She was a woman who felt her psyche was under great emotional stress. On this particular night, her ability to handle anymore responsibilities, solve anymore problems, and give anymore had been drained dry. A tiny, helpless, completely dependent, totally trusting newborn baby was on the other side.

Dorothy was bent over the railing of the crib, her hands inches away from Jessica's body, when the crying started again. She immediately slid her hands under the tiny pair of shoulders and gently picked up her newborn. Before she had snuggled the crying infant against her bosom, the crying suddenly stopped.

Quickly, as if she was ridding herself of a repulsive object, Dorothy put Jessica back in the crib. The moment the body touched the mattress, the crying started. This time, it was louder. Dorothy reached into the crib, but she put Jessica back down a few seconds later when the crying stopped. This happened a few more times. When the baby was up, the crying immediately stopped. When she was down, the crying started just as quickly. Every time Dorothy picked up Jessica, she did so with a little more of a jerk until she did not make any motion to pick her up. Instead, she glared at the little creature with her own will. Memories of her struggle to cure Ellen of crying flooded her mind.

"You're spoiled," she snapped. "I can't hold you every time you want me to. I have to take care of your sister and your father as well. I don't have enough time to just hold you!"

Dorothy's angry words triggered another bout of crying. Her hand shot into the crib and tightly clamped over the tiny mouth.

"Stop crying!" she commanded. The crying did not stop. Muffled shrieks escaped from underneath her hand.

She felt the lid starting to come off long-suppressed, very intense feelings. When the shrieks kept coming, Dorothy's face twisted into a mass of frustration and rage. She forced her hands under Jessica's shoulders, jerked the frail body through the air, and pulled the little face directly in front of her own, just inches away.

"You're a bad girl," the big mouth snarled. "I didn't have this problem with your sister. There's something wrong with you!"

The massive, twisted face, which was filled with rage and bulging veins, stayed inches away from Jessica's face. The unspoken message—"Don't you dare open your mouth again!"—crackled through the air.

Dorothy held her breath. The tiny mouth started opening, wider than Dorothy had ever seen. A shriek of infantile terror filled the air. The shrill sound pierced the quiet and pummeled Dorothy's mind, unleashing a flood of long, pent-up feelings and memories. Her arms started vibrating. Dorothy felt she was a second away from completely losing control. Every ounce of giving had been squeezed from her. The screaming infant demanding attention this instant rubbed raw every nerve in her body. The weight hanging from her trembling hands was no longer human. Dorothy felt her arms losing strength. No longer herself, she was a bystander watching what was happening to her body. She felt the infant slip from her fingers and tilt backward before beginning its fall through empty space. One last terror-filled cry filled the air before the human form landed once more on the bedsheets, back-first.

At that same instant, Dorothy spun around and hurried toward the doorway. Her fists were clenched, and her teeth were grinding together. The following thoughts pounded in her head, "There isn't anymore I can do. She'll just have to cry herself to sleep."

Before Dorothy took no more than a few steps, she came to a sudden halt. A look of amazement was on her face. Her breath was frozen in her throat. Her ears scanned the horizon like giant radar dishes. She had just been holding a screaming infant. High-pitched wails had filled the air. Now there was a tomb-like silence. No shrill sounds broke the still night air. The instantaneous change seemed miraculous to Dorothy. She remained standing in the darkness, straining her ears. The loudest sound was Jessica's breathing. It flowed quickly but rhythmically, in and out. It was the pure sound of life. Dorothy felt her own feelings loosening their grip on her. The utter frustration and helplessness that overwhelmed her were quickly fading away. For Dorothy, a silent infant had never sounded so welcome, so peaceful. She tuned into Jessica's breathing again. It was also slowing down as Dorothy left the room.

Jessica lay on her back while she fixated on the ceiling. Her whole body seemed lifeless. No movement came from her legs, arms, hands, or fingers. Her eyes also seemed to have stopped blinking. They stared straight up, frozen in position, as if someone had painted a pair on her. Except for the faint sound of her breathing and the heaving motion of her little chest, anyone looking at her would have thought a lifeless, wooden doll was in the crib.

When Dorothy came into Jessica's room the next morning, she found the infant lying perfectly still, absolutely quiet. There was no crying, whimpering, or fussing. This contrasted with every morning until now, when Dorothy found a wet, hungry, crying baby. Total silence was in its place.

While Dorothy busied herself with changing and dressing Jessica, she did not notice the little, human form in front of her offered no resistance to anything she did and never looked her in the eye. When their eyes happened to meet, there was no sign in Jessica's eyes that she was looking at another human being. She seemed to be looking right through Dorothy, as if she did not exist. When Dorothy finished, she covered Jessica with a blanket and left to fix a bottle in the kitchen. The baby did not even whimper.

In a few minutes, Dorothy returned. She reached into the crib and put the nipple to the infant's mouth, but the mouth would not open. The face was a blank stare. Her eyes stared at the ceiling. This had never happened before. Jessica had always been eager to suck, and her mouth popped open as soon as she saw the bottle coming toward her.

Now it lay against her lips. Dorothy gave the bottle a slight jiggle, but there was no response. Dorothy jiggled it again. She then did it again a few more times in quick succession. Jessica's mouth finally opened very slowly, as if she was not quite sure what to do. The tiny lips slowly inched their way around the rubbery surface, and she took a tiny suck. Then she stopped. Dorothy jiggled the bottle. She then did it again a few more times. Jessica then took another little suck. A third followed a few moments later. Then she gave a hesitant swallow. Her mouth was then motionless. Dorothy had to jiggle the bottle again. This time, Jessica sucked slightly harder and did not wait as long to swallow. During this time, Jessica never took more than a hesitant swallow or two on her own. Dorothy always had to jiggle the bottle to get her started again.

After twenty minutes, Jessica had only managed to finish one-third of the bottle, much less than she usually drank. She used to suck and swallow like a hungry baby who was not afraid to act on what it needed.

Dorothy jiggled the partially empty bottle a few more times, but there was no response. If that was all she wanted, Dorothy was not going to push it. She would probably make up for it at her next feeding. Taking care of an infant who was not crying felt like a blessing, especially on this morning after. Her senses basked in the quiet sounds of the early morning. She was not about to do anything to disrupt the stillness. Once again, she found herself hoping for a good baby.

Starting with the next morning, Dorothy's wish came true, far more than she ever imagined. She never believed for one instant she would get an infant who never cried. She just hoped for one who cried less than most—and a lot less than Ellen. However, this imaginary, perfect baby was now lying in front of her. For the rest of Jessica's infancy, Dorothy never heard her cry. Not at night. Not in the daytime. Never. Even when Jessica was hungry, she did not cry. The only way to tell if she was hungry was to put a bottle to her mouth. Even then, Dorothy had to coax her, though not quite as much as on that morning after. Jessica did not cry or fuss if she needed a changing either. Instead, she lay quietly until Dorothy came, unlike the night when her crying demanded someone come quickly. In the morning, Dorothy had to go into Jessica's room to make sure she was even alive.

This baby that never cried and never seemed to need anything from anyone was more of a good baby than Dorothy had ever hoped for. Maybe some babies did not need to cry or be held as much as others. She wondered if some babies were just naturally independent.

Some months later, when Jessica could crawl, Dorothy could only conclude she was probably right about Jessica having an independent nature. When Jessica was taken outside in warmer weather and placed on a blanket in the backyard, she ran her little hands back and forth in the grass. She slowly, rhythmically rubbed her fingers in the dirt. The little explorer then crawled to the flowerbeds to savor the fragrances. She then went to the nearest trees to feel the bark. On sunny days, she sat with her face toward the sun. On windy days, she sat with her face into the breeze. Any bird that came to visit only held her attention as long as it chirped away or flitted through the branches.

Somewhere in her mind, Dorothy noted to herself that Jessica did not cry like other infants. She sometimes wondered why Jessica did not seem excited when someone touched her. However, she did not think of these as problems and, therefore, did not worry about them. She was feeling too fortunate. For years afterward, whenever babies were the topic of conversation, Dorothy never tired of proclaiming, "Jessica was such a good baby! She never cried and never wanted anything!"

Dorothy also found comfort in the prevailing attitude about infants in the mid-1950s. Newborn babies were primarily interested in eating, sleeping, and feeling safe and comfortable. They only cried to let you know if they were hungry, wet, or scared. It did not matter how you sounded or looked in front of them. They weren't really human.

Despite what the experts thought, Jessica had entered the world with definite feelings about what she needed, what felt good, and what did not feel good. Her instincts told her that she needed to be held for long periods, have her skin caressed, be smiled at, be spoken to softly, and be handled gently. She needed to feel she, as a fellow human being, could bring a smile to other people. She needed to feel she was a good baby and had added one more good thing to the world.

When Jessica looked at her mother, she usually saw a grumpy, unsmiling face with eyes blazing resentment. She heard an angry, loud voice; hurried breathing; and loud sighs of frustration. How Dorothy's eyes and face looked, how her voice sounded, and how she touched her newborn was how the world spoke to Jessica.

What was happening to Jessica did not feel very good. It was deeply hurtful. Her personality's core, her sense of who she was as a human being, was being determined. It was not being determined in the way she hoped for.

Dorothy first noticed it a few weeks after the battle of wills. It happened when she gave Jessica her bottle in the morning. While Jessica was sucking, milk was going through the nipple, but it was spilling out of her mouth. From what Dorothy could see, Jessica was not swallowing. She eased the bottle out and opened Jessica's mouth. She could not find anything wrong. An hour later, the exact same thing happened.

Dorothy sprang into action. A neighbor agreed to watch Ellen. Another drove Dorothy and Jessica to the emergency service at the hospital where Jessica was born.

A tumor was discovered deep in Jessica's throat. The doctor had never heard of a tumor in an infant. He urged Dorothy to go to a larger hospital in Detroit, the only medical center in the area with radiation therapy, the very latest treatment for tumors. There, with one radiation treatment, the tumor quickly dissolved.

With that, Jessica returned to being the perfect baby. Dorothy returned to enjoying the baby who never cried and never wanted anything.

4

The Healing Journey Begins

I first met Jessica when she was twenty-three and married to Roger Page, who was two years older. They had attended the same high school and had married less than a year after Jessica had graduated. They had a three-year-old daughter, Melissa. They were living in Bayport, a small, quiet community at the very edge of suburbia south of Detroit. It was nestled alongside one of the waterways that ran between the Great Lakes.

I had just opened my office in a suburb closer to Detroit after seven years at Family Service, a non-profit agency for individual, marital, family, and group counseling on the other side of town. Being on my own as a psychotherapist was the fulfillment of a childhood dream, one I had been quite secretive about for many years.

Before I even knew what the word psychotherapist meant, I was practicing being one (in my own surreptitious way, of course). One of my favorite pastimes was watching people, especially when an emotional force seemed to energize their behavior. This seized my attention in a way that nothing else seemed to do. By my teens, this yearning to understand what made people tick had become a bit of an obsession. In high school, I would go to any library I could find. When I thought no one was looking, I grabbed any book with the word "mind" in the title. I hoped to find the answers to human behavior there, even if I only understood a few words in every third sentence. I also devoured any psychology books I could find. In those years, psychoanalysis was the best the mental health field had to offer. I quickly realized that was not what I was searching for. Were our minds at the mercy of irrational instincts? Were our personalities formed by the age of six? If true, who would want to be a human being?

At the time, the only other people I knew who studied the mind were psychiatrists. However, I thought they went to school for what seemed like forever; so I naturally believed you had to be a certifiable genius to be one. While most people thought I was highly intelligent, I was most definitely not a genius. My strengths were perseverance and intuition. I had control over the former; I did not have control over the latter. I could only influence that part of my mind by pouring enough information and experience into my head through perseverance. I then sat back and waited for the creative processes I felt I had been fortunate enough to be born with do their thing. Those natural processes were like my own personal guru. It was something I could always count on for a sense of direction, even if the voice from my unconscious did not always speak to me as quickly as I hoped. Whatever therapeutic brilliance I had was entirely due to my commitment to being the best therapist I could be and working as hard as I could at it.

With great reluctance, I put my earliest dreams about what to pursue in life on my "what if" shelf. I turned my attention to solving problems in math and physics. However, shortly after I started graduate work in physics, an image of myself fifty years in the future haunted me. While gripping my white hair and wondering where my brains had gone to years earlier, I exclaimed, "Why hadn't I acted on what I had felt in my blood?" The longer I studied physics, the more this image haunted me. At the end of a year of graduate school, I said, "Enough!" I then waved good-bye to physics.

By the age of twenty-eight, I was working as a therapist. Finally, I could officially do what I had started doing furtively as a child. After seven fruitful years at Family Service, where I learned a great deal, I was eager to try more challenging cases. Such cases usually required a more innovative treatment approach than a publicly funded agency, with a corresponding public image, was too skittish to allow.

Perhaps fate presented me with an opportunity to see what kind of a challenge I could handle on my own. Jessica was my first new client. One day, a week or two after I opened my office, Gloria, a client who started with me at Family Service, said a friend of hers, Jessica Page, was going to call. They had known each other since early childhood and had been a winning, canoe-racing team in their early teens in competition on the nearby St. Catherine's River. Gloria and Jessica had not had much contact with each other since graduating from high school five years before. Both had married shortly after, but their mothers remained close.

When Gloria called her longtime friend, she simply said, "Call him! He's different!" This was a reference to both women seeing therapists in the past. Gloria knew about Jessica seeing a psychiatrist for a few months at the local country health center a month after graduating from high school. Dorothy had made the appointment. Jessica had stayed home for a few days and had not said a word to anyone, even Roger, her boyfriend at the time. She did not even call the restaurant where she worked as a waitress to say she was not coming in. Dorothy did not have any idea why her daughter seemed to be wasting her life away. She tried to motivate her by reminding her she had just graduated and was at the peak of her life. When it appeared Jessica was going to miss a third day of work, Dorothy was at her wit's end. She called the county health center and made the appointment. Gloria had gone to the same county psychiatric center shortly after Jessica stopped going there. In one session, her psychiatrist abruptly left the office as soon as she started crying. He said he would come back when she was done.

A few days after Gloria mentioned her friend to me, the phone in my office rang while I was updating my records.

After I identified myself, the person on the other end said, "This is Jessica Page."

Without waiting for her to say anything else, I hurriedly said, "Oh, yes. Gloria said you'd be calling." I did not ask, "Could you tell me a bit about why you're calling?" (I customarily did this when someone new called.) I was too ecstatic about getting my first new client. Until the new phonebook came out in another six months, where I would be listed in two separate headings, I had to rely on word of mouth as my primary means of obtaining new clients. I also assumed Jessica had spoken with Gloria and had checked out whatever she needed to know about me. Immediately after she identified herself, I asked, "When would you like to make an appointment?"

"How about a few days from now, on Thursday, at four?"

"That's fine, I'll see you then."

The day before the appointment, Jessica called to say she and her husband were remodeling their kitchen. It was taking longer and costing more than they had anticipated. She would call again.

A few weeks went by. Jessica had not called back. At the end of a session with Gloria, I asked, "What happened to your friend?"

As soon as Gloria got home, she called Jessica and simply said, "Do it!"

Jessica called the next day. We made an appointment for the end of the week.

On the day of the appointment, a few minutes before the appointed hour, I left my office in the secluded corner of the building and walked down a carpeted hallway to the waiting area. One person, seated at one end of a large, black sofa, was there. Dressed in fashionable jeans and a short-sleeved, blue- and yellow-checkered shirt, a touch of eye shadow darkened her eyes a bit. Some rouge gave a slight reddish glow to her cheeks. Her long, brown hair lay in flowing waves down her shoulders. Her erect posture made her appear as if she was poised for a business appointment, not someone seeking help.

I later learned my initial suspicion was right on target. Jessica really wanted to present herself as someone who did not need therapy, even though she felt she was on the verge of losing complete control of her life. She was so petrified of anyone discovering her secret that she did everything she could to give the impression she was a confident person in complete control of her life.

With the traffic in the late afternoon, the trip to my office from where they lived took about twenty-five minutes. Jessica and her husband had arrived a few minutes early.

In the waiting area, I took a step or two in her direction.

"Mrs. Page?"

Jessica nodded her head smartly.

I smiled and said, "Hi, I'm Jeffrey. Did you have any trouble in finding your way?"

"No," she said. "My husband, Roger, drove. He knows the area. He's waiting in the car with our daughter."

With a wave of my hand and an inviting smile, indicating for her to follow, I said, "My office is this way."

Jessica initially thought, even though I looked about ten years older than she was (thirteen actually), I was not too old or too young. My unhurried movements, brown, doe-like eyes, and soft voice produced an immediate thought in her mind.

"He wouldn't hurt a flea."

Inside my office, I indicated one of two typical office chairs facing each other. After we were seated (a bit more than an arm's reach apart), I pointed out the box of tissues the small table alongside her chair. Several color enlargements of photographs I had taken of idyllic mountain scenes hung from the walls. They were vivid reminders of long, summer backpacking trips to national parks in recent years.

Jessica settled herself in her chair and expectantly stared at me, as if she was waiting for a direction.

I said, "What can I help you with?"

There was the briefest pause before she spoke. "When my husband works nights, I have to take my daughter and spend the night at my mother's house."

When her mouth closed around the escaping sounds of the last word, she abruptly stopped talking and stared at me. Her face was a complete blank. Her eyes were expressionless, and her hands were folded in her lap. I waited to see if she was going to provide more details, details that seemed painfully obvious to me. Why exactly couldn't she stay home at night? Was she too afraid? I assumed she was, but I noted she had not said so. If she was, was this the first time in her life she had been so afraid? When had she started going to her mother's house? What was happening in her life when it started? Had she sought help for it before?

I kept hoping she would volunteer more information, details I thought any person seeking help would eagerly want to provide or at least make a start on. However, for whatever reason, she was not. In her fleeting statement, she had only stated a problem. She had not even said what she wanted to do about it. For all I knew, maybe her mother was frightened at night and needed company. As she continued sitting like a meditating Buddha, I was fearful her face would freeze in place if I did not say anything.

I began asking the questions I did not have answers for. "Can you tell me more about why you have to stay at your mother's house?"

With a sideways tilt of her head, Jessica squinted at me from the corners of her eyes.

"What do you want to know?" she managed to squeak out, looking like a trapped animal trying to appease its attacker.

Many months later, I learned why my question had terrified her so.

◆   ◆   ◆

The night air lay quiet. The Pages lived on the east side of Bayport, a bulge of land jutting into Hansen's Bay. On the other side of the bay, an uninhabited, wooded island, officially a state wildlife preserve, shielded the small, horseshoe-shaped body of water from the St. Catherine's River. Farther out in the river nearer the Canadian shore was the main shipping channel for the huge freighters that worked the Great Lakes. At night, from certain vantage points along the shore, the running lights high on the superstructure of the ships gave the only sign of their noiseless passage. Inlets from the bay cut into the peninsula and divided it into randomly arranged, slender strips. These islands were connected to each other by quaint, one-lane bridges that were built years ago from small boulders found during the construction of the paved road that traversed the boundary of the peninsula. Larger homes snuggled closely together along the shores of the bay and the inlets. Their lawns stretched to the water's edge. Smaller, more modest homes lined the tree-lined dirt streets that connected the winding sides of the elliptical-shaped, paved road. Seagulls, ducks, and birds spilled over from the wildlife preserve. They nested safely for the night along the shore of the bay and the inlets and secluded themselves under bushes. In the day, the ducks wandered all over the peninsula. They were considered a community asset. Motorists could be ticketed for hitting one. Dogs were scolded for chasing them. Nests were protected. The only gas station in town—located by the only traffic light, which was a flashing caution—closed not long after the supper hour. So did the only restaurant and all-purpose drugstore. Away from the huge auto, steel, and chemical plants and busy shopping centers in nearby communities, all in Bayport in the middle of this particular early spring night seemed quiet and peaceful. This was the same as it was every night of the year, except for the first warm weekend announcing the start of the boating season. However, on this particular night, one person in one of the modest homes on one of the dirt roads was having a decidedly different reaction. Jessica Thomas Page balanced on the edge of her chair in front of the television. All the muscles in her body were taut like a coiled spring. Her breath came rapidly. Her chest heaved up and down. Her hands flew after each other in an endless chase through the ends of her long hair that fell over her shoulders in front of her. It was a purely mechanical reaction, repeated many times.

The characters on a late-night movie paraded across the television screen. Jessica's eyes were glued to every action, and her ears took in every sound. However, nothing registered in her mind. The action on the screen was not important. It was only an escape, something outside of herself to force her attention away from what was happening inside of her. Her fear of something getting her had erupted with a far greater intensity than she had ever known.

While the fear lay quietly inside of her like a caged animal at rest, the television worked as a diversion. However, when the fear erupted and struck at her in a surging wave, she felt as if she was being electrocuted. Her muscles snapped. Her body jerked in the air. Her frenzied pace carried her from one side of the room to the other. Her fists clenched like claws to strike out at whatever the something was. Her face was frozen in terror; her heart was racing.

As soon as she reached one wall, she spun around and headed for the other. She hoped her racing steps would keep her away from whatever it was. Her eyes darted into the darkness in the next room and outside the windows. Maybe something was hiding out there. Her nerves were so tight that the slightest unexpected sound, even a twig from the big tree in the front yard landing on the roof, made her want to jump out of her skin.

While Bayport lay quiet in the night and people, ducks, seagulls, and birds slept peacefully, Jessica frantically paced back and forth. After about twenty minutes, the volcanic eruption of raw terror subsided. Her racing heart slowed down.

At least for the time being, she did not feel the something was one second away from ending her life.

She sat down again. Her eyes riveted on the television in front of her. Having missed twenty minutes of the movie did not matter. The movie worked as a distraction for only a little while. Then the panic returned with all of its roaring intensity and shot her into the air.

When she sat down after another fifteen or twenty minutes of frenzied pacing, she reached for a paperback novel, a woman's story, she had been reading. She hoped the combination of the television and book would be enough to keep the panic at bay.

Before long, she was into another bout of pacing. Her great wish was to be peacefully asleep, just like her three-year-old daughter in her room on the other side of the house.

Every night for the past two months had been like this. It started when Roger went back to the night shift at the St. Catherine's Iron Works. As soon as he stepped out of the house, the panic began growing inside of Jessica. She locked the doors, checked Melissa, put out the lights, and went to bed. She closed her eyes and lay quietly, waiting for sleep to come. Sleep did not come. She waited and waited. The night dragged on. The furniture took on a sinister appearance. The darkest corners hid horrifying creatures. Something was lurking in the bedroom. She moved to the couch in the living room. Sleep did not come there either. She was soon watching television or reading a book. She would try doing both at the same time. Then the panic erupted. She started frantically pacing the floor.

Sheer exhaustion usually caught up with Jessica an hour or two before dawn. She fell asleep wherever she was, usually in the chair with the television on and a book in her lap. She never slept for more than a few hours, sometimes one or two. She did not know how she functioned on so little sleep. She did not care.

During the day, her panic stayed dormant enough for her to do what was expected of her as a wife and mother. Her only problem in the day (and the only problem anyone outside her family knew about) was being unable to drive. Whenever she tried driving, she felt her mind was about to plunge into chaos the instant the car started moving. She could only be a passenger if Roger or her mother drove and she sat in the front seat.

After struggling with her nocturnal demons for another month, Jessica admitted defeat. She had never given in to any of her mysterious problems before. She had always tried finding a way to live with them and carry on as best she could.

Now she felt she did not have a choice. The panic was stronger and more powerful than any resource she could find inside of her. Struggling with her panic attacks and trying to subdue them night after night was a losing battle. It was one she had yet to gain an inch of ground on.

On the day she admitted defeat, she simply said to Roger, "I don't like spending the nights alone with Melissa. You'll have to take us to my mother's house on your way to work."

Roger quietly agreed. So did Dorothy. Neither asked a question or raised any objection. Dorothy's house was on the other side of Bayport, only a minute out of Roger's way. It seemed like a simple request. In the morning, Dorothy drove Jessica and Melissa back home by seven-thirty. Jessica watched two neighborhood children in her home. Roger slept at Dorothy's house.

Having her mother in the same house with her at night was enough to keep Jessica from pacing the floor, though she continued to sleep fitfully.

◆   ◆   ◆

Despite asking—in as many ways as I could think of—why she sought the sanctuary of her mother's house, all Jessica could say was that she felt "too scared…too upset…I can't be home alone at night." She then blankly stared at me. All of my attempts to discover what exactly made her feel too afraid or too upset (for example, being alone, the night, the dark, being harassed by a neighbor, or bad dreams) only caused her to say, "I don't think so" or "No." Jessica started going to her mother's a few months ago. The only reason she could think of was that Roger had started working nights a few months before that and she "just had to." She could not think of any other time in her life when she had felt the same way.

Not definitely knowing why Jessica was being so secretive, I hoped a slightly different approach might elicit more helpful answers. "Can you tell me what made you pick up the phone the first time a few weeks ago and call me? Did something happen that made you feel you had to do that?"

Jessica hesitated for a moment or two. This was the first time she had done so in a response to my questions. "Roger and I had an argument," she said weakly.

Based on how Jessica sounded, my immediate thought was that, even though they may have had an argument, this was not the reason she had called me. If she said, "Gloria told me to call," which I was expecting, I would have said, "Yes, that's true. Can you tell me what it was about her telling you to call that made you do it?"

I did ask a few questions about the supposed argument to let her know I took seriously anything she told me as well as give her a chance to collect herself. Even so, just like my other invitations, she was not able to provide more useful information about the supposed argument or her overall relationship with her husband.

While I listened to Jessica, my mind kept superimposing images from another first interview from earlier in my career. A forty-year-old woman, who called because a friend of hers (and my client) had urged her, sat down in my office.

"What can I help you with?" I asked.

She said she had a fear of heights. On her own, she described the first time it had happened. Ten years ago, she had started a new job on the twentieth floor of the biggest skyscraper in Detroit. Sometime during the day, while she was counting the number of sheets in a stack of paper, she began feeling an irresistible pull toward a window on the other side of the room. The pull felt so powerful and terrified her so much that she was forced to wrap both arms around a floor-to-ceiling post to keep from being mysteriously pulled over there and thrown out. When she could get enough of a grip on herself, she collected her belongings and fled the building in an intense state of anxiety. It mystified her that she had gone for an interview in the same office suite the day before. Her boyfriend accompanied her as far as the waiting room, just outside the room she was now working in. After describing this first attack, she spoke for a few minutes about previous therapists who had failed to help her.

After relating all of this in about ten minutes in response to my opening question, she asked, "Can you help me?"

I said, "I don't know yet. I need to know more about what was going on in your life at the time it started."

She said, "Okay." She then told me about her abortion, which was illegal at the time, two days before her first anxiety attack. In giving a detailed account of the experience, she identified the act of counting that had triggered her phobia. The doctor had asked her to count backward from 100 when he injected her with anesthesia. She also said, in her childhood, her father had been a fundamentalist minister, who threatened her with passages from the Bible and preached abortion was a great sin. Within twenty minutes, we were making significant progress. In a few sessions, buried memories from her childhood surfaced. Every session was exciting. There was definite progress every week. We accomplished a great deal in several months.

For whatever reason, Jessica was not able to be as open. Perhaps later in the session or in the next one, I thought she would feel more at ease. After all, she was talking to total stranger, and we had been together for a total of ten minutes.

I asked about other areas in her life, including marriage, being a parent, her mother, other family members, her childhood, friends, and interests. Those who seek therapy rarely, if ever, have an isolated problem.

I discovered she did have disagreements with Roger, but they did not seem to worry her very much. She and Roger were not sleeping together. Though she felt afraid of Roger hurting her, she could not understand why as she had always thought of him—and continued to do so—as the gentlest man she had ever known. She had not explained any of this to him. She just avoided the subject. If Roger suspected anything, he apparently did not notice or did not care. She did wonder if the two of them not sleeping together was a sign of their marriage breaking up. She did not seem frightened about that possibility. Moreover, from the information I gathered, Roger did not seem to be either.

Jessica also had upsetting interactions with her mother. They seemed to bother her much more than anything happening with her husband. Describing a few, she ended her discussion of each with the same comment, "She's just doing the best she can!"

Jessica said she was too scared to drive. She stopped driving sometime after she married. She could not think of anything that had happened to make her fearful of driving. It was all a great mystery to her because she had started driving at fourteen on a special permit for day-use only due to her mother's arthritis and only in the small community they lived in.

Another problem involved her daughter, Melissa. Though Jessica seemed to dearly love her, she could not play with her. She could not get down on the floor and participate in whatever activity Melissa found entertaining. Jessica's only thought was that her mother had not played with her. She did not know how this caused her to not play with her daughter, but it was the only clue she spoke of. This bothered her because she did not have any problem playing with the two neighborhood children she watched. Both were about her daughter's age.

Jessica did not spontaneously volunteer all this information. I only learned about it because of persistent questioning.

As this first session ended, the only thing I knew about why Jessica had come for therapy was because she was not able to stay home alone at night. I did not know why she could not stay home at night, and I didn't know what she wanted to do about it. I just assumed she wanted to, even though she had not said so. Although there were other problems in her life, she did not say what she wanted to do about them either. I assumed, for example, she wanted to be able to drive, but I noted she had not said so.

At the end of every first session, I give a brief explanation of how I believe psychological problems occur and can be resolved. The basic message is very simple: Unresolved feelings from hurtful experiences cause any such problems. The cure is to release those feelings. This remedy does not apply to any problem that can be resolved by a conscious decision. When that can be done, it simply means the problem in question is not being driven by strong, unresolved feelings.

After I explained this to Jessica, I added, "We may not know the reason why you have to go to your mother's at night, but the reason has to be unresolved feelings from some past experience. Sometime in the past, you were hurt, and no one gave you the opportunity to get rid of the upset. It wasn't anything you did to cause the past experience or the present problem."

While I spoke, Jessica seemed to listen more attentively than she had at any other time. My message was a tremendous relief to her. It was a direct contradiction to the message she had heard throughout her childhood from her mother about not trying hard enough.

After I finished, I asked her what she thought.

"Sounds fine!" she immediately replied.

"Would you like to come back?" I asked.

"Yes!"

I was glad. If people did not come back, I could not help them. I was relieved, too. I did not know if she had come only because Gloria, with my urging, had pressured her into it.

5

Tears—But "I'm Not Upset!"

Even though Jessica continued coming for further sessions (never canceling and always punctual), she was just as reluctant to reveal her feelings. All of our sessions began the same way. She silently stared at me, and I asked the same question, "Well, how are you doing?" I started each session with this question, hoping she would seize the initiative and talk about an upsetting event that had happened since we last met or add information about something from a previous session. However, the only response I ever heard was, "So-so." Then she would stare at me. To get things going, I had to ask very specific questions.

"Did you have any disagreements with your mother?"

"No."

"Did your mother say anything that made you upset?"

"No."

"Did you talk with your mother today?"

"Yes."

"What did you talk about?"

After pausing a few seconds, with the barest hint of a pained look on her face, Jessica said, "She wanted to talk about the plants I bought for her."

"What did she say?"

"She thought I could have done a better job of picking them out."

"Is that what she actually said?"

"No."

"What did she actually say?"

"She said something about them not looking very fresh."

Even when I asked Jessica to quote her mother exactly, she continued to soften the effect of whatever her mother had said. "Did she sound critical when she said it?"

"She was just expressing her opinion?" Another softening.

"Did it seem she was blaming you for not having made a better choice?"

"Well, she said she needed plants and didn't have time to go. So, I said I'd get Roger to drive me, and I'd pick them up for her."

"Did she ask you to do that?"

"No."

"So you just offered to do her a favor?"

"Yes."

"And now she doesn't seem to appreciate your efforts?"

At this point, Jessica's face turned stone-cold. After she stared over my shoulder for a few moments, she exclaimed, "My mom's just doing the best she can!" She stared over my shoulder and continued until I broke the silence.

The first crack in Jessica's reluctance to reveal her feelings happened after we had been meeting for just over a month, but it left me even more bewildered about who was sitting across from me.

In a session three days before the Fourth of July, I asked Jessica about her plans for the holiday. Because holidays are usually a time for family gatherings, I thought I would take advantage of it being on the calendar and see if she was having any particular feelings about it. By this time in her therapy, I knew, if she was upset about anything, I would have to gently pry the details out of her.

She said no one in her family—her two sisters and two brothers in the area, who were all married—had made any plans for the approaching holiday. She tossed the comment out and waited, just like her response to my opening question in our very first session. Just like then, I was forced to jump to the task of trying to learn more.

For years, Dorothy had hosted a family get-together for the holiday. For the past few years, she had called Jessica first. However, Dorothy had not called anyone yet. Jessica decided she would have to call her mother. If she had not made any plans, she would host the event. Jessica emphasized how willing she was to invite everyone and make all the preparations.

At her next session a week later, my first question was about the holiday. As soon as Jessica heard my question, she started talking.

"I called my mom right after I got home last week." For the first time since I had known her, she kept talking. Her voice was filled with more emotion than I had ever heard. "She hadn't made any plans yet, and no one had called her to see what we were doing. I had to call everyone, make all the plans, and have it at my house. I had to do everything!" With her final words, she suddenly stopped talking and stared at me.

At this point, there was only one obvious question to ask, one I had not yet felt gun-shy about asking. "And how did you feel about having to do all that?"

Jessica first shrugged her shoulders before exclaiming, "My mom's just doing the best she can!"

I waited patiently to see if she was going to say more in order to see if she was finally aware that, by making excuses for her mother, she was avoiding a very upsetting feeling of her own. For the next thirty seconds, she just stared over my shoulder. Then little pools of water started forming at the bottom of her eyes. I watched them grow bigger. A few tears spilled over each eyelid and trickled down her cheeks. She sat perfectly still the entire time with her hands folded in her lap. A few more tears then trickled out. They ran down her face, merged with the first ones at the bottom of her chin, and moved in little rivulets down her neck. She continued staring over my shoulder, hoping it would all magically disappear if she ignored it.

"What are you upset about?" I softly asked.

With a perfectly blank facial expression and while continuing to stare over my shoulder, she said, "I'm not upset."

I could not believe what I had just heard. I wanted to shout, "What do you mean you're not upset? What's that stuff running down your face?" I managed to keep quiet and waited for my surge of impatience to diminish. When it did, I realized my question had not been specific enough. There was undeniable evidence. "What's making you cry?" I asked in my most sympathetic voice.

"I'm not crying!" she shot back even more quickly than when she had asserted she was not upset. She somehow managed to maintain her composure, even though a few more tears surged up and trickled down. She remained immobile. The box of tissues on the small table next to her remained untouched.

Jessica's mystifying inability to acknowledge she was upset with her mother raised a whole host of questions. What really motivated her? Was she trying to please her mother? Was she trying to be good? Was this how she felt loved? That she belonged? That she was accepted? More importantly, why did she seem a million miles away—psychologically—from the fact she was crying?

Whenever she struggled with making excuses for her mother's behavior, I started asking these questions. After I asked several and she seemed on the verge of saying something like, "I just want my mom to say that she appreciated all the work I did" and have a good cry, she would suddenly exclaim, "She's just doing the best she can!" A new rush of tears would then run down her face while she sat stone-faced. She would not reach for a tissue or say another word.

Obviously, the painful emotion the Fourth of July had triggered was not about to be resolved. Reluctantly, I placed her relationship with her mother in the same "to be solved later" category as her initial request and the several other problems I learned about.

A few sessions later, after I heard "My mom's just doing the best she can!" for what seemed like the umpteenth time, I said, "When is the first time in your life that you remember thinking that about your mother?"

Jessica immediately responded, "When I had to stay at my aunt's house for three years to take care of my grandmother."

One day, when Ellen was ten and Jessica was nine, Dorothy explained to her two oldest children that their Grandmother Thomas had a stroke. She was bed-ridden, could only make unintelligible sounds, and had to be fed and washed. Their grandmother was living with one of her daughters, Iris. Iris owned an auto repair shop. At the time, it was quite possibly the only female-owned shop in southeast Michigan, which was definitely the Auto Capital of the World then. She worked six days a week. She left well before seven in the morning and returned, quite exhausted, about twelve hours later. No one else in the Thomas family was available to help.

Dorothy reminded Ellen and Jessica—in case they had forgotten—their grandmother had unselfishly (at least in Dorothy's eyes) helped provide for them while she was struggling to survive as a single parent. Despite her best efforts, Dorothy was always desperately short of money and barely able to support her five children. Henry stubbornly refused to pay child support. Whenever Dorothy filed a motion for what was unpaid, the court allowed him to pay a paltry amount. Henry's mother gave her money quite often.

When Dorothy learned about Henry's mother, she told Iris that Ellen and Jessica could take turns staying at her house, one week at a time. Dorothy reassured her two daughters that they could continue to attend the same school, although they would have to take a different bus. Dorothy sent all of her children to the same parochial school. She helped pay for it by working in the school cafeteria.

Ellen was the first to spend a week at Iris's house. On her first day back home, she complained about not liking her aunt. After a few more weeks of staying there, she threw a tantrum and screamed, "I hate it there! There's nothing to do. It's so lonely!"

Dorothy then turned to Jessica. On a Sunday afternoon in the middle of the school year, Jessica moved into Iris's house for an extended stay. Even though the house dated from the mid-1930s, it had yet to be finished some thirty years later. Some of the walls were bare drywall, never having been painted or wallpapered, and there was no indoor plumbing. An outhouse sat nestled among some trees in the backyard. Her grandmother's bed was in a partitioned part of the dining room. She had to be helped to a makeshift chair alongside her bed that served as a commode. Water had to be hauled in buckets from an outside faucet at a relative's house across a small field or large drums in the back of Iris's pickup truck, if she remembered to fill them.

Before Jessica left for school in the morning, she made and fed grandmother breakfast. A neighbor prepared lunch. Jessica also made supper for herself and her grandmother. Even at close to ten years of age, she knew how to navigate her way around a kitchen and safely operate a gas stove. When Ellen and Jessica had been tall enough to reach into the kitchen sink, they had helped with the preparation of fruits and vegetables for canning and baking bread. Jessica's only companion, aside from her grandmother's little dog, was a male cousin. A year younger, he lived in the relative's house across the field. He was a regular visitor and came nearly every day, always with a full bucket. The two children had great fun together, mostly playing with the dog. Ellen thought he was too young.

Dorothy's last words to Jessica before she left on what would be a nearly three-year assignment were to "be good" and "do your homework." Jessica took the instructions to heart and decided being good also meant housecleaning, which her aunt sorely neglected.

One Saturday morning in early spring, Jessica decided the inside of the house was in severe need of an overhaul. She spent the whole day dusting, cleaning, scrubbing, vacuuming, and making everything as sparkling as she could. Iris arrived back in the evening with a girlfriend. When they entered, they suddenly stopped, looked around, and exclaimed the place had never looked so clean. As they stood admiring the new look, no one said a word to the small figure with bruised knuckles, sore knees, and aching muscles sitting off by herself. The two women ignored the agitated sounds coming from the bed in the dining room.

Jessica also did the laundry. Every Sunday, Iris drove her to the nearest Laundromat, about a mile away, with the week's load, detergent, and a pouch full of coins. When she was finished a few hours later, she called Iris. One Saturday morning, Mrs. Peters, the neighbor who helped with lunch, barged in and took the week's laundry to her place. She returned hours later with all of it freshly ironed.

On a sunny, summer Saturday, when Jessica went across the field with an empty bucket, she found her cousin on his way to a small park just on the other side of his house. He invited her to come along. She said she would go for a short while.

At the park, they met a few of his friends, a small group of boys and girls. Within a few minutes, two of the boys were pushing Jessica on a swing. They suddenly pressed harder against her back. She lost her grip, flew off, and landed awkwardly on her left arm. Sharp pain ripped her arm, but she acted as if nothing had happened. Managing to get to her feet, she hid her use of only one arm to get up. She yelled to the others that she had to get back home. Her cousin explained why.

At her cousin's house, she carefully filled the bucket and carried it with her good arm. Jessica was only supposed to call her aunt at work if there was an emergency with her grandmother or the house. She called her mother instead, but she was not home. Jessica left a message.

When her grandmother noticed Jessica was favoring her left arm, she squeezed out a noise that had the telltale sound of a question. Jessica just said she had hurt it and went about her chores, just more slowly. Her grandmother could only shake her head and make imploring sounds that Jessica ignored.

About two hours later, Dorothy called. She came right over. With Mrs. Peters agreeing to watch grandmother, Dorothy left with Jessica for the local hospital. There, Jessica's arm was put in a full cast. In a month, it could be replaced with one just for her forearm.

As they walked slowly out of the hospital into the late afternoon sun, Jessica waited—she could not somehow bring herself to ask—for her mother to say where they were going. She thought they might go home, but she was not sure. As they walked to the car, she did not say anything. After they were seated and Dorothy started the car, she said, "Well, at least it wasn't your good arm."

With that, they headed back to Iris's house. In Dorothy's mind, it seemed all Jessica had to do was to be good, keep an eye on her grandmother, do her homework, and stay out of the way.

When Dorothy let Jessica out, she said she would try to reach Iris later that night. If she couldn't, she would try in the morning after she got back from church. As Jessica squirmed her way out of the car, Dorothy's parting words were, "Now don't go lifting anything too heavy and cause further injury."

As Jessica made her way up the front walk, Mrs. Peters opened the front door. Dorothy waved from the car and drove away—without a word. Jessica and Mrs. Peters chatted for awhile about what had happened at the hospital. Before she left, Mrs. Peters made Jessica promise she would call if she needed help. Jessica thanked her, but she knew it would take two broken arms before she would ask for help. When she stepped into the dining room, a shrill shriek came from the bed on the other side. Jessica explained what had happened.

Later in the evening, Dorothy called and talked to Iris. After Iris hung up, she just repeated what Dorothy had said about not lifting anything too heavy. Iris never said what "too heavy" might be. That was left to Jessica to decide. She somehow found a way to do all of the chores. She even managed to help her grandmother to her chair with the use of her one good shoulder. She continued doing the laundry, even though Iris carried the baskets in and came back to help fold clothes. A month later, Dorothy took Jessica back to the hospital. The large cast was removed; a smaller one replaced it. A month later, that was removed, and her arm was pronounced healed.

Jessica's enforced captivity ended when one of the major auto companies hired Iris in a technical capacity. She then received enough medical insurance to hire a visiting nurse.

About ten years later, when her grandmother knew she had a short time to live, she profusely thanked her granddaughter for all of her tireless efforts from years ago in the halting speech she had since regained.

Over several sessions, I had to bombard Jessica with constant questions to overcome her reluctance to tell me all the heartbreaking details. At times, a few tears ran down her cheeks, but she never raised a hand to flick them away. Whenever I interrupted to ask Jessica about what seemed to be a very upsetting moment (for example, when Dorothy took her back to Iris's house from the hospital) and implored her to express her feelings, all she could manage was, "Someone had to help with my grandmother…My aunt couldn't quit her job."

When I heard all of these details, I was nearly overcome with contempt. This was slavery, or something very close to it. Whatever mix of feelings Dorothy had toward her mother-in-law had been played out in a macabre ritual with Jessica as the innocent victim. Maybe it all went back to Dorothy losing her mother at the age of six and being trained by her needle-tongued grandmother to be the woman of the house and mother to her sisters. What could be said about Iris taking shameless advantage of Jessica's goodness? No wonder this had been Jessica's immediate response to my question about her earliest memory.

"My mom's just doing the best she can!"

6

No Progress at Twice a Week

For three months, Jessica came for weekly sessions. She was always on time, poised confidently on the couch in the waiting area, and waiting for me to start the session. At the end of our first three months, I knew a lot more facts about her, only because I acted like a bloodhound sniffing out the tiniest leads. However, the real Jessica, the needing and wanting Jessica, remained as elusive as a mirage of water to someone lost in the desert.

When Jessica's therapy reached the three-month mark, she asked at the end of a session, just when I was expecting her to rise up and start to leave, if she could come twice a week. I almost fell off my chair. This was such an unexpected request. My experience with clients who did not like to discuss their feelings and seemed to regard that task as a thoroughly distasteful subject or unwelcome burden was not good. When someone decides to see a therapist, you would think the person would expect upsetting feelings (the main reason why most people see a therapist, even though most do not directly say it) to be the major focus. However, when these wannabe clients finished telling me about their problem and I started to ask about their feelings in order to begin the process of trying to help them, I usually saw a curled upper lip, eyes doubling in size, or even a flash of outright hostility. Obviously, these people were quite upset with me for not focusing on what they insisted was the problem, which was usually someone else's behavior or a situation neither one of us could realistically do anything about. I categorized all such people as *feeling-phobes*. I knew (in fact, I would bet a large sum of money on it) they would not stay in therapy for very long. Most never came back for a second session; others only came a few more times. I was surprised Jessica stuck it out this long, was always punctual, and never missed an appointment. I was not used to seeing this behavior from a feeling-phobe. Her request for two sessions a week only added to the mystery of who was sitting across from me.

Unsurprisingly, she did not say why she wanted to come more often, and I was not going to ask. I just knew, even though I was certain she would do her best to explain why, her answer would only add to my confusion about her. I just took her request at face value and assumed she knew better than I did about what she needed. I earnestly hoped her request signaled a readiness on her part to be more open about herself. That, however, quickly turned out to be wishful thinking on my part. I had to be as doggedly persistent as I had been, but now for two sessions a week.

After a few months of biweekly sessions, I decided a different approach—role-playing—was necessary. Role-plays are contrived situations meant to resemble real-life events. Because they are structured to make the person feel closer to such an event, they tend to evoke more emotion than when a person just talks about an experience that has already happened. They have the great advantage of allowing the therapist to make changes if an attempt at eliciting emotional release is not productive.

Nearly all of the present-day events Jessica talked about involved her mother or one of her sisters. The feeling that seemed to upset Jessica the most was other family members not doing their share. Whenever she spoke about such an event, she always shed some tears, just as she had when discussing the Fourth of July, but the tearing never progressed to anything more productive. While it was probably true that other family members were not doing their share, a deeper, unresolved issue must have made Jessica shoulder more than her share of the responsibility.

Whenever I asked Jessica what she thought the deeper feeling might be, some tears always trickled out. She could only say she was upset. After a minute, the tears ended, and the rush of emotion diminished.

Instead of asking her to talk, we stood, facing each other, while I asked her to imagine me as a family member. She was to say, "Do your share!" while simultaneously pushing me backward by my shoulders. After a few steps backward, I stepped right back in front of her, and she did it again. After a minute or two, her voice was a bit more indignant, her shove was a bit more vigorous, and bigger tears ran out in a steady stream. However, after ten minutes, the tears stopped, and the indignation lessened.

Role-playing was a part of every session for a month. I often tried it twice in the same session. The result was always the same: a steady trickle of tears and an indignant-sounding voice for ten to fifteen minutes.

Another role-play focused on Jessica's relationship with her mother. Jessica often felt her mother was criticizing her. Within a minute or two after she started talking about a recent incident with her mother, tears would roll down her cheeks. At that point, she always seemed on the verge of exclaiming, "I just want her to see me as a good person!" or something similar and have a good cry. Instead, she would suddenly end it all with, "She's just doing the best she can!" Then a new rush of tears ran down her face while she sat stone-faced. She did not reach for a tissue or say another word.

While I could only guess about the deeper feeling these words covered, their intensity was made unmistakably clear to me one day when I took the part of Dorothy. When I gave my best imitation of the look I imagined was on her face when she was in her criticizing mode, Jessica immediately shot up from her chair. With her face white and terror in her eyes, she exclaimed, "I have to get out of here!" She then headed for the door.

I immediately said, "Wait!" I quickly became myself, and Jessica stayed.

Her reaction completely surprised me. I had imitated a significant person in a client's life many times with many clients, but I had never seen anyone look as terrified as Jessica. I had no idea why she was so scared. I could not understand how a stern look (and I did not think I had overdone it) could terrify an adult human being so much.

Jessica gave another idea for a role-play. She described an upsetting interaction with another person. Details about who said and did what rolled effortlessly out of her mouth, usually accompanied by a steady but trickling flow of tears. After awhile, I realized, although she went into extensive detail, I had never heard her say what she needed or wanted from the other person. Always implied, but never stated, it was just like her answer to my very first question to her.

I modeled a beaming face and outstretched arms for her. Fully confident, I said, "I need you!" I encouraged her to imitate my performance and do it as if she really meant it. Her eyes immediately glazed over. She could only manage a wooden, "I can't do that." I tried it every session for a few weeks, but I got the same result every time.

I finally had to ask directly, "What do you want from your mother?"

Her immediate response was, "Nothing!" Then she stared over my shoulder with a blank look.

A surge of frustration rose in my body. I wanted to wave my arms in the air and exclaim, "What do you mean you don't want anything from your mother!"

I waited for my frustration to lessen so I could respond in a more helpful way. "Does your mother ever give you a compliment or say something nice?"

After a few moments, Jessica mumbled, "She usually says thank you if I've done something."

"Is that enough for you?"

In a subdued voice, Jessica could only say, "I don't know."

I again wanted to exclaim, "What do you mean you don't know?" Instead, I said, "Does your mother ever do anything or say anything that makes you feel really good?"

In a subdued voice, she again said, "I don't know."

"Don't you ever hope she'll say something like 'I really appreciated you're doing that' or 'That was a really thoughtful thing you did.' Does she ever just give you a hug because she just feels like giving you a hug?"

For my efforts, she only quietly said, "I don't know."

I suddenly felt very sad for Jessica. Didn't she know what she needed from her mother? Didn't she want to feel loved, wanted, or appreciated? Didn't she want to feel she belonged? Didn't she want to be seen as a good, worthwhile person? Didn't everyone want this?

Even patients with long-term serious psychological difficulties I worked with in psychiatric hospitals let me know what they needed. When I was in graduate school, I worked as an aide on a psychiatric ward to supplement my schools loans. Avery was in his fifties and had been in the hospital for most of his adult life. Other staff that had known him far longer could not remember hearing him say a word, although he seemed to understand whatever was said to him. Whenever I first saw him during the day, I always said, "Hi, Avery." He always stared directly into my eyes for a bit. He never said a word, but he blinked his eyes a few times before walking away. If he was near me, I would sometimes say, "Avery, could you sit over there for a minute? I need to sweep here" or, "Avery, could you hold the dustpan?" I always said his name when I spoke to him.

After a month, I was transferred to another floor for two months and did not have any contact with him, although I am sure he saw me when we took the patients outside for their recreation time. On my first day back in Avery's ward, I stepped just inside the door at the end of a long corridor. The day room, where most of the patients spent their time, was at the other end. When Avery spotted me, he immediately got up from his chair and slowly walked down the hallway toward me. He stopped a few steps away from me. I took that as a sign that we were close enough, and I stopped walking. I said, "Hi, Avery." He stared at me for a few seconds, blinked his eyes a few times, turned around, and walked back.

This was Avery's way of saying he missed me. I expected this very indirect, awkward attempt at communicating needs from people with severe psychological conditions. Jessica obviously was not like that. Yet, she was more secretive about what she needed than anyone I had ever worked with. I had to assume she was doing the very best she possibly could, even if it was the equivalent of using her elbow to point to the back of her neck to say, "This is how I hurt." It was my task to figure out what the underlying hurt was.

7

Dorothy Tries to Help

One day a few months after Jessica asked to come twice a week, I was sitting in my office catching up on my records when Dorothy called. She was about the last person in the world I expected to hear from.

In the same breath she used to identify herself, she asked if she could come in and tell me about an incident from Jessica's childhood "because it may have something to do with why she can't stay home at night." My interest was piqued. Even so, there was a momentary urge to quickly interrupt her with, "I know you want to be helpful, but I'm wondering if you should get Jessica's permission?" However, my urge to follow standard protocol was not nearly as strong as my curiosity to learn something that might make Jessica less of an enigma.

Two days later, in the morning of the day I was to see Jessica again, I found Dorothy in the waiting area. She was perched somewhat precariously on the front edge of the couch. I knew immediately it was she because of the striking physical appearance to her daughter. Both were about the same height. They were somewhat on the large-boned side and had a broad face and high cheekbones. When I walked over and introduced myself, she quickly explained she was afraid she would have too much difficulty getting up if she had let herself sink into the soft cushions because of her arthritis.

"Give me a moment or two to get up," she said.

She leaned forward a bit, pushed against the edge of the cushions with her hands, and slowly stood. I led the way to my office. Behind me, I heard the faint shuffle of one shoe against the carpet.

I held the door open for her and motioned to a chair. I watched her favor one side of her body as she maneuvered her way over there. She slowly turned around and sat down.

"It's my right hip," she explained.

Her words then and in the waiting room did not have the tone of an apology or seem to be an implied request for any assistance. She was simply stating a fact about her physical condition, and this was the best she could do. If she needed any help, she would ask.

When Dorothy made herself as comfortable as she could while sitting with a slight sideways lean, she looked me straight in the eyes.

"Something happened to Jessica when she was thirteen years old you need to know about. I'm sure she's never told you because I've never heard her talk about it since." With a sad shaking of her head, she added, "Jessica never talks about anything that upsets her. The child guidance clinic I took her to at the time couldn't get her to talk either. Maybe you can."

With that, Dorothy launched into her story. One day, she found her lying on her back on the small throw rug in her room. Her hands rested protectively on the sides of her lower abdomen, and her eyelids were squeezed tightly shut.

"I knew immediately what the problem was. I told her I was taking her right over to Bayview."

Dorothy helped her daughter up and guided her out of the house and into the car. She did not hear a whimper. In ten minutes, they were at the small hospital, one town over from Bayport, more into suburbia. Dorothy drove right to the emergency entrance. She escorted Jessica inside and told her to have a seat in the small waiting area. In a few minutes, she was back.

"They said about fifteen minutes. I couldn't get them to see you right away."

Jessica nodded her head and closed her eyes. A nurse came about ten minutes later and asked Jessica to follow her.

"I piped right up and asked to go in with her, but the nurse said the doctor wanted to see Jessica by herself, and he would talk to me afterwards. I didn't see Jessica again until they told me I could go back there. When I walked in, Jessica was getting dressed. She said the doctor had just left and the nurse had left a few minutes before that. I asked if the doctor wanted to talk to me. Jessica said, 'He told me to tell you he had an emergency and he would call you later.'

"I asked what he said, but Jessica repeated what she had just said. She added he came back after the nurse left and gave her a shot. The doctor didn't explain what the shot was for. I thought that was very strange. I really wanted to talk to him, but I wanted to get Jessica home. Even though she said she felt okay, I thought she looked very tired. I know my daughter well enough to know she never complains about anything. She's always been the exact opposite of Ellen."

An attendant came with a wheelchair. With Dorothy leading, they made their way to the car. By the time Jessica was situated in the front seat, Dorothy noticed she was struggling to keep her eyes open.

"I pumped her for more information as quickly as I could. Before she fell asleep, she told me the doctor had nicked her skin with one of his instruments. My God! She wasn't there for surgery! He had asked if she had a boyfriend and, would you believe it, if she was pregnant. I told Jessica to stay put. I opened the windows a bit to let air in, locked the doors, and rushed back. I could walk at a normal pace back then," she added, as if to reassure me that she had not wasted precious time.

Dorothy pounced on the first employee she saw sitting behind a desk and demanded she page the doctor. That employee paged him several times over the next few minutes, but the doctor never answered. After a few more phone calls, the person reported that Dr. Woods had left the hospital. Dorothy asked to speak with the hospital administrator, but a quick phone call revealed he was at an out-of-town conference. Dorothy found the nearest pay phone and called Dr. Frank, the Thomas's longtime family doctor, to explain the situation. He offered to call the hospital administrator in the morning. Later that morning, the administrator called Dorothy and asked her to tell him what had happened. Two days later, he called back to apologize for the way Jessica had been treated and to let her know that Dr. Woods had been dismissed because of the hospital receiving too many complaints about his behavior with young, female patients.

"They should have never hired that doctor. No one should be allowed to practice and treat patients like that, especially young girls. The reason I think more happened than Jessica ever told me is because she started acting strangely that evening."

Early that evening, Dorothy told Ellen and Jessica, who were in their room doing homework, she was going across the street for just a little while to visit a neighbor. As she started to walk away, Jessica suddenly exclaimed, "Can I come?"

"I didn't know what to make of it. Jessica had never acted like that. She had always been so responsible and did whatever I asked her to do, usually more than I asked. I reminded her that I was only going across the street and I wouldn't be long. But she insisted on coming.

"I told her this was the safest neighborhood we'd ever lived in. If anyone knocked, first ask who it is. If you don't know the person, don't open the door. Call Christine's house, and I'll be right over."

However, when she kept insisting, I reminded her again I would be back as soon as I could.

"I was back in a half hour. When I stepped into the living room, Jessica was sitting in a chair, staring at me. She looked like she had seen a ghost. I had never seen her look so frightened. Before I could catch my breath, she said, 'Are you okay?'

"I…I didn't know what to say or why she was even asking. I just said, 'Of course, I'm okay.' I asked if she'd finished her homework. I never graduated from high school, so I made sure all my children got their homework done."

Over the next week, there were several more episodes of Jessica pleading to go with her mother when she visited her neighbor. By this time, Dorothy had stopped trying to reason with her and simply said, "I don't want to hear anymore!"

"Later that evening, I came upon Jessica in the bathroom. Her hand was slightly cupped and heading toward her mouth. I asked if she was okay. She said she had a headache and was taking an aspirin. I thought I had seen more than one pill go into her mouth. I just reminded her not to take too many."

◆   ◆   ◆

Starting at age six, the morning after the night Dorothy hired a male babysitter for the only time in her life, a neighbor's sixteen-year-old son, Jessica had suffered from body-headaches. A throbbing pain was deep in her head, as if a malevolent spirit was living inside of her and was trying to split her skull open with a jackhammer. For seconds at a time, her vision became blurry. She felt sick to her stomach, but she rarely threw up. Her skin felt on fire whenever anything rubbed against it, even her clothes. Thoughts raced around in her head, making her mind feel as if it was careening around a racetrack and about to spin off into chaos. Just when she felt she was about to lose all control and scream in unbridled panic that she could not stand it any longer, a blank countenance appeared on her face.

Jessica was prone to having these attacks once or twice a month. They could last as long as three days. She often snuck into the bathroom and gulped up to six maximum-strength pain pills at once. Jessica never told her mother about these strange symptoms. She was well-acquainted with Dorothy's reaction when any of her children complained about anything.

"God never gives people too much to handle. If you're having a problem, you're not trying hard enough to solve it. I'm doing all I can to help you kids. If you're not happy, there isn't anything I can do about it."

◆   ◆   ◆

A few days after Jessica pleaded with her mother to go with her when she visited her neighbor, the school notified Dorothy that Jessica was having episodes of staring off into space. She was also having difficulty concentrating on her work. Dorothy could only remind Jessica she was sending all of her children to a parochial school so they could get a good education, which she did not have, and she was working in the school cafeteria to help pay for it.

A week later, Dorothy took Jessica for a regular checkup with Dr. Frank. In the waiting room, Dorothy had just finished exchanging little smiles with another mother when Jessica leaned toward her and whispered, "I don't want to go in!"

"I was completely shocked. Jessica had never been afraid of Dr. Frank, nor had my other two daughters. I chose him because I completely trusted him. He would never do anything to hurt or embarrass any female. I didn't want to have a scene in the waiting room, so I told Jessica I'd go in with her. When we were called, Jessica didn't stand right away. She had this horrified look on her face, but she followed me in.

"Dr. Frank was his usual, friendly self. He spoke to Jessica directly and expected her to answer for herself. When he was finished with his questions about her health since her last visit, he said, 'Well, let's go inside and have a look at you.' He then got up and headed for the examining room. Jessica sat where she was. Then she nearly hissed at me, insisting she didn't want to go.

"I don't mind telling you that I was fed up. I grabbed her under the shoulder and yanked her forward. She insisted I go first. So I did, anything to get her in there.

"When Dr. Frank touched Jessica with his hand or an instrument, I swear her body shrank back ever so slightly. That horrified look came over her. If Dr. Frank noticed anything, he didn't say so. When he was finished, he pronounced her healthy, and we left.

"In the car, I started scolding her. I admit that I couldn't help myself. I didn't know what else to do. I said, 'What is the matter with you? You've seen Dr. Frank since you were an infant. He's never hurt or embarrassed you. I don't understand what you're afraid of. What has got…' Then it suddenly dawned on me. Dr. Frank was a man. Dr. Woods was a man. He must have done something that Jessica wasn't telling me. Maybe that was why he gave her that shot, to make her forget."

As soon as they were home, Dorothy called Dr. Frank, explained Jessica's behavior since her experience at the hospital, and asked if he knew of a psychological clinic for teenagers. Dr. Frank thought counseling was an excellent idea. There was a child guidance clinic in a small building behind Bayview hospital.

"That evening, I told Jessica I had made an appointment for her. Both Dr. Frank and I thought she needed to talk with someone about what had happened with Dr. Woods. I reminded her that, even though we had to go back to Bayview, we'd be in another building and Dr. Woods wasn't even there anymore. I told her she would be seeing Ms. Haskill, a social worker. I'd already spoken with her on the phone, and she sounded very nice. I told her it was in two days. I'd pick her up after school."

◆   ◆   ◆

With Dorothy's last words, emergency alarms went off in Jessica's mind. Her mother was very worried. She had even called other people for help. Whatever Jessica was doing had to stop—immediately. It felt like her life depended on it.

While Jessica was nodding her head in agreement, she was already deciding on her reason for agreeing to see a counselor. It was not a reason that Dorothy, Dr. Frank, or Ms. Haskill would approve of. In fact, if they knew, they would have seen it as a sure sign that Jessica did need counseling.

One thought consumed Jessica's mind: be good. If her mother was upset, there could be only one reason. She was not trying hard enough. She would have to try harder. She was very sorry she was causing a problem for her mother and making her worry. She did not mean to.

◆   ◆   ◆

"The moment I told Jessica about the appointment, she changed back to the responsible-acting child I had always known. She stopped worrying about me. That horrified look went away. She was more helpful around the house. She went back to asking me if she could do anything and doing things before I even asked her. It was like magic.

"When I picked her up at school, she slid right into the front seat, looking eager to go. I reassured her anyway and said, 'Now, Jessica, there's nothing to worry about. All that...' She cut me off before I could finish. She said, 'I'm not worried. All that Ms. Haskill is going to talk with me about is Dr. Woods.' I can't tell you how relieved I was to hear that."

◆   ◆   ◆

While Dorothy was ecstatic about how relaxed her daughter seemed, Jessica was deep in thought. It was time for the next step in her plan. She was trying to figure out how to be a good client. She was only going to counseling so her mother would stop worrying about her. She did not want to be the cause of anyone feeling bad. She did not even want Ms. Haskill to worry about her.

◆   ◆   ◆

Dorothy parked in front of the small building behind the hospital. Jessica jumped out and led the way. She reached the entrance first, opened the big glass doors, and walked in. Dorothy was a step behind.

Jessica quickly surveyed the area and went directly to the receptionist. She said, "I'm Jessica Thomas. I have an appointment with Ms. Haskill."

The receptionist smiled and said, "I'll tell her you're here. You and your mother can sit over there if you'd like." She pointed to some chairs on the other side of the room. "Ms. Haskill should be out in a few minutes."

In this waiting room, Jessica was the exact opposite of how she had been in Dr. Frank's office. Poised confidently on her chair, she gave her mother a reassuring smile. A few minutes later, a middle-aged woman dressed in a pantsuit, a sign of the times, came into the waiting area.

"I'm Ms. Haskill," she said first to Dorothy. As she shifted her attention, she then said, "You must be Jessica. Would you like to come with me?"

◆   ◆   ◆

Jessica stood quickly. Without looking at Dorothy, she followed Ms. Haskill. Inside her office, she pointed to a chair alongside her desk. Jessica smoothed out her blue, school-regulation skirt as she sat down and smartly folded her hands in her lap. She kept her feet and knees close together. She looked directly into Ms. Haskill's eyes and waited.

Ms. Haskill was fully prepared to discharge her professional responsibility of assessing the problem and helping her client feel better. She was unaware the client sitting alongside her desk was secretly poised to do exactly that for her.

An experienced counselor, Ms. Haskill started slowly, "Well, how are you doing this afternoon?"

Jessica confidently said, "Fine." Silence followed.

Ms. Haskill proceeded to ask questions about Jessica's present life. In this first session, she did not ask for any information she had learned from Dorothy. Jessica readily answered all of the questions. She did not give simple yes or no answers, but she did provide as complete of an answer as she thought was expected. She did not volunteer information Ms. Haskill did not ask for. Jessica spoke calmly, as if she was having a pleasant conversation.

At the end of the session, Ms. Haskill said, "I'd like to have another chance to talk with you. Would you like to come back?"

Jessica smiled and said, "Yes." Whatever Ms. Haskill wanted was fine.

◆   ◆   ◆

In the waiting room, Ms. Haskill said to Dorothy, "Can you bring Jessica back the same time next week?"

"Certainly."

Reassuring smiles were exchanged.

As soon as Dorothy and Jessica were in the car, Dorothy asked, "Well, how was it?"

"Okay." Jessica glanced at her mother and smiled.

Dorothy accepted the answer and the smile.

◆   ◆   ◆

Over the next few sessions, Ms. Haskill asked Jessica many questions and invited her to talk about different areas of her life. She was a patient listener and tried understanding fully what Jessica said. She did not interrupt or criticize.

Having another person relate to her in this way was a new experience for Jessica. However, it did not change her goal of being a good client. Ms. Haskill's patient listening and nonjudgmental attitude only made this an easier task, much easier than with her mother. It was easier for Jessica to figure out what Ms. Haskill wanted, and she did not have to try as hard to be good. With her mother, both were a constant struggle.

A month of weekly sessions went by before Ms. Haskill asked Jessica about her mother's concerns. When she said, "Tell me what happened with Dr. Woods?" Jessica was well-prepared.

"Dr. Woods examined me while a nurse was present. He nicked my skin and made it bleed for a few minutes. He thought I had a boyfriend and I might be pregnant. I didn't—and don't—have a boyfriend. He gave me a shot, which made me very sleepy." Finished, Jessica stared at Ms. Haskill, waiting to discover what else she wanted to know about.

Ms. Haskill had to ask, "Did Dr. Woods hurt you?"

"Only when he nicked my skin."

"Did any of his questions frighten you?"

"No, I just didn't understand why he was asking some of them."

"Did he do anything that made you angry?"

"No, I just didn't think he was a very nice person."

"How did you feel after the exam was over?"

"Sleepy."

"You didn't feel afraid of anything?"

"No."

Ms. Haskill feared Jessica was giving these short answers because the questions were making her too anxious. So, she returned to issues that did not cause anxiety: school and friends.

Several weeks later, Ms. Haskill returned to Dorothy's concerns. She said, "When your mother called us, she was worried that what had happened with Dr. Woods had made you afraid." Ms. Haskill looked at Jessica expectantly.

Jessica stared back. She was waiting for a question.

"Did Dr. Woods make you feel afraid of men or anything else?"

"No."

"Your mother thought you were afraid of being examined by Dr. Frank." Ms. Haskill stared at Jessica.

There was no response.

"Were you afraid of Dr. Frank?"

Jessica had a ready answer, as if she had been anticipating the question. "Dr. Frank always says what he's going to do before he does anything. Dr. Woods never explained anything. I wasn't sure if Dr. Frank was going to start acting like Dr. Woods."

The experienced Ms. Haskill quickly noted her client had not answered her question. She tried again, "Were you afraid Dr. Frank was going to hurt you?"

Jessica was ready with a reply. "I really didn't think he would because he never had."

Again, Ms. Haskill made the same mental note to herself. She tried a slightly different approach.

"A day or so after seeing Dr. Frank, when your mother left the house in the evening, why did you want to go with her?"

"I don't like being with my sister, Ellen, when my mom isn't there. She and my mom yell at each other a lot. When my mom is gone, Ellen rants and raves about how much she hates her. She yells at my brothers and other sister the same way my mom does."

Ms. Haskill saw Jessica a few more times.

◆   ◆   ◆

After four months of weekly sessions, Ms. Haskill called Dorothy and said she did not need to see Jessica anymore. She had not been able to find any fears of any kind. She thought Dr. Woods had probably frightened her, and some fears just seem to go away on their own.

A letter arrived a few days later. When Dorothy showed it to Jessica, two sentences jumped out at her: "We were unable to find any problem that required counseling" and "We think Jessica is a well-adjusted young lady."

◆   ◆   ◆

Jessica was greatly relieved. She had accomplished her goal. She had been the perfect client. She had not made anyone worry about her.

◆   ◆   ◆

Dorothy told me this in about thirty minutes. She spoke quickly, as if she had often thought about this since it had happened. I mainly listened, made a few supportive comments, and asked a few brief questions. She did not seem to need anymore from me to continue.

When she was finished, she said, "Well, that's all I wanted to tell you. I still think more happened with that doctor than she has ever told me or anyone else. Why else would a female be afraid of being alone at night?"

With that, Dorothy gathered her purse and started to leave. I thanked her for coming. Obviously, she was genuinely concerned about Jessica. She tried doing what she thought was best for her children. It was also obvious why Jessica was reluctant to confide in her. Because these details were news to me (Jessica had not mentioned a word about them) I filed them away in my mind for future reference. I did not intend to tell Jessica that I had seen her mother and assumed Dorothy would not tell her either.

8

Jeffrey's Delusion

Two sessions later, the instant Jessica sat down, she said, "Did my mother call you?" I knew from her tone of voice she already knew the answer.

"Yes, she did," I quietly acknowledged, while I held my breath. If Jessica was not going to ask if her mother had come to my office, I was not going to volunteer that information. She was already quite irritated over the situation.

"Okay, what did she say?"

I spoke very briefly and only gave the basic facts. Several times during the short time I spoke, she shook her head in disgust, as if to say her mother must have been mistaken. She was quite annoyed at me for not telling her immediately. I did not blame her. I knew I should have politely, but firmly, interrupted Dorothy. However, at the time, I was torn between learning some useful information about Jessica (information she was not willing—or ready—to reveal) and talking behind her back.

After Jessica was over her initial rush of anger at both her mother and me, she filled me in on her own version.

"That intern was nothing more than a robot with an attitude. I was nothing more than a body he had to fix."

"After he grunted his name at me, he ordered me to get on the table and put my feet in the stirrups. When he cut me, all he did was mutter something unintelligible. While he held a piece of cotton against the spot, he asked if I had a boyfriend. He made it sound like having one was a crime. I didn't say anything because I couldn't understand what that had to do with my being there. When I didn't speak up right away, he demanded to know what my boyfriend and I did when we were alone. He didn't wait for me to give an answer. He then asked if I was pregnant! All I could think to say to that idiot was, 'You should know the answer to that!' Then he told me to get dressed, and he excused the nurse. He came back a few minutes later with the biggest syringe I had ever seen. He didn't say a word. He just swabbed a spot on my arm and stuck it in. That must have been what made me so sleepy.

"I think my mom had every right to go back in. If it was my daughter, I would have done the same thing. But she's way out of line in thinking the doctor made me afraid of men or being away from her at night. My mom's arthritis was getting worse, especially in her hands and knees. She could barely drive anymore, and she stopped doing upholstery work. I was worried about her all the time, more so at night. Ellen was very serious about living with our dad because she and my mom were having really awful fights. If my mom got hurt and Ellen wasn't there, I'd be left to take care of everyone. I was also worried I might have to quit school, just like my mom did."

Without pausing, Jessica moved onto her appointment with Dr. Frank.

"When we were in Dr. Frank's waiting room, I may have been a little afraid of seeing him, even though he'd never done anything to make me feel that way. But I wasn't afraid of him in the way my mom made it sound. I just wanted to make sure Dr. Frank wasn't going to start acting the way that idiot doctor had. That's why I asked my mom to come in with me.

"When she told me she had made an appointment at the child guidance clinic, I knew I had to go. It was useless to argue with her once she made her mind up. I saw a woman social worker once a week for four months. I don't remember much about what we talked about. We just chatted about everyday things. She was a nice person to talk to. The only thing that sticks in my mind was the letter she sent to my mom. In it, she said she couldn't find any evidence of my being afraid of men or being away from my mom. I was also a well-adjusted young lady."

When Jessica was finished, she stared at me. While I was certain she was being as open as she could be and she was not deliberately trying to deceive me about anything, I tended to believe what Dorothy had told me. Back then, all of this had continued for a few weeks. I did not think Dorothy could be that mistaken about Jessica's behavior over all that time. While I did not think the incident with the intern was traumatic enough to account for Jessica's intense level of anxiety over being away from her mother or not wanting to be alone with Dr. Frank, I was certain it triggered unresolved feelings about an earlier experience in her life. So I did not question her about it. Ms. Haskill's conclusion certainly did not surprise me. Jessica had become an expert at concealing upsetting feelings a very long time ago.

This new information about Jessica was definitely interesting. It troubled me that she had not volunteered any of it. She had been forced to tell me because of her mother. After a few sessions of following our usual format of me asking questions and Jessica taking her direction from that, the events from ten years ago were not obviously going to cause any dramatic change in her therapy.

While we settled back into our predictable (and increasingly frustrating) routine, I knew I had to do something about Jessica continuing to be so guarded about herself. A foolish urge to ask her about this flew out of my mind even faster than it entered. After a few weeks of keeping this in the forefront of my mind, I finally developed what I thought was a rather creative idea. In acting on it, I made an unexpected discovery: I had been laboring under a delusion about who was sitting across from me all these months. I had been deluded from the moment she first stepped into my office.

I knew the key to resolving any fear Jessica had was, at least in words, quite simple. I had to help her release enough of the unresolved emotion that had been locked in place ever since the upsetting event happened. In actual practice, it usually took persistence, patience, and creativity on the part of the therapist. My only success at gaining access to the place in Jessica's psyche holding unresolved feelings was prodding into the relationship with her mother. I never thought her fear of staying home was rooted in any experiences with Dorothy, at least any I was aware of. However, that was the only avenue I had for getting into Jessica's huge reservoir of untapped feelings, a reservoir I often pictured as an impregnable, bombproof shelter. I was growing weary of incessantly questioning her about her mother and getting nowhere. Hopefully, making use of another ongoing relationship in her life might be more successful. It was one I could monitor as we talked about it. That other relationship was ours. After all of these months, she must have some kind of feeling about me trying to get to know her. After all, she was a human being. Human beings have needs, don't they?

One day, after Jessica finished venting her feelings about whatever had troubled her since the last session, I gave her a warm smile and said, "How do you feel about me trying to get to know you?"

I sprang this tactic on her without any warning for a very specific reason. Hopefully, it would force her to react on the spot before her defenses had a chance to get organized. I was tired of listening to reports of incidents that had already happened, after her psyche had transformed the whole experience into a sterile, emotional account.

There was a potential risk. Most people who make the decision to seek therapy have suffered from a large amount of emotional neglect in their lives, as do many who do not seek therapy. While such neglect is not usually the reason people give for seeking therapy, the psychological effect of such experience is apparent to any skilled therapist. The specific danger in asking this kind of a question is that the client, particularly someone of the opposite sex, might interpret it as an invitation for a personal relationship, something that is an aching hole in the psychological makeup of anyone who has suffered from a large amount of emotional neglect. I most definitely would not ask this question of certain clients, especially the woman who was unhappily married and invited me to her home for lunch. When I tactfully explained why I could not, she brought me a homemade lunch the next week. I would have not asked the woman seeking a divorce who invited me to her birthday party to be held on a Saturday night. I later learned the invited guests totaled one—me. However, because Jessica was so far removed from her basic needs, I thought the chances of her misinterpreting my question were about the same as a match igniting in a hurricane.

Even though I never asked Jessica anything even remotely similar to this and did surprise her, she had an immediate reply, as if she had been expecting my question from the very start and had been steeling herself for this eventuality ever since.

"You're simply a computer," she quickly began. She sounded like a professor who was impatiently explaining a fundamental point to an obtuse student. "You're just a thing I put information into and get a program back. You can't be human. You can't have any feelings." Then her words stopped as abruptly as they had started. She blankly stared at me.

A million lightbulbs went off in my head. I immediately thought, "No wonder I've had such a hard time reaching her. In her mind, I'm not a person. I'm just a pile of electrical parts!"

When Jessica looked at me, did she see that I was a human being? Of course she did. That reality was not enough for her to overcome her fear about relating to me as a human being. Why she was not able to do that was beyond my comprehension. I just could not understand how she could see me as something other than human after months of unrelenting effort on my part to reach her. Her chilling answer was one I would have expected from a robot, not from someone who functioned in society, talked face-to-face to me, and, aside from her inability to stay home at night and fear of driving, behaved like an ordinary person. I had never felt so estranged from a human being in my life.

I was certain no one in her life had ever asked her the question I had just asked. If anyone had, Jessica's answer—cold, crisp, and fired like bullets—would certainly have driven that person out of her life forever.

Despite her icy reply to my question, I did take some solace in the fact that my attempt to jump-start her therapy had at least caused her to spew out her startling response. I had to ask one more question, even though I was almost certain I would not receive any answer from her, at least any relevant answer.

I asked, "Why can't I have any feelings?" I hoped she would not say the obvious answer, "How can you? You're just a computer." She didn't.

She had another immediate reply, "Because humans have hurt me. If you have feelings, it means you're human. If you're human, you could hurt me."

She spoke with the certainty that this was a condition she had known all of her life, so it seemed there was no reason in her mind to even consider an alternative. I encouraged her to tell me more about people hurting her. For once, she did not have a ready answer.

She hesitated a bit before saying in a subdued voice, "People have just given me a hard time." A few tears then trickled out, which she let dribble down her face. She ignored them and the tissue box. She stared at me.

Although this attempt to inject some movement into Jessica's therapy had not produced a breakthrough, I was not finished with taking more active measures. Her interminable responses of "so-so" or "about the same" to my opening question of "How are you doing?" and her waiting for me to suggest a topic had finally reached the limit of my frustration. At the start of sessions, I began waiting a little after she gave her usual reply to my opening question. I just pleasantly stared at her, silently inviting her to say something.

The first time I did this, she gave a quick, impatient response. "Well, what would you like me to talk about?"

The first few times she did this, I sprang to her invitation. I was relieved to have any initiative from her and suggested something. Jessica talked for awhile about each suggestion. She sometimes even shed a few tears toward the end of the time. She then stopped talking shortly after the tears appeared and stared.

When I again sat silent, she came right back with, "Well, what else would you like me to talk about?"

When she came to the end of whatever I mentioned, I knew exactly what was coming if I did not suggest something quickly. After a few weeks, my new idea had only created another monotonous, repetitive, unproductive way to start a session. I finally had no choice except confronting her obvious dependence on me. The next time she fired the question at me, I was armed with several responses: "What are you feeling that makes you ask me what to talk about? What feels hard about you picking a topic? In what way is it easier if I do the choosing?"

To these questions, which I tried over a few sessions, Jessica could only respond with her habitual, familiar "I don't know" or "I don't know how to answer that." She then stared at me. When she did, I had no choice but suggesting a topic.

I began dreading the start of a session. From the instant I rose from my chair to walk down the hallway to see if she was perched in her usual spot on the end of the couch, my nerves started feeling like a plucked, piano wire. A sense of dread descended like suffocating, volcanic ash over my spirit. An impulse to say, "Well, are you going to ask your question again?" nearly overcame me. Despite this emotional torment, I was not about to acknowledge defeat. Whatever I struggled with paled in comparison to whatever Jessica was doing battle with. In always showing up and being punctual, she was asking for help in the only way she knew how. I always greeted her with a cheerful, "Hi!"

While I escorted her to my office, I had to make a conscious effort to keep my urge in check. Even before we sat down, I fantasized what might happen if she asked the question again. One scenario had me jumping straight up from my chair, throwing my hands in the air, and pleading, "Stop! I can't stand it! Please! No more!" In another scenario, I suddenly excused myself and dashed for the bathroom down the hall. Inside, I would bang my head against the tile walls, trying to exorcise my feeling of utter frustration.

When the weariness in Jessica's voice whenever she asked me the dreaded question began speaking louder than her actual words, I knew I had to do something. We—I—could not possibly continue this way. I could only think of one idea, a last resort. If our next session began with her usual question, I would not say a word or nod my head. I would simply stare at her with an interested, inviting countenance and wait.

For all its seeming innocence, this idea entailed a great risk. I was going to force her to directly confront the fear that was causing her to robotically ask, "Well, what..." It could cause her to be so anxious that she would not come back.

I was certainly aware of all this, but I did not know what else to do. I was desperate, and I knew it. As a partial rationalization, I reminded myself that I was only asking her to make a decision about what she wanted to talk about. I fully expected this would indeed make her anxious. How anxious could she be? After all, what could possibly be so frightening about deciding what to talk about?

When she next promptly sat down in her chair and, after a few moments of my warm, silent stare, she began, as I had feared, to ask the dreaded question. I kept smiling and stared back. I continued doing that when she asked her question a second and a third time.

With a hint of aggravation in her voice, she finally said, "I saw my mom yesterday. Do you want me to talk about that?"

I said nothing. After a bit, she proceeded to talk about a disagreement with her mother. She spoke for several minutes without any tears and a lot of emotion. She stopped. I said nothing and stared, invitingly.

After several seconds, with a slight rise in anxiety in her voice, she said, "I had an argument with Roger. Do you want me to talk about it?"

I remained silent. She then proceeded to talk about the incident for a few minutes in the same mechanical, non-feeling way she talked about her mother. She then stopped. I waited.

A few moments later, with more of a rush to her words, she declared, "My sister did something the other day I didn't like. Do you want me to talk about it?"

I said nothing. She talked about her sister in the same way. She then stopped. I waited. She volunteered another topic or two and talked about each for a few minutes in the same way. All the while, I said nothing and maintained an inviting expression.

When she was finished with her last idea, she stared at me for what felt like an eternity, although it was probably no more than a few moments.

"What do you want me to do?" she finally exclaimed.

Fear saturated her voice in a way I had never heard. A part of me wanted to jump in and give her something to talk about. It was so heartbreaking to see her struggle with something so basically human. Nonetheless, I kept silent, restraining myself from even saying, "Anything you want!"

The pupils in her eyes then suddenly multiplied in size. There was a sharp intake of breath, and her face froze in terror. I was on the edge of my chair. Holding my breath, I hoped and prayed I would finally be given a clue to the source of the terror. Without a word, she ran out of my office, leaving the door open. I wanted to hurry after her, but I did not want to cause an embarrassing scene.

Instead, I waited in my office. Maybe she would return when the rush of emotion lessened. I heard her hurry down the hallway. I then heard faint footsteps across the slate floor of the waiting area. The front door opened and closed. My worst fear had come true. I had frightened her. Badly. The terror lurking behind her inability to simply decide what to talk about was beyond my comprehension.

When I called my answering service the next morning, there was not any message from her. Later in the afternoon, when she was finished with childcare, I called. Roger answered.

"Can I speak with Jessica?" I asked.

He said, "She doesn't want to talk to you." He spoke calmly, not angrily or defiantly. He did not hang up to end the conversation.

I quickly asked, "Can you put her on the phone?"

She came right away. I immediately apologized for scaring her. Nearly as quickly, she said she wanted to come back. However, I had to promise I would not do that again. I promised.

Jessica did come for her next appointment and was punctual as usual. I was not surprised. Even though she had initially not wanted to talk to me when I had called, she had come to the phone quickly. Clearly, she had been thinking about what had happened and what reassurance she needed. From somewhere deep inside, she was asking for help and saying it as loudly as she could. Her coming was just another indication of how determined she was. As soon as she was in my office, I apologized again for having made the last session so difficult for her.

Although we weathered a crisis in our relationship, there was a fracture in its foundation that needed to be healed. For progress to happen, Jessica had to experience one feeling above all others: safety. That is, I would not do anything to make her too frightened or too anxious. That had been seriously compromised. It had to be restored at least to what it had been.

We settled back into our old routine of me asking questions and directing the session. All I could do was wait for a sign from her that safety had been restored.

9

Panic Rising

At the time, I was oblivious to the fact that Jessica had always been petrified of making a decision based on what she felt she needed. In fact, Jessica had no memory (at least for as far back as she could remember) of ever having made one. Whenever anyone expected her to do so (for example, asking what she wanted or needed), her mind felt like it was about to be engulfed by chaos. She was never more aware of the terror that struck at her than throughout her senior year in high school.

◆　　　◆　　　◆

As Jessica prepared for bed on her last night of summer vacation before the start of her senior year, she placed the small clock radio as close as possible to the edge of the nightstand and carefully aimed its tiny speaker at the space just above the pillow where her head would soon come to rest. She set the alarm, took off her slippers, and nestled them under her bed. She turned off the light, crawled under the covers, and gently lowered her head onto the inviting softness.

Before a hint of dawn even beckoned in the sky, soft music from an all-night station drifted into her ear and slowly sparked her slumbering brain into wakefulness. The volume was just loud enough for the music to penetrate her senses. Her mother, brothers, and younger sister, who were in their rooms just down the hallway, were not expecting nor prepared to be awakened before six in the morning. Jessica's school day started at seven. The new high school was not finished. The senior high students used the junior high building in the morning. At the end of World War II, Bayport was an isolated hamlet beyond the Detroit metropolitan area, a pleasant Sunday drive to the country for city folk. The town planners had been slow to respond to the baby boom after the war. Jessica's brothers and younger sister were in junior high and left later.

In the dark of night and with her head still resting on the pillow, Jessica slid an arm out from under the covers and slowly raised it in the direction of the sound. Carefully lowering her hand until her fingers touched the hard, plastic surface, she searched for the rounded bulge of the off button. Finally feeling it under her fingertip, she gently pushed it down and slid the hard, plastic object away from the edge.

She eased her body out of bed to minimize any squeaks, pulled her slippers from underneath the bed, and slipped them on. With a few quick, silent steps, she was at the door to her room. She cradled the knob with both of her hands, slowly pulled upwards, and quietly opened the door. A big step out into the hallway avoided the soft spot in the floorboards just outside her room. Nightlights in the bathroom and the kitchen cast an eerie, shadow-filled glow throughout the house. After a step or two to her right, she cut through a corner of the carpeted living room and stepped onto the kitchen's linoleum floor. She glided past the yellow kitchen table on her left and reached the sink on the other side of the room, in between the avocado stove and refrigerator. She carefully turned the faucet to a trickle and washed her face. She had taken her shower the night before.

She fixed the quietist breakfast she could think of, cereal with milk and sliced banana. She nudged her fingertips under the edges of cupboard doors and gently pried them open. Dishes were handled as if they were priceless antiques. The refrigerator door was eased open to soften the sound of the rubber seals coming apart. A chair was lifted away from the table as if it was a crystal chandelier.

Finished, she gingerly placed the glass bowl and spoon in the metallic sink and retraced her route to her room. She dressed in the clothes she had laid out on the chair next to her dresser the evening before, jeans and a long-sleeved blue shirt with little colored flowers. She exchanged her slippers for her brown loafers. She then stood in front of her dresser. Behind her, on the other side of the room, a small lamp on a nightstand next to her bed cast a pale yellow glow. Pictures of dogs with soulful eyes hung from the sky-blue walls.

She reached for her hairbrush on the dresser and slowly raised her arm until her hand was poised just above her head. She then locked her arm in place. With her eyes glued to the silhouette of her head directly in front of her, she tightened her grip on the brush. With a slow, deliberate stroke, she guided it through her long, brown hair. As her arm moved downward, her eyes tracked the moving shadow on the wall. Her mind automatically cemented into place the trace of the brush. The mental image of the slightly curved arc on the wall was her only guide, besides a sixth sense based on touch, to judge where to comb next. After several minutes of concentrating on her silhouette, Jessica decided she had run her brush through her hair the number of times it usually took to get a compliment. She quietly placed it back on the dresser.

Jessica had always been terrified of mirrors. As far back as she could remember, mirrors only existed to torment her. Any reflecting surface was nothing more than a torture chamber inhabited by a sinister being whose only goal in life was to take great pleasure in her misery. Whenever her antennae failed to warn her and she unexpectedly caught a glimpse of herself in one, a terrifying, instinctive urge to rocket backward about a million paces while shrieking, "Who are you!" overcame her. As with all the other mysterious happenings taking place inside of her, she kept this one a secret as well.

When the Thomases moved into their present house five years ago, Dorothy hung a mirror for her two eldest. No one noticed that Jessica never used the mirror. Although all would swear that Jessica was frequently seen carrying her hairbrush into the bathroom just across the hall and ask, if anyone was nearby, "How do I look?" when she came out with her hair neatly combed. Perhaps they thought she was being thoughtful of her sister, who spent a long time in front of the mirror in the bedroom.

Jessica disposed of the sinister object hanging ominously above the dresser the day Ellen had left home at sixteen to live with their dad, two states and a few hundred miles away. Dorothy had always had a difficult relationship with her oldest daughter. Over time, arguments became more frequent. Voices grew louder, and words were more cutting. When Ellen announced she was leaving, while holding up the money her dad had sent for the bus trip, Dorothy did not voice any objection. Whatever feelings she had, she kept them to herself. On the day Dorothy drove Ellen to the bus station, Jessica sprang into action as soon as the car disappeared from sight. She marched into what was now her bedroom and snatched the menacing thing off the wall. She stiff-armed the haunting object that seemed to drip with malevolence every time she entered the room into the closet next to the dresser. She leaned the reflecting surface against the wall. All the while, her eyes never met another pair staring back.

Jessica settled in an armchair in the living room. With a view of the driveway, she wanted to know exactly when her mother returned. As soon as Dorothy pulled in, Jessica rushed to the front door. She had to speak first before Dorothy noticed the missing mirror and hurled an accusation, "What happened now? Don't tell me you broke it?"

Before her mother had taken more than two steps into the living room, Jessica said, "I put the mirror in my room in the closet. I'm tired of hairs getting all over the dresser and the floor." Jessica knew it was a bit of a lie. She held her breath.

"Well, if that's what you want," Dorothy replied. Nothing more was ever said about the matter.

After deciding she had run the brush through her hair enough times, Jessica tiptoed back into the kitchen. She again gently opened the refrigerator. She snatched her lunch bag from inside, also placed there the night before, and quietly stepped back into the living room.

Jessica's noiseless movements on this particular morning were not any different from her usual behavior. She had always been acutely sensitive to the needs of others. She had always thought of it as a built-in part of her nature, something she did automatically and instinctively. It was something she did without wasting an instant of her time or an ounce of her energy thinking about it.

She soundlessly made her way to the front door. She found her purple shorts and baton for band practice. She folded her shorts into her purse and grabbed her baton. She quietly turned the deadbolt on the front door and stepped out into the chill of the early dawn. After locking the door, she tightly held her lunch bag and baton, jumped down the front steps, and skipped along the front walk to the street. Her feet felt like they barely touched the pavement.

The cool, early September air infused Jessica's senses with an eagerness to absorb the sights, sounds, and smells around her. Nature was the only place in world where her antennae could relax. Nature did not hold any surprises. Nature did not have any expectations. Nature did not care who or what she was. Nature did not ask she be more of this or less of that. Nature did not care what she did or did not do. If nature was her only concern, she would not have to prove a thing or convince anyone of anything.

As Jessica made her way along the edge of the road, her eyes surveyed the ground for the few dried leaves that had already fallen. Whenever she spied one, she stomped on it to hear the crunch and see the little tendrils of powdered dirt erupt.

After a few minutes of romping with nature, she rounded a curve in the road and spied two girls, one a bit taller than the other, standing farther down. They were waiting for the school bus where the dirt road ended and met the short, paved spur from Bayport Road, the only link between the east and west sides of town.

Jessica knew one of the girls, Dawn, the taller one. She was a year behind her. Jessica had not seen her all summer. She lived some distance on the other side of Bayport Road.

As soon as Dawn spotted her, she waved and yelled, "Hi, Jessica!"

Jessica waved back and yelled, "Hi, Dawn!"

Jessica quickened her pace. As she approached them, she veered to the other girl. Without waiting to cover the final steps, she did the expected and introduced herself. As soon as the girl finished saying, "Hi, I'm Linda," Jessica asked all the appropriate questions. Linda's family had just moved to Bayport a few weeks ago from another state. This was her first year in high school. She had a younger brother who needed to be watched after school. She seemed nervous and asked questions about the school, teachers, and students. Jessica reassured her and invited her to call if she had any more questions.

When Jessica and Linda finished their chat, Dawn touched Jessica on the shoulder and started speaking. Jessica only caught a few words, something about Dawn wishing she was a senior. Jessica could not tell if Dawn was asking her a question or not, so she did not say anything.

They heard the sound of the bus chugging its way toward them after crossing over the interstate. They quickly formed a line. Jessica made sure she was last. The bus pulled onto the paved spur and came to a stop. The three trudged up the steps. Only a handful of students were on board, mostly girls. Jessica greeted the ones she knew and kept heading farther back. Dawn was behind Linda. She tapped her on the shoulder as they approached an empty row of seats. They sat down together. Jessica was ecstatic. She walked a few rows past them and slid into an empty seat. She always prayed no one would sit with her. The only thing to do on a bus was talk.

Less than a minute later, Dawn glanced back at Jessica, said something to Linda, and suddenly jumped up and walked back to Jessica. She plopped down beside her and immediately picked up where she had left off about wishing she was a senior. She was so enthused. She had so many ideas for what she might do after graduating.

Jessica listened, smiled, and asked an occasional question to keep Dawn talking. The bus made a few more stops. More students got on. Jessica nodded and smiled to a few of them. Dawn ignored everyone and kept chirping away.

Just as the bus pulled away from a stop, Dawn looked at Jessica with a spark in her eyes and asked, "Well, what are you going to do after graduation?"

The words penetrated Jessica's skull like a rocket-launched grenade. She had always dreaded anyone asking her a question about what she thought, how she felt, what she wanted to do, or hoped to do. She had always hated these personal questions. Whenever she tried answering, she felt her mind was about to shatter into a million pieces. Early in life, she learned, if she did not respond quickly enough, people gave her a funny look. Despite the chaos swirling in her head, she always managed to force out what she hoped was a reasonable answer. She always kept it as short as possible. The quicker she could get her attention and her interrogator's attention away from herself, the better she felt.

Dawn was the first person to ask her about plans for after graduation and then wait for an answer. Over the summer, a few people had talked about graduation in general or had suggested what she might do without waiting for her to answer.

She would usually say, "That's an interesting idea." She hoped it was enough.

In her imagination, she was screaming at Dawn to disappear, along with her uninvited question. Jessica averted her eyes and stared out the window. She fixed her eyes on the sun barely peeping over the horizon. Dawn's eyes seemed like they were boring into the back of her head. She did not dare wait more than a few seconds. She glanced back at Dawn and shrugged her shoulders, hoping she would get the hint. Dawn immediately turned to another senior girl two rows away, asked the same question, and quickly jumped over to her. Her words were still reverberating in the caverns of Jessica's mind.

The bus continued on for a few more stops. More students got on. Jessica's eyes were staring out the window, concentrating on the scenery while trying to block Dawn's voice from a few seats away. Although other students were busily chatting, especially the two in front of her, Dawn's voice sounded like it was coming from a loudspeaker.

Before the bus came to a stop in the schoolyard, Jessica was edging off her seat. The panic was still swirling in her mind. The side door was just a step away. The instant the bus came to a stop, she flew out and rushed toward the building. If someone said "hi" or called her name, she just gave a quick "hi" back and kept on going. School could not start fast enough. No one would be able to ask that question once it did. She left her baton and lunch in her locker and sought the sanctuary of her first class.

None of her classmates did ask that question, but all of her teachers started class by reminding the students they were seniors. They would be graduating, and the class would be important to them after high school. Jessica felt as if the teachers were talking directly to her, as if they were saying, "You'd better know what you want to do after graduation!"

The whole school day was a psychological nightmare for Jessica. She barely stumbled out of her last class because of the severe pounding in her head. In her last class of the day, she had to keep staring at the words on the blackboard until her vision cleared before she could decipher them.

With tiny steps so her clothes would not chafe against her skin, she shuffled her way to her locker. She snatched the sandwich from the bag and tossed it into the nearest wastebasket. She feared what would happen if she ate it. She then changed into her shorts in the girl's room.

She continued shuffling to the athletic field on the opposite side of the building from the parking lot. She stepped up into the stands and went to the highest row. She prayed it was far enough for no one to bother her. She dipped into her purse and popped some pills for her headache. She slowly munched on the apple, took a few sips from the thermos, and waited for practice to start. The sun's warmth and the fresh breeze on her face helped soothe her.

As the band members trickled onto the field, some noticed her way up in the stands and waved. She waved back, but no one came up. She did not join the others until the band director was ready to start. Band practice was an immense relief. For the next hour and a half, her eyes were glued to the director. She twirled her baton, marched smartly to the music, and did not talk to anyone.

Over the next few days, Jessica made a gratifying discovery. When she was forced to concentrate on something outside of herself (for example, being in class or band practice, helping her mother at home, doing homework, or actually doing just about anything), the question did not haunt her. Even though each bout with the panic always seemed like a distant memory once it subsided, she could feel it lurking around. Fortunately, it never felt on the verge of erupting, which it threatened to do if she let more than a few minutes elapse without having her attention riveted on being busy. The panic then gathered itself together, as if it had a mind of its own. Fearful of letting her guard down, she frantically tried finding enough ways to stay in robotic motion.

Dorothy was quickly tiring of Jessica pestering her for things to do. If she could not think of anything, Jessica volunteered to vacuum, do the laundry, iron clothes, freshen the bathroom, wash walls, shampoo rugs, make clothes on the sewing machine, knead dough, bake bread, prepare fruits and vegetables for canning, polish silverware, mow grass, dig weeds, or check her siblings' homework. Anything!

One day after band practice, Jessica was deep in concentration as she walked from the practice field to the bus. A list of chores to do at home was quickly filling her mind.

At first, she was not sure if it was her imagination. The voice then kept growing louder and more insistent.

"Jessica."

"*Jessica.*"

As she was about to spin around, she felt a hand on her arm. It was Julie. They had twirled together since junior high. Jessica started twirling in grade school when a girlfriend pleaded with her to take a class. Others then urged her to try out for the school band. She had been a majorette since the eighth grade.

"I've been yelling your name for the past minute!" Julie exclaimed, as she took her hand off Jessica's arm.

"Sorry," Jessica quickly reassured her. They resumed walking.

"I just got accepted to Rushmore," Julie exclaimed, "and the band director wants me to be in the marching band."

"Congratulations!"

"Thanks. My parents will be able to come and watch. It's not that far. How about you? Are you going to be in a band in college?"

"Don't know," Jessica mumbled. She felt the panic starting to gather itself together.

"Well, if you don't go to college, what do you think you will do?"

Jessica's head was starting to feel like a racetrack. Thoughts were starting to spin out of control. She silently screamed at them to stop, but they kept flying around. All she could do was mumble a weak, "Don't know." She kept her mouth shut and listened to Julie prattle away.

The panic quickly died down. They chatted about other things. Julie did not ask anymore questions Jessica could not answer. When they got on the bus, Jessica said she was not feeling well and wanted to sit by herself. Julie did not make a fuss and sat with someone else. Jessica found an empty row in the back. As the bus rumbled along, she knew exactly what she had to do as soon as she saw her mother.

When the bus stopped at the end of the paved spur, Jessica jumped off and hurried down the road. She waved to a few neighbors. Dorothy was not home yet, so Jessica busied herself with cleaning the kitchen and tidying other rooms. As soon as she heard her mother pull into the driveway, she bounded out the front door and jumped down the steps.

"Mom!" she yelled as Dorothy was getting out of the car, "Can I get a job after school?"

"Jessica! For goodness sakes, be careful! Now tell me what you were yelling about." She shuffled slowly along the walk.

"I want to get an after-school job," she began breathlessly, "at Richardson's and…"

"Now look what you've done to yourself. Calm down first so we can talk about it."

Jessica took a deep breath before plunging on. "One of my friends told me Mr. Richardson was looking for a part-time waitress and…"

"But you've never worked as a waitress!"

"My friend said that didn't matter."

Dorothy gave her a stern look before speaking. "What about your homework?"

"I don't have any more than in past years, and tomorrow is the last day for band practice."

"If you work at Richardson's, you'll have to use the car some of the time. I don't think I'd be up to driving you there every day."

"I'll be careful."

Dorothy was silent for a bit.

"Besides," Jessica began hesitantly, knowing she was about to hit a sore spot, "we could use the extra money."

"Well," Dorothy began, "I don't want you working too many hours."

"Can I drive over to Richardson's now? I cleaned up the kitchen."

"Well…okay."

"Thanks, Mom."

Jessica jumped in the car. The restaurant was a few miles away, farther into the country and away from the creeping edge of suburbia. Mr. Richardson had owned it for years. He had renovated a big, old house near an interstate exit when the road had been built some years ago. It was the only place a restaurant could survive in this area of small towns. He lived upstairs. Jessica knew him and most of the people who worked there. The Sunday brunch specials were the only time the Thomas family ate out. Mr. Richardson was glad to see Jessica. He asked about her mother and her siblings. He hired her right away. Someone was needed for the supper hour. She could start on Monday.

At the restaurant, Jessica was in constant movement from the moment she walked in to when she left. There were preparations for the dinner hour, then a flood of customers, and then cleaning up. She usually stayed until seven-thirty or eight when a part of the seating area was closed off and truckers were the main customers.

The rest of Jessica's day away from the restaurant was just as frantic. When she arrived home from school, she grabbed a snack and did as much of her homework as she could. She then hurried to work. After work, there was always something to do at home if she had not finished her homework.

After a few weeks of this frenetic pace, Jessica clung to the hope she had beaten back the insidious panic. But it had not gone away. It was still lurking around, but it did not feel like it was about to erupt. All she could wish for now was to prevent it from taking complete control of her life. If it did, she was certain she would completely lose her mind and do something irrational, something crazy, maybe something not human.

One day at work, she hurried down the darkened hallway off the kitchen to the bathroom at the back of the building. Warped, aged floorboards creaked with each step. The bathroom door hung at a slight angle, as if to say it had been in that position for too many years. It protested loudly when pushed open. Jessica stepped in and flipped the light switch. The single bulb in the ceiling filled the windowless space with a dingy, white light. She closed the door behind her and slid the latch in place.

The instant she turned around and faced the room, her heart felt like it was about to explode. Cold perspiration spewed from every pore in her body. Her breath came in short gasps. One thought overwhelmed her mind. *Something* was in the room. It felt like a cold, sinister, terrifying presence. Survival instincts immediately spun her body around. In the same motion, one of her hands flew to the latch while the other grabbed the doorknob. She flipped the latch, yanked the door open, and jumped out into the hallway. As terrified as she was, she first had to see if anyone was coming. She had no idea what explanation she would offer for her behavior if someone had seen her flying out of the bathroom. There wasn't anyone.

A moment later, she realized the *something* had not followed her and she had left the light on. She was not about to step back in. A plastic calmness quickly settled over her face, an automatic response whenever something greatly upset her. She headed to the kitchen. She hoped she looked like she always did, calm and in control of herself.

She stepped into the kitchen and picked up an order. She spoke to the cook and another waitress and chatted with the couple at the table. No one said anything to her or looked peculiarly at her.

From that day, Jessica never put another foot into the bathroom or any other windowless bathroom. The gas station next door had a bathroom, and one with a small window. No one working there ever said anything.

The bizarre experience left her with a constant feeling that *something* was about to jump out from the nearest hiding place and terrorize her. Whenever she approached a corner of a building, a big tree, a car she could not see behind, or the next room she could not see into, she held her breath and hesitated a second, just long enough to have the quickest peek.

Jessica bounced around in this nervous state for a few days, waiting for the overwhelming fear to diminish. Barely eating, she lost several pounds in a week. Because she always had a few extra pounds on her, no one seemed concerned. She only slept for short periods and awoke with a panicky feeling. It took a long time for her to get back to sleep. In the morning, makeup took care of the bags under her eyes.

After nearly a week, Jessica was just as jumpy and panicky about something getting her. She could only think of one remedy, more mindless, repetitive work.

Dorothy was initially against it. "Too busy of a schedule," she insisted initially. "It won't leave time for anything else, even your homework."

She finally relented when Jessica promised she would quit if her grades dropped. She started working forty hours a week, adding ten- to twelve-hour days on the weekend when she also spent a few hours as one of the cooks. She was spending more time at work than any place else. She did not know what else to do.

10

Dorothy's Accident

One evening at the restaurant while the hectic pace of the supper hour was ending, Jessica was in the kitchen, carefully loading a big, round metal tray with dishes and drinks. She slowly hoisted it into the air and carefully rested an edge on her shoulder. After a few measured steps to check for balance, she nudged open the swinging half-door with her hip. As she twirled through the opening and looked through the spacious front window, she saw Roger Page stepping out of his car. He leaned his slender body into the chilly, windy gusts that were announcing winter's arrival. After a few steps, he grasped the heavy front door with both hands and stumbled inside.

He had graduated from Bayport High two years ago. She had last seen him the past summer at the nearby park along the river, only at a distance then. The only other times they had seen each other, aside from passing in the school's hallway, were at postgame football parties or occasionally at the park with groups of friends they had in common. They had never spoken more than a minute to just each other. They were usually part of a group conversation.

Their first meeting had etched itself into Jessica's mind. At the park, a group of boys Roger was with merged with the group of girls she was with. Roger trailed over, a few steps behind the others. On the way, a bright, blue butterfly suddenly took flight. He stopped and followed its graceful, pulsating movements. When he joined the group, he cautiously inserted himself into an open space among the other boys. He did not interrupt the ongoing conversation to announce his presence.

Whenever Jessica saw him, warm, safe vibrations coursed through her body. It was the same feeling she had with nature. No possible harm could come to her. She was completely safe. She had no idea how he felt about her.

While Jessica made her way to her table with the tray balanced on her shoulder, she stole a few glances. Roger stood where he had landed just inside the door, surveying the restaurant. He did not see her. An older couple on their way out was heading directly toward him. He opened the door for them. The woman said something to him as she went by. He then made his way to the nearest booth and molded his slender frame to the seat.

After delivering her order, Jessica hurried back to the counter for a menu and a glass of water. Roger was staring out the window. When she was a step or two from the table, he turned his head. He smiled. His eyes doubled in size. Jessica smiled, too.

"Hi, Roger."

"Hi, Jessica. Gosh, I didn't know you worked here."

"Have been for a month or so, only for the dinner hour during the week. I added the weekends a few weeks ago." She quickly changed the subject. "What are you doing these days?"

"I just quit my job," Roger quietly said, sounding somewhat embarrassed. "Didn't like the place," he quickly added. He glanced away for a second or two and then said, "I had been working afternoons." It was as if he was explaining why he did not know she had been here.

Jessica lingered for a few minutes. They chatted about mutual friends. Whenever she went back to his table to bring his meal, refill his coffee, or bring his check, his eyes picked her up on the way over. While she waited on other customers, she glanced over at him. When Roger left, he looked back into the restaurant. She was behind the counter, watching.

Over the next week or two, Roger came into the restaurant a few more times and always sat in her section. It was always a bit later than the first time—when fewer people were there. Whenever she came to his table, they made small talk, but never for very long.

One evening, when she left his check, she finally said, "Find any work yet?"

He held her gaze briefly before looking away. "No," he said quietly.

She flashed her best smile. "That's not good. Your mind needs to be active!" This was Jessica.

He shot a surprised glance back at her. When he left, his step was quick. Nearly a week passed before he came in again.

As Jessica walked over to him with the menu and a glass of water, an energy was in his eyes that she had not seen before.

"Well, I'm working at St. Catherine's Iron Works," he said proudly.

"Good for you!" She gave him her best smile again. "What are you doing?"

Roger worked the night shift on the shuttle train that transferred iron ore and other materials from the main railroad track to the plant. She knew a number of men who worked at St. Catherine's. It was in a nearby community, closer to

Detroit. She was glad he worked outside. Corrosive chemicals and hot furnaces were inside.

When she went back to his table for a refill, Roger asked her to go to the movies on Saturday night, a few days away. She accepted. She had not been on a date since school had started. A few boys had asked her out, but she had avoided getting to know anyone new after her first day of school. Postgame football parties were the only socializing she had done. Being in a group was safer. People did not ask personal questions.

Roger called her at home two days before their date, just to chat for a minute or two. Jessica already sensed that sitting and chatting was not one of his favorite things to do. That was fine with her. They dated the next few Saturday nights, and they were soon a steady couple. On most days, they only saw each other when he took her to or from work or came to the restaurant. If they did not see each other, they talked on the phone, usually late in the evening and not for very long.

Jessica related to Roger in the same way she did with everyone else in her life. She bombarded him with questions about what he did and did not like. She then did whatever she thought would bring a smile to his face and make him feel good. If people were happy with her, they would not ask probing questions. Because Roger was not very talkative, they went places where they could watch or do something, so their attention was not on the two of them, their relationship, or what they needed from each other. When she was with Roger, she discovered she was much less afraid of the *something* suddenly jumping out from behind a hiding place and attacking her, just as she was with her mother.

Even so, she was not going to stop working or work less to spend more time with Roger. They were fine as long as they were doing something. When they ran out of things to do, she could feel the panic lurking in the background. Even watching television with Roger was not enough of a distraction.

Although the icy blasts of winter had long disappeared, warmer weather was coming to Michigan. As it usually did, it was slowly tantalizing. Two rainy days in the low forties or even an overnight frost could easily follow a sunny day in the high sixties.

Hopes and plans for postgraduation began filling the air again. This time, the haunting question did not fade from Jessica's mind as quickly as it did at the start of the school year. Now, the panic was sharper, and it penetrated more deeply into the core of her being. When anyone asked her the question, despite her best efforts to steer everyone away from it, she wanted to grasp the sides of her head and scream, "Why are you asking me? How am I supposed to know what I want?"

Every second she was awake, her whole body, her whole being it seemed, trembled with fear, except when she was with Roger or her mother or when she stayed busy with mindless, repetitive work. The panic was then under control, though just barely. Thoughts did not spin in her head. Chaos was not going to overtake her mind. The *something* was not going to make a sudden appearance.

Roger and Dorothy were now Jessica's umbilical cords, her lifelines, and she was terrified of losing either one. When she was with Roger, she had to feel his body touching hers. When they went anywhere, she held his hand or entwined her arms around one of his. When they sat, she guided him to a chair that was big enough for the two of them and then snuggled as close as possible. People saw it as being in love.

When Jessica was home, she was terrified when her mother had to leave, even if just to visit a neighbor for a few minutes. Whenever Dorothy announced she was going next door or across the street, Jessica wanted to plead with her to stay, but she could only manage a whiny, "Are you sure you'll be back in a few minutes?"

The first time Jessica asked her mother, Dorothy gave her a funny glance. When Jessica pestered her with the same question a few days later, her mother scrunched her face, as if to say, "Stop acting so weird!" Jessica stopped asking.

Her nights were just as restless. She tossed and turned for hours. Her mind was attuned to any sound—the bark of a dog, the roar of the trucks on the interstate, the chirps of the crickets, or an airplane's roar. Only sheer exhaustion eventually subdued her mind. However, too much nervous energy was seething through her body. After only a few hours of sleep, she was wide-awake. Her brain was galvanized for any emergency.

When she got home after work or after a date with Roger, she felt just as energized as when she woke up in the morning. She was not eating much either. The most she ever had was a small glass of orange juice for breakfast and never more than a sandwich or sometimes just a piece of fruit for lunch. At home after school, she would have a sandwich, if she had not eaten one at lunch. At the restaurant, she could only manage a few mouthfuls of whatever was left. After work, she just did not feel like eating. She was thinner than she had ever been, but thin was in. Many people told her how great she looked.

At work, a maniacal urge to stay constantly in motion drove her. She filled in for people on their break, cooked, washed dishes, and cleaned tables. She did anything to keep herself in motion. Others kept telling her, "Slow down...You don't have to work as hard…You're doing too many favors…Others are taking advantage of you." She knew they were right, but she did not care. From when she awoke to when her brain finally surrendered at night, her life felt like a movie run at fast-forward without any pauses.

One day at work, while she was ringing up a customer's bill and asking if everything was okay, her knees buckled, and her body slumped to the floor. When she came to, she was lying on her side. She quickly got to her hands and knees. A waitress who had been a few feet away was kneeling beside her. Her hand was on Jessica's shoulder and she was asking if she was hurt.

"I'm fine," Jessica insisted.

She did not feel any pain anywhere. Even if she had, she would not have said so. Another waitress hurried over. Someone called Mr. Richardson and asked about smelling salts. Voices urged her to sit down and rest. Jessica heard several offers for a ride home.

Just hearing someone suggest she should rest or leave work was enough to make Jessica struggle to her feet. She initially felt a little dizzy, but that did not stop her from insisting, "I'm fine, really. I don't need to sit down." She waved away a glass of water and glanced at the cash register.

"I need to finish ringing up that guy's bill!" she said.

Another waitress said she would finish it, but she did not make any motion to do so. All around her, people were just standing and staring, like zombies. Jessica suddenly waved her arms in the air to emphasize she was fine. She gently pushed someone out of the way and marched into the kitchen. For the rest of the evening, she acted as if it had never happened.

About a week later, while she was taking a couple's order at a table and holding her pen poised in one hand ready to write on the pad in her other hand, she fainted again, just as unexpectedly as the last time. Just as she was losing consciousness, she caught a glance of the husband of the couple rushing toward her. When she came to, she was slumped over at the waist. Only his arms held her up.

A second time in a few days was not only embarrassing but frightening as well. She was more determined than the last time to pass this off. She quickly reassured everyone that she was okay. To prove it, she dropped to the floor to find her pen and pad. She quickly grabbed them, stood up, and wrote the order down. Another waitress rushed over.

Before she could say anything, Jessica interrupted, "I've hardly had anything to eat all day." When she got to the kitchen, she quickly threw some food in her mouth.

She did not dare let this happen again. The only thing she could do was force herself to eat more. Over the next two weeks, she even gained a few pounds and did not embarrass herself.

One evening in early May, a few weeks after she had fainted the second time, there was a phone call for her when the dinner hour was just slowing down. She assumed it was either her mother or Roger. No one else ever called her at work. It was from Bayview hospital.

The female voice began in a professional, reassuring tone, "Your mother was in an auto accident. Her life isn't in any danger, but she did sustain some injuries. She has quite a serious whiplash to her neck and her left arm is broken. She will probably be here for about two weeks, and she'll then have to finish recuperating at home."

Panic engulfed Jessica's mind. One-half of her lifeline would be in the hospital for two weeks. She had no idea what she was going to do. She could not ask Roger to move in. While she stood at the front desk, the pile driver was starting deep in her skull. Blood drained from her head. Her legs felt like jelly. With an act of sheer willpower, she put down the phone. Her mouth moved mechanically. Sounds came rushing out, to everyone near and to no one in particular, "My mom's been in an accident! She's at Bayview."

The waitress closest to her suddenly exclaimed, "Oh, Jessica!" She reached for her purse under the cash register, "Here's my keys. Bring my car back tomorrow. Jack can come and get me."

Jessica mechanically held out her hand and felt the keys plop into it.

The woman offering the car said, "Do you want me to drive?"

Jessica suddenly realized she must look far more upset than she thought. "No, that's okay," she quickly asserted. "I'll be all right. It was just the initial shock."

The hospital was ten minutes away, but Jessica drove slowly. Objects around her were already beginning to shift in and out of focus. By the time she arrived, her head was pounding. She stopped at the front desk for directions. She marched right to the ward and found a grandmotherly-looking nurse with white hair sitting behind a desk. She stepped right over and drilled her with questions. The first few came out so fast that the nurse did not have time to answer. Instead, she reached over the countertop, patted Jessica's arm, smiled, and started talking in a reassuring voice. "There really isn't anything to worry about. Besides the whiplash and broken arm, there are some internal injuries. There usually are in car accidents, but they aren't serious. She does have some bruises. She will probably be here for fourteen days. When she leaves, her neck will be in a brace, and her arm will be in a cast. I'm sure she'll be fine after she's recuperated at home.

You can see her, but she may not be awake right now. She was in a lot of pain. The doctor gave her something. Her room number is 115, down that way on the right side. Oh, by the way, someone from the hospital called your home just after we called you and spoke to one of your brothers. He said he'd try to find a neighbor to bring them."

With quivering legs and her breath stuck in her throat, Jessica tiptoed into her mother's room. Dorothy was asleep. Jessica's eyes focused on the bulging neck brace and the cast on the arm. She then spied an ugly bruise above one eye. All of it only made her more panicky. After just a minute or two, she hurried out and made a beeline for the white-haired nurse behind the desk.

"Are you sure my mother will be okay?" She couldn't help herself.

Again, the nurse patted her arm. "Don't worry, dear. I'm sure she'll be fine. I know she looks like she's been beat up, but all of it will heal." She spoke slowly and calmly. Jessica knew she was trying to reassure her, but it was not working.

She hurried to a phone and called Roger. The instant she heard his voice, her mouth started moving. "My mom was in an accident and she…Yes, in the car…No, not that serious…Her neck is in a brace, and her arm is broken. She has a big bruise above one eye…I was at work and borrowed a car…The nurse said she has some internal injuries and everything will heal and…No, I didn't speak to her. She was asleep…The nurse said she was in a lot of pain and the doctor gave her something…What?…The nurse said about fourteen days…Yes, can you come here? I don't think I can drive. I'm in the front of the parking lot in a red car."

She was afraid she had been screaming at Roger. He had never heard her sound so upset.

She then called home and spoke with one of her brothers. No one had been able to take them to the hospital yet. She told him everything and said she would be home after she went back to the restaurant.

Jessica stumbled her way along the hospital corridor, lurched through the doors, and tottered her way to the car. She tumbled in and waited. Roger pulled up about ten minutes later. By that time, she thought she could drive back to the restaurant if he led the way. If all she had to do was stare at his car, she thought she'd be okay.

As soon as she stepped into the restaurant, everyone swarmed over, even a few of the customers. Mr. Richardson came down. She could take some time off if she wanted or cut back on her hours. Jessica thanked him and said she would have to see. She was only being polite. Working less was simply out of the question. After she told everyone about her mother's condition, she thanked everyone and left with Roger. She dropped him off at his house and kept his car.

Jessica went to the hospital every day right from school, usually by herself, and on the weekends after work. Roger came with her a few times. He took her brothers and sister a few times.

Aside from Roger accompanying her to the hospital, Jessica only saw him if he came to the restaurant or came over after she got home from work. Dorothy wanted Jessica to stay home on Saturday and Sunday evenings to watch her brothers and sister. When Roger came over on school nights, he had to leave by ten. He could stay until eleven on Friday and Saturday night. He usually helped her with chores. The neighbors took turns watching her brothers and sister if she was not there and helped with chores as well.

At night, after Roger left and everyone else was in bed, Jessica was utterly alone. Her mother's room was an aching emptiness that seemed to permeate the whole house. As soon as the noise of Roger's car faded away, Jessica was terrified of having a full-blown panic attack, just like the one in the bathroom at the restaurant a few months ago. She could barely sit in one place for more than a minute of two. When she tried studying, the words on the page seemed to float in the air. Thoughts raced around in her head. She desperately wanted to call Roger and ask him to spend the night. She had never felt so terrified and helpless in her life.

11

Final Exams

Ten days after Dorothy's accident, the hospital called the restaurant during mid-afternoon. Jessica could take her mother home in a few hours. Jessica spoke to the head waitress, who said she could leave whenever she needed. She called Roger, just to tell him the news.

Jessica initially found herself looking at the clock every few minutes. The time in between each peek seemed like an eternity. She then willed herself to pay more attention to her work. She did until about an hour after the call and at least two hours before her mother would be ready. She grabbed the wrong order from the kitchen and did not realize it until her customer pointed it out. The head waitress saw her bring the order back to the kitchen and overheard enough of Jessica's explanation to the cook to determine what happened. A short while later, Jessica filled a glass with milk instead of water.

"Damn!" she muttered when she realized her mistake.

The head waitress stepped over. "Why don't you just leave now," she whispered. "We can cover for you."

The comment shocked Jessica back to reality. All she could say—or dare-say—was, "I'll be more careful." For the next hour, Jessica's only thought was to be the best waitress possible.

The next time she glanced at the clock, she only had ten minutes left. The head waitress had been watching the time as well. It only took a pleading look and a vigorous nod of a head in return. Jessica finished taking her last order and collected her things. She was going to start on her time card when the head waitress grabbed it and told her to leave. As she hurried out, a few of the employees sent their regards. She hopped in Roger's car and drove off.

When she arrived on the ward, she pounced on the nurse behind the desk. While Jessica desperately wanted her mother home, she also wanted to ensure she was getting all the help possible. She knew how much her mother hated being confined. She feared her mother had fooled the doctor into thinking she was ready to come home.

"My mom's been here for only ten days. She was supposed to be here for fourteen. Are you sure she's ready to leave?"

The nurse tried to be reassuring. "She's recuperated a lot quicker than we expected."

Jessica prayed she was right. She went to her mother's room. Dorothy was seated on the edge of her bed.

As soon as she spotted Jessica, she exclaimed, "Where have you been? I can't stand it here another minute. Get me out of here!"

Dorothy's words carried out into the hallway. The nurse reassured them that an attendant was on his way. About five minutes later, he came into the room.

"I thought you were going to be here minutes ago," Dorothy scolded the young man.

"Sorry ma'am. Got held up with my last patient. We'll have you out of here in no time."

"Hold that chair steady while I get in," she snapped. She was unwilling to wait for the orderly to do something.

Jessica stepped over to the chair and put her arms out for her mother.

"Jessica! If I need help, I'll say so!"

Sliding her body a few inches at a time along the edge of the bed and using her one good arm and both of her feet for support, Dorothy finally made it to the chair, accompanied by a few sharp cries of pain.

When they emerged from the room, as Jessica led the way, the white-haired nurse rushed over. She first spoke to Dorothy, "We've all gotten to know Jessica very well. You're very lucky to have such a responsible daughter. Now you be sure and let her take good care of you." She then turned to Jessica, patted her on the shoulder, and said, "Don't worry, dear. Your mother will be fine. Just make sure she stays in bed and doesn't strain herself."

The nurse smiled and walked back to her station. When Dorothy was convinced the nurse was out of earshot, she said, "Come on! Get me out of here!"

The threesome made their way along the corridor to the entrance. They went through the double doors and into the parking lot. When they reached the car, Dorothy scorned all offers of arms and hands.

"Ma'am, I'm supposed to help you," the orderly pleaded.

"You can stand by if you like," Dorothy relented. She then twisted, squirmed, and winced her way out of the chair and into the front seat.

"Jessica, you're going to have to put the seat belt around me. I can't reach it."

Jessica hurriedly did so, but Dorothy insisted on snapping the buckle into place herself. She fumbled with it for more than a minute. When Jessica reached for the buckle, her mother snapped, "Don't! I can get it. Just because I've been in the hospital for ten days doesn't mean I'm an invalid."

With her mother securely strapped in, Jessica slid behind the wheel and slowly drove off with her precious cargo. From the hospital grounds, she turned onto St. Catherine's Highway, a divided road with two lanes on each side of a very wide, grassy strip. The speed limit was fifty-five. Jessica stayed in the right lane and slowly nudged the car up to thirty. There was little traffic at this time in the evening.

Dorothy quickly urged her to go faster. Jessica slowly inched the speedometer up to thirty-five. A minute later, the same command filled the inside of the car.

"I have a lot of work to catch up on!" Dorothy then said.

Jessica sped up to forty. A few miles later, they came to the intersection with Bayport Road, near the paved spur the school bus turned onto. Jessica continued driving as if she was giving a lesson in the ultimate in safe driving. Dorothy did not urge her to go faster, although Jessica could hear her impatient breathing. On the dirt road to their house, Jessica slowly maneuvered around any dip in the surface.

As they approached the house, Jessica saw her brothers and sister sitting on the front steps. A few neighbors were standing in the driveway, chatting with each other. As Jessica pulled in, the women hurried to Dorothy's side. Jessica jumped out and went to her siblings. Her brothers carried the luggage in. Jessica and her sister joined the women, who chatted with Dorothy for awhile. All offered to help and urged her to get plenty of rest and to let everyone take care of her. The women were only a few steps away when Jessica spoke to her mother through the open car window, "Now, wait 'til I open the door and help you out."

One of the neighbors spun around. "Dorothy, do exactly what Jessica says. You're very lucky to have a daughter like her." Dorothy smiled and nodded her head.

Jessica opened the car door and held her arm out. Dorothy peeked at the women to see how far away they were.

She then hissed, "Jessica, back up!"

"But Mom!"

"Don't but me, young lady. Doctors tell you not to strain yourself because that's what they're supposed to say. Now step back so I can get out."

Dorothy had already unbuckled the seat belt and was starting to slowly twist her body around. She then let out a cry of pain.

"Mom, please!"

"Jessica, I said back up! If I had been afraid of pain, none of you would have ever been born. It's not as bad as it sounds. I just haven't figured out yet which motions hurt and which don't."

In a series of tiny movements, using her one arm and both feet to maneuver, Dorothy turned her body sideways and very slowly edged her way off the seat.

"Here, grab my arm." Jessica stood in front of her.

"Jessica, please!"

With a few more groans and sharp cries, Dorothy was on her feet. With tiny steps, she shuffled her way up the front walk to the porch steps. With her head held stiffly, she looked robotic.

Jessica hovered over her the whole way. "Now watch the step!"

"I can see the step! I'm not blind!"

Jessica went up the first of the two steps just ahead, holding her arm out. But Dorothy never reached for it. She managed the two steps by placing both feet together on the same surface before stepping up. Jessica held the front door open. Dorothy stepped up a tiny bit once more and inched her way into the house. The figure holding the door rushed in behind her and hurried to the far end of the hallway, to her mother's room. She pulled back the covers on the bed and waited.

Sounds of shoes shuffling across the kitchen floor drifted down the hallway. Jessica rushed out. Dorothy had the fingers of her free hand wrapped around the handle of the refrigerator door. She slowly leaned backward. As the rubber strips started to peel apart and the door slowly opened, Jessica heard a sharp cry of pain.

"Mom! Don't! You're supposed to be in bed! You're going to hurt yourself."

Jessica rushed over to her. "Is your neck brace still in place? And your…"

"Don't play doctor with me, young lady! I'm not going to lie in bed for a month. Get a piece of paper and write down what I tell you. We're going shopping when you get back from school tomorrow. You'll have to drive. I can't turn the wheel with one arm."

"I'll take an hour or two off from work and do the shopping," Jessica pleaded.

"There's no need for that!"

"But you should be resting."

"Go to work tomorrow! I'll be here when you get back. I'm not going anywhere."

Dorothy remained planted in front of the refrigerator, announcing what to write down. The words came rapidly, and Jessica had to scribble to keep up. They then rummaged through the cupboards.

When Dorothy was finished in the kitchen, they roamed about the house, checking every room, before going outside. There was just enough daylight. While her mother had been in the hospital, Jessica had not been able to maintain the grounds. When they were finished in the yard, they went back inside. Dorothy reluctantly let Jessica make a cup of tea for her while they sat at the kitchen table and Dorothy went over the list Jessica had made.

After Dorothy finished her tea, she announced she was going to bed. Jessica popped up from her chair and rushed to help, but she had learned her lesson from earlier in the day. Her only offer of help was to now hold her mother's chair to prevent it from moving as Dorothy twisted and turned her body and finally stood up. Jessica was never more than a step or two behind as her mother made her halting way down the hallway to her room. Jessica stepped in behind her. Once inside, she hurried past her mother to the head of the bed and finished pulling the covers back.

"Jessica, what do you think you're doing?"

Dorothy's cold stare was enough. Jessica released the blanket and quickly added, "Please let me know if you need me."

"I will…if I need you!"

Jessica scurried to the kitchen. She went over the shopping list and reorganized the list of chores. She liked making lists and organizing things. It made her feel, at least in her corner of the world, there were not any surprises and everything was operating like it should. While she was sitting at the kitchen table staring at the list, the nurse's words about her mother having to stay in bed for several weeks still rang in her head.

Jessica knew the nurse or anyone else at the hospital was not aware of the largest obstacle to her instructions, Dorothy's pride in being self-sufficient. Probably more than anything else in the world, she hated the feeling of being dependent.

Fully aware of her mother's yearning for self-sufficiency, Jessica realized she did not have a choice. She would have to be at home as much as her schedule would allow. She would have to be ready at any instant to leap to her feet. Roger would just have to understand that they could not go anywhere.

After Jessica got home from school the next day, she went shopping with her mother. At the supermarket, Dorothy moved slowly and winced whenever she got impatient and tried moving too fast. She let Jessica lift the heavier items.

When they got home, the other children had just arrived from school. Dorothy had never expected them to be as helpful around the house as her two oldest. Before Jessica left for work, she told her siblings to make sure they kept an eye on their mother.

On her way to the restaurant, she arrived at a decision, one she would have considered unthinkable until now. She asked Mr. Richardson if she could take him up on his offer to cut back on her hours. She would go in an hour later, leave an hour earlier, and not work more than six hours on Saturday or Sunday.

Jessica now had a new mission in life, being her mother's shadow. If Dorothy was in the kitchen, Jessica anchored herself to a chair at the kitchen table. Her schoolbooks were open on the table in front of her. If Dorothy sat in the living room to watch television, Jessica sank her body into a chair in a corner across the room from her, holding her books open in her lap. When her mother went to bed, Jessica tiptoed down the hallway as close to her mother's room as she dared. When she heard her mother getting into bed, she breathed a sigh of relief, went back to her room, and left the door open while she sat at her desk and stared at her books.

When Jessica brought her mother home from the hospital, her final exams were about a month away. When she tried studying, she glued her eyes to any movement her mother made. Her ears scanned the air for any unexpected sounds. Dorothy urged her to go to her room and study, promising to call if she needed her help.

"Don't you remember the nurse telling us that you needed to stay in bed?" Jessica pleaded once again.

Dorothy shot back, "I'm not going to spend all day in bed! I'd go out of my mind!"

"But the doctor must have told her to say that," Jessica insisted.

"I'm not staying in my room, and that's that."

"What if you have an accident? What if you fall? What if you can't get up? What if you hurt your neck? If I'm in my room, I may not get to you in time!"

Dorothy sat stone-faced, and the discussion ended. Jessica continued shadowing her mother.

She only saw Roger, besides when he came to the restaurant, when he visited in the evening. Saturday evening was the only time they were together for more than an hour, but they did not go anywhere.

When the insurance money arrived, Dorothy bought a car from friends of Roger's parents. In the few weeks since Dorothy had come home, she showed small signs of improvement in her mobility. She could reach a bit higher, twist a bit further, walk a bit faster, bend a bit more, and lift objects a bit heavier.

While Jessica was greatly relieved that her mother's condition was showing definite signs of progress, her behavior was causing Jessica's anxiety to go sky-high. Dorothy's desire for self-sufficiency did not know any bounds. She started acting as if she no longer wore a neck brace or had her arm in a cast. There were more gasps of pain than before. Jessica's mind and body were galvanized for any emergency.

The day of Jessica's final exams descended on her harried life before she realized it. She had three, all on the same day. On that day, as she was getting ready, a body-headache erupted. When she left, Dorothy said, "Good luck." By the time she drove off, her head was pounding, but her vision was clear. She drove carefully over the dips, passed the bus stop, and turned onto Bayport Road. She stayed to the right and drove slowly. In a short distance, she came to St. Catherine's Highway. The school was less than a mile down the road.

During the drive, her vision slowly worsened. During the last minute, she nearly sideswiped another car as both pulled into the school's parking lot. She immediately veered to the back of the lot and parked there. She had to will her body to get out. Her head felt like it was about to split open. With each step, the pounding pain vibrated through every fiber in her body. Her skin felt like it was on fire.

She kept repeating to herself, "You're here to take finals!"

If she did not command her body like a drill sergeant, she was afraid it would just collapse. She stared straight ahead, walked with robot-like stiffness, and ignored everyone.

She propped herself against the school building, just outside the doors, until the last minute. She turned her back to the students streaming in. The thought of bumping into anyone greatly frightened her. She hurried into the room just as the teacher was starting to write the exam questions on the board. Exam booklets were on the desks.

She extracted her pencil from her purse, held it poised in her fingers, arranged the booklet, and stared at the first question. The words were a mass of jumbled swirls, like a foreign language she had never seen. She rubbed her eyes, squinted, and waited. After a minute, some of the words slipped into focus. In another minute, all the words were clear—or at least so they seemed. She continued staring. After another minute or two, she thought she understood the question and began writing. She wrote whatever thoughts appeared in her mind. She then stared back at the board and waited for more thoughts to appear, even if it was only a few words. She quickly wrote down whatever appeared in her mind. She did not waste any time reading what she had written. She just stared at the board and waited for thoughts (or bits of thoughts) to appear.

"Time is up!"

The booming voice broke her concentration. She had no idea how much she had written, but she did not care. She had lost all sense of time. If someone asked her how long she had been sitting there, she would have exclaimed, "Oh, five or ten minutes."

She passed her paper up to the front, put her pencil back in her purse, and went to her next exam. Her eyes fixed straight ahead, but her head was pounding. It was all she could do to keep from ripping off her clothes. She avoided bumping into anyone.

She went through the next two exams in the same numb, mechanical state and stopped writing when she heard, "Time's up!"

When the last exam was over, other students were jumping, yelling, and running through the halls. She avoided everyone. She darted between clusters of people. If anyone yelled, "Jessica!" she yelled, "Have to check on my mom!"

She stumbled through the school doors. When she finally found sanctuary in her car, the world was a big blur. She was grateful she had parked in the back of the lot. Everyone else had parked much closer. For a few minutes, she sat perfectly still until her vision cleared enough for her to very slowly drive. Once or twice, she was forced to pull over on the shoulder and wait for a few minutes because of her fluctuating vision.

At home, she found her mother at the sewing machine in the living room. She held her head stiffly. If she rested her arm in the sling on the table, she could use those fingers. As soon as Jessica stepped into the room, she stopped sewing and looked up.

"Well, how did you do?"

Jessica shrugged her shoulders and mumbled, "Okay."

From the second Jessica had handed in her last final, it was like the whole experience had never happened. Dorothy nodded and went back to her sewing. Jessica busied herself around the house until it was time to leave for work.

By the time she was in the car and on her way to the restaurant, she was doing her best to fight a full-blown panic attack. She knew why it was happening. Tomorrow morning and the early afternoon, the hours when she was used to being in school, were opening before her like a gaping abyss in her day.

As soon as Jessica arrived at the restaurant, she pounced on Mr. Richardson and asked if she could start working every day, starting tomorrow, and for as many hours as he could fit her in. He probably thought she was trying to save money for college. One of the waitresses wanted to cut back on her hours to have more time during the summer for her children. Jessica could start tomorrow, twelve to fourteen hours a day, seven days a week, if she wanted that much work.

On this day, she stayed two hours longer. When she got home, everyone was in bed.

In the morning, she was at work by 6:00 AM. She left a note for her mother about her new hours. A few hours after Jessica left, the phone in the Thomas house rang. Dorothy was at the kitchen table. The phone was on a small table at the other side of the small dining area, at the hallway's entrance. She reached it after a few rings.

"Mrs. Thomas?" It was Mr. Carter, Jessica's school counselor ever since she started high school. Dorothy had met him at school functions, and she liked him.

"Mrs. Thomas, could you possibly come to school today? I'd like to talk to you about Jessica's final exams."

"Jessica has my car, but I'll see if one of my neighbors can give me a ride. I'll let you know in a few minutes." After two calls, Dorothy found an available neighbor. She called Mr. Carter, "I'll be there in a half hour."

"Good. I'll be waiting. Just come right to my office."

Forty-five minutes later, Dorothy shuffled into Mr. Carter's office. He was in his chair behind his desk, reading some papers. With her first step into the office, Dorothy started apologizing for being late. He abruptly interrupted her words.

"What happened?" Mr. Carter exclaimed as he jumped up from behind his desk to pull out a chair. "Why didn't you tell me? I wouldn't have asked..."

Dorothy made a small wave with her one free arm. "If it's about Jessica's finals, I want to be here."

She eased herself into the chair and brought Mr. Carter up-to-date. His call had not surprised her. She knew Jessica had not been concentrating on her studies as well as she could have.

"I think she was in a state of shock over my accident. When she saw me in the hospital, she badgered me with questions and kept pestering the nurses about how serious my injuries were. From the minute I walked into the house, she wouldn't let me out of her sight. Every time we went anywhere, she wouldn't let me get more than a few feet away. She's been my shadow! I kept telling her to study. She never studied in her room, always in the kitchen or the living room, where I was. I was getting most of my work done. It was just taking me longer than usual. Sometimes, I did try things I probably shouldn't have and moaned a bit. Whenever I did, she jumped up to run over to me. There were only one or two things I really needed help with, like getting the vacuum cleaner out of the closet and washing the bath tub."

Mr. Carter's head bobbed up and down the entire time. "I'm so sorry this happened. Jessica must have been a big help. It's just like her to be so responsible.

She must have been sick with worry. She has only you, and she's now the oldest child at home." He flashed Dorothy a knowing smile and glanced at some papers on his desk. He then looked at Dorothy. "Well, all this now makes a lot more sense. We were all…that is, Jessica's teachers as well as myself…just at a complete loss in trying to understand this. Jessica's always been an excellent…"

"You don't understand what?"

"These are Jessica's final exams," Mr. Carter began. "She…well…she did answer all the questions and wrote a fair amount, as you can see." He held up the sheets of paper. Dorothy recognized Jessica's writing. "But what she wrote…well…" he gestured helplessly, "well, it just doesn't make very much sense!" Having finally said it, he visibly relaxed. "Her answers, or what she wrote for answers, are mainly isolated thoughts, like separate pieces of information all unrelated to each other. One of her teachers even said, 'It's like she wasn't in class the whole year.'"

Dorothy paused to catch her breath. Her eyes pleaded with Mr. Carter to understand. "Jessica has never been like this! She's always been so responsible, so good, for as long as I can remember. It seemed like she was born that way." After peering at Mr. Carter, she forced out the words, "Will Jessica graduate?"

"Oh, of course…Well, that is, if it was just up to me. But, it's really up to Mr. Porter, the principal." Mr. Carter's face then broke into a reassuring smile. "I'm sure he'll work something out once he learns about Jessica's reaction to your accident. We all want to do what's best for her. Her teachers were so shocked by all this." His eyes shifted to the papers. "Let me talk with Mr. Porter and the teachers. I'll call you as soon as I can."

Dorothy struggled to a standing position, thanked Mr. Carter for his concern, and shuffled off to find her neighbor. A few hours later, Mr. Carter called. Jessica's teachers would base her final grade on her work before the exams, and the principal agreed. She would graduate.

While Dorothy was elated over the school's decision, she was also panic-stricken. She feared what she had dreaded for a long time and tried shoving to the back of her mind ever since her children had been born, especially her daughters, was now becoming a reality.

Dorothy's three sisters were the nervous type. Two had breakdowns within a year after graduating from high school. One had been in a psychiatric hospital for a few months. The other, the oldest, had stayed married to a domineering husband. After getting married herself, Dorothy began hearing rumors that her mother had died in a mental hospital, not from spinal meningitis complicated by pneumonia, as she had always been told.

The dreaded question haunted Dorothy: Was there mental illness in the family? If so, it seemed to afflict the females. Dorothy had never spoken to her daughters about this. She had not wanted to worry them unnecessarily. Dorothy decided, if Jessica did not say anything about her final exams, she would not either.

After the talk with Mr. Carter, Dorothy realized that Jessica had been far more worried about her accident than she had suspected. All she could do was to keep a sharp eye on everything Jessica did and pray.

On the second day of her new schedule, Jessica worked fifteen hours, until 9:00 PM. She and Roger then went for ice cream. She did not see her mother until the next morning, and then for only a few minutes. Dorothy wished her luck with her new schedule and breathed a sigh of relief. If Jessica was working so hard, how could she be the nervous type?

With final exams over, the next big event in Jessica's life was graduation. While she was losing herself in near perpetual motion at the restaurant while Dorothy met with Mr. Carter, an unsettling thought struggled to form in her mind. The words "on my own" kept pressing into her consciousness. She tried in vain to ignore them. When she was unable to push them to the back of her mind, her heart started to race. Beads of perspiration stuck to her forehead. For an instant, her mind felt like it was starting to spin out of control.

Jessica had never given much thought to what she would do after graduation. She just assumed she would find a way of maneuvering her way through life as she had always done, that is, by doing what was expected. However, no one seemed to be telling her what to do. Dorothy had not said one word about what she would like Jessica to do. Mr. Carter had told her that she seemed to have an aptitude for certain kinds of work or particular subjects, if she wanted to go to college. He emphasized that decision was hers.

On the night before graduation, as Jessica stood in front of her dresser and stared at the blank wall with brush in hand, the intrusive words, "on my own," with their message of foreboding reverberated in her mind. The thought of going to the graduation ceremony petrified her. The official act of graduating seemed to mark the division between doing what others expected and deciding on her own what to do. She would have much rather preferred working the whole day. She knew there was not any way of getting out of it. Last week, Mr. Richardson, thinking he was doing her a favor, scheduled her for the day off. Even so, before she left the day before, she agreed to work for another waitress who wanted Sunday morning off. Jessica worked the breakfast shift and did not get home until the last minute. Everyone else was practically ready. Roger had already arrived.

She let her hair down, freshened up the little makeup she used, and changed her clothes. They then all piled into Roger's car.

At the ceremony, she walked to the middle of the platform and shook hands with Mr. Carter and Mr. Porter. Both gave her a reassuring smile. She accepted the mock diploma in her other hand and finished walking across the stage. She said, "Thank you" to "Good luck." She smiled during pictures. When asked about future plans, she simply said, "I don't know."

When Roger brought her home after the last party they had gone to and she kissed him goodnight, she felt the panic gathering itself together, like a demon that had lost the last battle and was ferociously preparing to continue the fight.

The next morning, she awoke just before the alarm was set to go off at five-thirty. She had volunteered to have the restaurant open at 6:00 AM. She could not get there fast enough. Working was the only way to keep her sanity. The world had never seemed so alien. Overnight, she felt she had been magically transported to a strange land. No familiar road signs guided her way. As she hurried from the house, she took her first trembling steps into this new territory.

12

Immobilized by the Future

Jessica plunged headfirst into this territory and stayed frantically busy. On most days, she worked at least fourteen hours. The earliest she ever left the restaurant was at eight o'clock in the evening. Usually, it was nine or ten before she went home.

For the first two weeks, Jessica only saw Roger when she was finished at the restaurant. He took her home, or she drove to his house. They could not visit for very long because he had to go to work on the night shift. When Jessica worked the first two Saturday nights after graduation until ten o'clock because someone wanted the evening off, Roger started dropping hints about the two of them going out on a Saturday night.

Two Saturdays later, they went to a drive-in movie. Although Jessica had agreed to go, just the thought of sitting in one place caused a surge of panic. She wondered where she was going to go if she had to get busy. Would she offer to work in the concession stand or march around the parking lot? She did not ask what was playing, and she did not care. Even though she would be glued to her seat for two hours, she thought she would be okay as long she was in physical contact with Roger.

They were going with another couple, Steve and Pat, Roger's friends. The three had graduated together. They were the only couple Jessica and Roger had ever gone anywhere with. They went bowling on one occasion and had pizza on another.

On Saturday, Jessica worked until 7:30, leaving just enough time to get ready at home. Roger came at 8:30, and they then picked up the other couple.

The drive-in was about fifteen minutes away, just off St. Catherine's Highway and about five miles past the high school. When they found a parking spot, Jessica removed her seat belt, slid closer to Roger, reached for his hand, and took a deep breath.

The opening scene practically jumped out at them. A teenage couple was walking hand-in-hand through the woods. Sunshine filtered through the branches. They were smiling and laughing. Suddenly, a hideous creature sprang out from behind a huge rock and savagely attacked both of them. Blood splattered everywhere. Heads rolled. Limbs were thrown about.

The instant the creature was catapulted into their world (right into the front seat it seemed to Jessica), she put a death grip on Roger's hand. While the air crackled with suspense, Jessica's panic started erupting. A bit later in the picture, after a few more teenagers had been dismembered, she was silently praying for this lunacy to end. Every time the creature attacked someone, she expected to be its next victim. In the next minute (the next instant), it was going to materialize alongside the car; reach in with its massive, ugly hands; dig its claws into her flailing arms and legs; haul her body through the window; and mercilessly snap it to pieces.

Roger, Steve, and Pat were cracking jokes and laughing loudly. For them, the creature's clumsy behavior and the antics of the boys and girls trying to flee were hilarious.

Jessica was oblivious to all of it. Thoughts spun around in her head. She felt like a spectator at a racetrack. She had lost all control over what was happening in her mind. It felt as if her head was about to spin right off her body. She was on the verge of flying out the window and running as fast as she could until she dropped.

All she could do was grit her teeth, tense all of her muscles to hopefully keep her head attached to her body, and put all of her energy into trying to stop the racing thoughts. She concentrated with all of her might, focusing all of her energy like a laser beam of light. She grabbed each errant thought with the force of her will and tried dragging it back down to earth.

Her efforts were useless. She felt her mind starting to descend into a bottomless pit of chaos. Her right hand groped frantically for the car door. At the same instant, her eyes spotted a brilliant, miniature rainbow. A tiny crack in the front window of the car caught the light from the screen and dispersed it into a brilliant array of colors. Her eyes focused on the radiant colors. They were hypnotic, and her mind lost itself in nature. The longer she stared at the display of colors, the more the panic faded. The racing thoughts started slowing down.

As she felt the last thought gradually spiraling down out of orbit and coming to rest, her tortured mind had no more than a moment's peace. She had a sudden, strange foreboding. The unspeakable question that had haunted her for months, the one she had frantically tried to prevent from preying on her spirit by staying perpetually busy, plastered itself like a large neon sign across the infinite space in her mind's eye. "What do I want?" seared itself into her consciousness.

She desperately wanted to scream back "That is the most ridiculous question I have ever heard! How am I supposed to know what I want?"

The question echoed through the caverns of her mind, seemingly taunting her and teasing her to find an answer. Every part of her—her emotions, mind, psyche, and spirit—was absolutely quiet. Silent. Lifeless. An urge or a desire to do anything was not inside of her. She felt absolutely dead. She no longer felt connected to the world. It was as if someone had opened the zipper of the world and tossed her out. She was no longer afraid of anything, even an attack from the *something*.

The fingers on her right hand released the door handle. It was a purely mechanical move. The object her left hand was holding felt lifeless and alien. She could see her left hand was attached to her arm and her arm was attached to her body. Only by this process of logical deduction, she knew her hand was holding this alien-looking object. The longer the movie lasted, the louder the other three laughed. Jessica was not laughing, saying a word, or moving a muscle. Her eyes were transfixed on the rainbow.

The movie finally ended. She had no idea how long she had been in this lifeless state. Roger turned around for one final joke with Steve and Pat. Jessica's head turned just enough for her to crack a little smile. Roger released her hand and started the car. They inched forward in stops and starts.

Jessica felt an overwhelming urge to be in her room. She wanted to scream at Roger to drive through a fence if he had to in order to get her home as fast as he could.

While they crept their way to the road, her attention was completely riveted on getting home. They finally made the road. After a few miles, they stopped at Pat's house and let the other two off. Jessica's mouth managed to say, "Goodbye." A few minutes later, Roger turned onto the dirt road leading to her house. Her fingers were already wrapped tightly around the door handle.

Before the car came to a full stop in the driveway, she shoved the door open. Without a word, she jumped out and rushed into the house. She caught a glimpse of her mother sitting in a chair watching television, but she did not slow down. She did not say—or even think of saying—a word. She hurried to her room and shut the door. She flopped down on her bed, crawled to the other side, turned her face to the wall, and closed her eyes.

A minute or two later, the door to her room opened.

"Jessica! What's the matter?"

Her mouth stayed shut. The only sound in the room was her mother's heavy breathing.

"Did you have a fight with Roger?"

It was not a question. It was an accusation. If she and Roger had an argument, it must have been her fault, either for starting it or for not smoothing it over.

Jessica said nothing.

"Roger is waiting for you!"

The prospect of talking to anyone, even Roger, left her cold.

"Jessica! Roger is waiting for you!"

After a few heavy sighs, Jessica heard, "I don't understand what's wrong with you! You've just graduated. Roger is a very nice, responsible young man. Your whole future is ahead of you. Why…You're at the peak of your life!"

Thinking about the future was the most frightening thing Jessica could imagine.

After the inert figure did not give a response, Dorothy said, "Jessica! I can't believe there's something wrong with you!"

The blaming voice awakened a part of Jessica's brain that had been locked in deep freeze for farther back in time than she could remember.

"There is! I've been trying to tell you that all of my life!" The words streaming out of her mouth, seemingly on their own accord, horrified Jessica. She immediately clamped her teeth down on her lips to make sure her mouth stayed shut. She could not believe what she had just uttered. She could not believe she had come so close to revealing her unspeakable secret.

Dorothy stomped down the hallway. Her neck brace had come off a week ago. Her arm was in a sling. She talked to Roger for a minute. The screen door opened and closed. A car started and moved into the distance. A minute later, Jessica heard the phone, just around the corner in the living room, being dialed.

"Dr. Frank, please?" Dorothy apologized for calling so late.

A few minutes later, Jessica heard a pleading voice come from somewhere on the other side of her room. "Will you talk to Dr. Frank?"

Just the thought of talking to anyone made her sick. However, if she didn't, she knew her mother would pester her with absurd comments about having the future ahead of her and being at the peak of her life.

Jessica rolled to the other side of the bed, swung her legs over the edge, and stood up. She made her way into the kitchen and took the phone from her mother.

Barely audible, she said, "Hello?"

She heard Dr. Frank's voice. He asked very simple questions: Was she sleeping enough? Eating enough? Working too many hours? Was she upset with anyone?

Yes and no were the only answers whatever part of Jessica's brain was operating could manage. She heard herself saying good-bye with the same weak voice she had said hello. Without saying anything or even looking at Dorothy, she handed the phone to her mother. She wanted to return to bed and shut out the rest of the world. Whatever Dr. Frank had said seemed an eternity ago.

She closed the door to her room and crawled back across the bed. Her face was inches from the wall. She closed her eyes, grabbed a pillow, stuck it over her head, and waited for the oblivion of sleep.

When she woke in the morning, her clothes were still on, and her face was still inches from the wall. The pillow had fallen off her head. She still felt completely separated from the world. She did not turn over to look at the clock. She had no idea what time it was. She did not care. She did not care if she stayed in bed and her body wasted away. She heard her mother and siblings moving about.

After awhile, her mother's heavy footsteps came down the hallway. She yanked open the door.

"Jessica, aren't you going to work?" Her mother's words were a challenge, not a question. "If you don't get up, you're going to be late for work."

Jessica tried blocking out the intruding voice. She was not thinking about work or anything else. She was not even thinking about telling her mother she did not want to go to work.

Her younger brothers started an argument in the kitchen. A few minutes later, her mother was back in the doorway.

"Do you want me to call the restaurant and tell them you're not coming in?"

Jessica did not care if her mother called or not. She did not care if she went to work or not. Whatever her mother wanted to do was fine with her.

She heard a long exhale clear across the room. She then heard heavy footsteps and the dialing of the phone. She put the pillow back over her head.

Her only desire was to isolate herself from the world. However, if she stayed in bed, she knew her mother would be back with more stupid questions, using the same impatient voice she had heard for years. The voice said, "I can't understand what's wrong with you! If you're having a problem, it's not my fault. I've helped you all I can. You're just going to have to try harder."

She changed her clothes, went to the living room, and sat down in an armchair opposite the large picture window. She sat perfectly still and stared at the sky, green lawns, flowers, and trees. Soon, her brothers and sister went outside to play. Her mother cleaned in the kitchen.

Awhile later, Dorothy came into the living room. "I have to go grocery shopping. Can I leave you alone?"

Ever since her first panic attack in the bathroom at work, Jessica had dreaded being alone, but she now welcomed that prospect. She stared out the window and did not say anything.

Dorothy spoke again, sharply. "If you don't have anything to say, I'm going shopping." With that, she grabbed her purse and left.

About two hours later (Jessica could only guess on the time), she watched her mother pull into the driveway. Dorothy got out, walked to the other side of the car, reached in, wrapped one arm around a bag, and snatched it.

Jessica watched her step onto the front porch and heard her fumble for the latch on the door. She continued staring out the window. Dorothy walked through the living room and into the kitchen. She made two more trips for the rest of the bags, wordlessly parading past Jessica each time. She put the groceries away, banging cans and slamming cabinet doors.

When her brothers and sisters came in for lunch, Jessica heard her name being loudly whispered. Her mother said, "She's not feeling well."

When lunch was finished and the others had left, Dorothy stomped into the living room. Her hands were on her hips. "Do you want me to make you anything for lunch?"

Jessica did not answer.

"Jessica, whatever this is, you can't let it get the best of you. Just sitting around doesn't seem to be doing you any good. I can't understand what could be troubling you so much, and you won't tell me. All I see when I look at you is a young lady who is at the peak of her life. I couldn't graduate with my friends from high school. I had to drop out to care for my sisters and take care of the big house we lived in when grandmother died. Then I married your father. You have so much more to look forward to. I just can't understand why you're letting yourself sit around like this."

Jessica kept staring straight ahead.

"If you're just going to sit there, I'm going next door for awhile."

Jessica sat. Dorothy left.

When she returned in what seemed to be an hour, Jessica was in the same exact position, staring straight ahead. Dorothy went to her room. In a few minutes, Jessica heard the hum of the sewing machine. Then the phone rang. Jessica did not move a muscle. After four rings, Dorothy answered it.

"Roger, she isn't feeling well. She didn't go to work today. She still isn't talking to anyone. Do you have any idea why she's like this?"

A minute later, Dorothy said, "I have no idea either. She won't say. She hasn't said a word to me all day. Maybe you can get her to talk. I tell her she has so much to look forward to, but it doesn't seem to do any good." A few seconds later, she said, "All right, I'll tell her."

From the hallway, she said, "Roger just woke up. He'll be over shortly...Did you hear me?" Jessica did not respond.

Roger arrived shortly. He came to the screen door, stood there, and said, "Hi!" Dorothy walked in from the kitchen.

"Hi, Roger, come in. I'll be in the backyard." Roger came in and stood right in front of Jessica. She stared at his belt buckle.

"What's the matter?" He spoke softly, but she did not say anything.

He stood in place for a minute or two before moving to the side of the chair. He dropped down on one knee and put an arm around her shoulder. Jessica knew his arm was there, but she could not feel it.

"Are you upset about something that happened last night?"

Silence.

"Your mom said you haven't spoken to her all day. Did she get you upset?"

Silence.

"She told me she was trying to convince you that you're at the peak of your life and she couldn't understand what you're so upset about and why you're not talking to anybody."

The only sign Roger was talking to a living being was the rising and falling of a chest and the occasional blinking of eyes. He stopped talking. He never spoke to Jessica in the blaming way Dorothy did. He just seemed to accept whatever she did or said. He never made her feel that she was not trying hard enough. That was a welcome relief. Still, Jessica felt no desire to talk to him. He stayed kneeling on the floor with his arm around her. She could feel him staring at her.

After five minutes, he said, "I'll call later tonight." He leaned over and kissed her on the cheek.

Shortly after Roger left, Dorothy came in the back door. She walked through the kitchen and into the living room's doorway. Silently, she went back into the kitchen and started supper. When the other children came in, she said, "She still isn't feeling well."

The others stayed in the kitchen through supper. When they were finished, Jessica's brothers and sister went out. Dorothy immediately marched into the living room.

"Aren't you hungry? I don't think you've eaten all day!" She used the blaming tone of voice that said Jessica had not eaten on purpose just to aggravate her. "I can't understand what you can be so upset about. You and Roger didn't have an argument. You have so much to look forward to. Much more than I ever did. Whatever this is, you can't let it get the best of you."

Jessica jumped from her chair and marched into the kitchen. She finished the remains of the salad bowl. She broke off a large chunk of meat loaf and shoved it in her mouth. She buttered a piece of bread and drank a half-glass of milk. She went out the back door and sat in a chair in the backyard. No one bothered her. When the sky turned dark, she went inside and went directly to her room. A few minutes later, the phone rang. A minute later, her mother stopped outside of her room.

"Roger will be over tomorrow afternoon about the same time."

In the morning, Dorothy knocked on Jessica's door. Jessica heard the door to her room being quietly opened. Her body was in the same position as last night.

"Are you feeling any better? Are you going to work?"

A minute later, Dorothy called the restaurant. "Jessica isn't feeling well again…I'm not sure, perhaps tomorrow."

Jessica spent the entire day in the chair in the living room, except for a few minutes after each meal when she dashed into the kitchen and threw some food into her mouth. She hoped it was enough to keep her mother from using her not eating as a reason for talking to her.

When Roger came over, he put his arm around her. She felt as she had yesterday. She could not understand why he was touching her because, as far as she was concerned, there was nothing to touch. He asked a few questions, none of which she answered. After awhile, he kissed her and left.

The next morning, when her mother came to her room, she found Jessica facing the wall. Without wasting another breath, she quietly closed the door. A short while later, Dorothy rushed down the hallway. The door to Jessica's room flew open, and Dorothy barged in. She marched all the way over to Jessica's bed.

"I…I just called the county hospital and made an appointment for you. It's with a psychiatrist. It's in two days. He said he could see you at eight in the morning. Will you go? Please. I…I don't know how to help you. You simply can't go on like this!"

Hearing her mother so upset triggered instinctive mechanisms. She had to do something to undo the terrible thing she must have done, whatever it was. As soon as Dorothy had finished, Jessica's head nodded up and down. She hurried to the phone, called the restaurant, and said she would be a bit late. She took the slip of paper Dorothy had written the psychiatrist's name, time of the appointment, and name of the building and put it in her purse.

She gave her mother a hug and reassured her, "Don't worry, I'll be okay."

When originally established many years ago, the psychiatric center of the county health department was located well beyond the then-existing Detroit suburban area. The property was now in the middle of suburbia. A modern, five-story medical center used by medical schools in the area as a training center stood at one end of the tract of land. On the opposite side of the property, across an expanse of open fields, the much older buildings of the psychiatric center sat under very large, gnarled oak and maple trees. A box-shaped, four-story building of very old, red brick served as the nerve center and housed the outpatient department. Smaller, two-story, L-shaped buildings with barred windows trailed off from the main building under the trees and housed the chronically ill. One of Dorothy's sisters had been in these buildings years ago. Jessica drove under the high ornamental arch of curved, iron bars and through a big, iron gate, now permanently open. All was part of the original black, spiked, iron fence that surrounded the area.

In the waiting room, Dr. Mung, a small man of Asian ethnicity, introduced himself in a quiet voice. He escorted Jessica to his office. She sat in a chair on the other side of his desk and waited. She felt his eyes scrutinizing her.

He smiled and spoke, "When your mother called us, she said you were staying home from work and weren't talking to anyone. How are you feeling now?"

"I'm back at work," Jessica confidently answered.

Dr. Mung nodded his head. "I'm glad to hear that. Could you tell me how you are feeling now?"

"Okay." It was purely a matter-of-fact reply. Jessica stared back at Dr. Mung and waited for his next question.

"You just didn't feel like going to work at the time? Or talking with anyone?"

Jessica did not speak. Instead, she just gave a little nod of her head.

"Were you feeling too depressed to go to work? To talk to people? Even your boyfriend?"

"I guess so," she replied.

Jessica's evasive answers were not good enough for the doctor. "What do you think made you stay home and not talk to anyone?"

"I don't know. I just didn't feel like it," Jessica said and stared back.

"I see," Dr. Mung said as he nodded his head. Not having much success with this line of questioning, he tried another approach. "How often do you work at the restaurant?"

"Every day."

"How many hours a day do you work?"

"At least twelve."

"That's quite a bit indeed. Are you going to continue working that much?"

"I guess so."

"After work, do you see your boyfriend?"

"Sometimes."

"Do you see him every day?"

"No."

"Do you have other friends you see? Girlfriends?"

"No." Ever since the fear of something getting her had become a part of Jessica's life, she had stopped seeing old friends, unless she was with Roger.

"You just go to work and see your boyfriend?"

"Yes."

"Have you ever thought of working less so you can be with your boyfriend more and make other friends? And do other things? I think you might feel better if you worked less and socialized more."

Jessica felt as if Dr. Mung was asking the impossible. Staying busy was the only way to keep her sanity. Jessica's socializing more became Dr. Mung's focus, his only focus. He did not bother to find out how his patient felt about anything else.

At the end of the first session, Dr. Mung gave Jessica some tranquilizers. She stopped taking them before her next session because they made her groggy. She did not tell him she was not taking them. Whenever he asked, she said they seemed to be helping.

Dr. Mung wanted to see Jessica every other week. Maybe he was impressed with her ability to quickly resume her demanding work schedule. Perhaps he believed she had not been that depressed or she did not have a serious problem.

Jessica saw Dr. Mung for the next three months. He only advised, "Loosen up! Learn to enjoy life! Don't be so serious! You and your boyfriend go out more and enjoy yourselves. Work less and be more active socially."

Every visit, Jessica would say, "I don't feel like it."

Dr. Mung did not seem to take her answer very seriously. He never tried to find out what was making her "not feel like it." He seemed to regard her "I don't feel like it" as a weak excuse. Once she was more active, she would like it.

Dr. Mung persisted with his single-minded advice. The more he harped on it, the more frustrated Jessica became. She later remembered the experience, "All he was doing was giving me this stupid advice. It was very frustrating!"

For one of her last sessions, Jessica came right from a twelve-hour day at the restaurant. She was wearing her uniform. She had never come directly from work before. She walked smartly into Dr. Mung's office. She sat more erect than usual. His eyes did a double take.

"Jessica! Is this you?" He stared at her in wide-eyed amazement. "You look better than I've ever seen you. Have you and Roger been going out more?"

Having her attention focused on something outside of herself had worked its magic again. Jessica forced herself to cheerfully respond, "Yes." She had had enough of this nonsense.

"Wonderful!" Dr. Mung beamed at her.

Jessica went for two more sessions. Dr. Mung continued to be impressed with how alert she looked. As far as Jessica was concerned, he was seeing things. She did not feel any better, and she did not feel any different about herself than she had ever felt. She decided that more sessions with him would be fruitless. It was obvious to her (if it wasn't to Dr. Mung) that she could not follow his advice. If anyone was ever going to help her, it was not him.

Jessica wrote Dr. Mung a letter, saying she did not think she needed to see him anymore and she was more active socially and feeling better. She told her mother about the letter, omitting the socializing more part. Dorothy was relieved.

Jessica continued working at the restaurant, seven days a week. Roger continued asking her to work less. Jessica said she enjoyed the work, which was a half-truth, and she was making good money, which was a whole truth. She reminded him that her family had lived in near-poverty for too many years.

A few months later, Roger proposed. Jessica initially hesitated. She knew she could not stop working, even though Roger said he did not have any problem with her working, but under a more normal schedule.

Roger continued asking and joked with others about trying to get her to say yes. Other people began asking Jessica when she was getting married. It soon seemed like everyone was expecting her to do so.

Jessica eventually said, "Yes." However, she was not sure how much she loved Roger. She hoped that being a wife and a mother, each with its own set of expectations, would give her some peace of mind. Working eighty to ninety hours a week was not keeping the panic at bay as it once did. She did not know what else to do.

13

Jessica's Daring Proposal

Unlike Dr. Mung, I was acutely aware that Jessica had a great deal of difficulty in deciding what to talk about, although I certainly did not know how terrified she actually was. If I had known, I would have never forced her to do something she was psychologically incapable of doing, such as deciding what to talk about based on her awareness of what she needed, and entirely through her own efforts without any hints or help of any kind from me. My ignorance of the depth of Jessica's fear over her doing exactly that had come very close to fatally fracturing our relationship. I had forced her to resort to a drastic step (fleeing from my office) to let me know how truly frightened she was. My only hope of repairing that fracture had been to return to our old routine of me asking questions and directing the session.

Two or three weeks after we settled into our old routine, Jessica began complaining of headaches. A complaint for her was to say, in her typical matter-of-fact way, "I've been having headaches." She made it seem as if it really was not a problem. She did not volunteer any thoughts about what might be causing them.

I was sorry she was having headaches. However, from the way she looked and sounded when she spoke about them, I just assumed they were the ordinary variety. She only needed an aspirin or two. In fact, as I would later learn, they were much worse.

◆　　　◆　　　◆

One evening at home, she was sitting on the living room couch watching Roger and Melissa playing a children's card game. Melissa was a fountain of excited chatter, but Jessica was oblivious to all of it. She was only pretending to watch because of the killing pain in her head, a pain that had started earlier in the day and had grown sharper and deeper.

With her husband and daughter still absorbed in their game, Jessica suddenly snatched a pillow off the couch, stretched out facedown on the floor, held the pillow tightly over her head, and screamed, "I want to die! I want to die! Please! Let me die!"

The air in the small house vibrated. Roger dropped his cards and jumped over to his wife. He shouted her name a few times. He shouted a few more times while he shook her by the shoulders. Jessica held tightly onto the pillow and kept insisting she wanted to die.

Roger was stunned. He—or anyone else—had never seen his wife in such a state. And talking of dying!

While Jessica was yelling, a part of her was shocked at how she was acting in front of her daughter. She quickly got a grip on herself. She sat up, crossed her legs in front of her, and proceeded to vigorously rock back and forth. Her eyes locked in a blank stare at the floor in front of her.

Roger said he wanted to take her to the hospital. Jessica did not seem to hear as she continued rocking. She stared straight ahead and did not say a word. After not hearing anymore pleas for her own death, Roger left her alone. Jessica rocked for awhile longer. Then she lay down on the floor, put her head on the pillow, and went to sleep. A few hours later, she woke up. A light blanket covered her.

◆   ◆   ◆

Along with more headaches, Jessica was also getting sick to her stomach. On her way home from a session, Roger had to stop the car a few times to let her out. Jessica threw up alongside the road every time.

When Jessica told me about getting sick to her stomach on their way home from the last session, I fairly exploded, "Why didn't you call me right away and tell me?"

Doing that seemed to me like the perfectly natural thing to do. All she had to do was pick up the phone. Then I quickly realized she had never called me in between sessions to say she was upset. Every client I had ever seen for this long of a time (by this time in my career, there had been quite a number) had called me at one time or another. Some called a lot more often than the others. One even called from a rest area on an interstate highway several states away. I just thought it was quite odd that Jessica had never called because she was upset. However, given what I knew about her, it made perfect sense.

Undoubtedly, Jessica's recurring headaches, even if I did not know the full extent of them at the time, as well as her being sick to her stomach were symptoms of inner emotional turmoil. I also thought I knew the cause. I was trying to relate to her as a human being, that is, a needing human being.

When I asked if she thought these symptoms were caused by her starting to feel she depended on or needed me, she could only weakly say, "I don't know."

While I was hoping for a more revealing answer, at least that was an improvement on her seeing me as a computer. If she did not know, I was certain I did, and I was going to give her an assignment to prove it. I told her, before her next appointment, she had to call and tell me how she was doing, even if nothing had upset her and even if everything in her life was just fine. It was probably better that she was not upset. In that case, I thought there was a much greater probability of her calling me. I wanted her to have the experience of calling in between sessions, in case she ever needed to.

When I gave Jessica a "homework" assignment for the first time, which I had done only two or three times with other clients in my career, I knew I was beginning to feel frustrated again, though not to the level as when she repeatedly asked her habitual question at the start of every session. I hoped I had made this request easier for her to follow than my last one.

Two days later, the day before her next appointment, Jessica called. "You're right," she said. "It was a lot scarier to call you than I thought it would be."

That was all she had to say. She talked for a minute or two about a few everyday things since we had last met. Nothing had upset her. By this time, I could tell if she was upset when she was not saying so. She did not say a word more about what "a lot scarier" meant, and I did not ask. I was only grateful that she had called.

After we hung up, I said a silent prayer. Fortunately, this was an exercise she had been able to complete. Over the next few weeks, I did not see any sign that her call had made any difference. We continued to meet and plod along in our old routine. I asked many questions and suggested a number of role-plays, which usually produced some tears and some light anger. I did not give her anymore assignments, and despite much prompting from me she did not remember anymore past experiences or volunteer anything. There was nothing new to focus on.

I did have hope. I continued believing that she was as committed as I was. She was keeping all of her appointments. She was always in the waiting area when I went there. If both of us persisted, I was certain we would find an answer.

A few weeks later, when Jessica sat down across from me at the start of a session, I immediately sensed a difference in how she looked. It was in her eyes. Some of her attention seemed to be on herself and not completely on me, as it usually was. It was enough of a difference for me to not say anything and wait.

In a halting, tentative voice, she spoke, "I think someone tried to rape me when I was six."

Despite the doubt in her words, the hint of anguish in her eyes said that someone had indeed brutalized her in this way. My hopes soared. Whenever other clients volunteered a traumatic event like this, a dramatic breakthrough always eventually followed. But I had never had anyone wait so long.

Without waiting to see if Jessica was going to continue on her own, I urged her to tell me about it. She slowly nodded her head a few times, as if to say she needed a few seconds to gather her resources, even though she knew she had volunteered the subject. She began in a halting voice, first providing events that had led up to the fateful event.

A week before, Dorothy had moved her five children to Oakwood, part of a line of older, suburban communities strung along the shore of the St. Catherine's River, stretching from the Detroit city limits to Bayport at the other end. Oakwood was near the middle. Their house was a few blocks from the downtown area that ran along the river. Most of Dorothy's neighbors in this older section of Oakwood were on fixed incomes. They were women on welfare with children, widows, and retirees.

Dorothy had separated from Henry a few years before. The final incident had been when he had come home late from work, drunk as usual. He smashed a pillow into her face while she sat on the couch. He jumped on top of her and swore he was going to kill her. Henry's brother, who was there for dinner, came running from another room, where he had been playing with the children, and yanked Henry off. Although Dorothy said nothing at the time, in her mind, she knew she did not have a choice. If something happened to her, she did not want her husband raising the children. A month later, with the help of her best girlfriend, she moved to the largest city in the southeast corner of Michigan, about thirty miles away. She hoped it was far enough so Henry could not find them by driving around.

The only area she could afford to move into with the meager amount of money she had been able to borrow was an old neighborhood within walking distance of the downtown business area. The only work she hoped to find was being a waitress. Even though she had never worked as one, she could not imagine it being more difficult than having been the woman of the house. She pleasantly discovered the area was quiet after the end of the business day, especially on Sunday, which had not yet become a regular business day, except for restaurants and gas stations.

True to what she felt was her nature, Dorothy tried making a go of it on her own. She worked the dinner hour during the week, the lunch hour if she could find a sitter, and often both on Saturday and Sunday. During the week, a sitter only had to watch three children because Ellen and Jessica were in school the entire day. On the weekends, those two were in charge, although a neighborhood woman or two popped in while Dorothy was at work.

Dorothy struggled for a few months to provide for her family. Then bags of groceries and clothes started appearing on her front porch, always off in a corner and always placed overnight. One morning, when she had used the last of the pancake mix, she called the restaurant to say she might be late. Her next paycheck was a few days away. The local department of social services office was about a half-mile away. She allowed enough walking time so she was there shortly before it opened. A neighbor had agreed to watch the children.

For whatever reason, the welfare worker immediately denied Dorothy's application. Upon hearing those words, Dorothy immediately shot up from her chair and announced she was going home to get her children. She was coming back with them. It might take while because they would have to walk. She was going to leave them with the worker because she did not have any food for them. When Dorothy was under a full head of steam, no one in earshot had any doubt that she meant every word she said. Before Dorothy had taken more than two steps, the woman gave in.

Dorothy knew she would have to rely on welfare until all of her children were in school. In the meantime, she learned how to upholster furniture in night classes at the local high school. Through word of mouth, she eventually had a steady income. About a year later, Dorothy learned that Henry had moved two states and several hundred miles away. She missed being closer to the rest of her family. With her savings from her upholstery work and weekend shifts at the restaurant, she could move to Oakwood. She quickly found work as a waitress.

Shortly after moving there, a neighbor invited Dorothy for a Saturday night get-together with other women in the neighborhood. She suggested her sixteen-year-old son as a sitter if Dorothy could not find anyone else. Dorothy had met the boy a few times. He seemed pleasant. Even though she had never hired a boy as a sitter, she soothed herself with the thought that this was only for a few hours and she would be just across the street. To ease his responsibility, she allowed Ellen, who shared a room with Jessica, to stay at her grandfather's house for the night.

Jessica first saw her nocturnal visitor when she felt someone shaking her shoulder after she had fallen asleep. She thought he was waking her because of a problem with her brothers and sister upstairs. But he smiled and said he had a surprise for her in the laundry room. Before she could say anything, he found her slippers under the bed. She just lay there. She was not sure what to do. Then he slowly lifted the covers off her and moved a slipper toward one of her feet. He slid one on and then put on the other.

He smiled again and said, "It's a very nice surprise, just what you like." He took a step and motioned for her to follow. Jessica slid out of bed and followed him to the other side of the house, through the kitchen, past the bathroom, and into the laundry room.

He then turned toward her and said, "I have to sit you on top of the washing machine."

He was still speaking softly and smiling. Jessica just stood there. She let him slide his hands under her shoulders and lift her up. He gently put her down on top of the machine as her legs dangled over the edge. He kept one hand on her shoulder.

He said, "To get the surprise, you have to do something first."

At the same instant he finished speaking, she saw his other hand start undoing his zipper. She squirmed backward. He squeezed her shoulder, which frightened her.

With urgency in his voice, he said, "There's nothing to be afraid of. I'm not going to hurt you. Come closer so you can see the surprise."

His hand disappeared inside his pants. She tried harder to get away. She kept staring at his hand. It looked like it was holding something big.

Practically hissing, he said, "Come closer!"

She put her hands flat against the top of the machine and pushed. He moved his cold, sweaty hand from her shoulder and wrapped it around the back of her neck. He started to pull her head down to where his hand was starting to come out of his pants. By that time, she could see what it was holding. She pushed as hard as she could and tried squirming backward as far as possible. He kept pulling her head toward him and down. She was nearly bent double.

He suddenly snatched her up in the air. He wrapped his arms around her and pressed her face against his chest. She could barely breathe. He rushed to the bathroom. After they were in, he shoved the door with his foot, but it did not close entirely. There were not any windows. The only light was the bit of moonlight that seeped in from the kitchen. He dropped to his knees, laid her down on the small rug, and pinned her there with his hand on her chest. With his other hand, he yanked off her pajama bottoms and pushed her top up. He slid his pants down and lay down on top of her. She felt something hard pressing into her stomach. She twisted her body in every direction she could manage. He slapped her on the side of the head. It hurt, but she kept struggling. He slapped her again, much harder. It stung her skin. Her body went limp. His body started to bounce up and down. She heard heavy breathing and animal-like grunts. With every downward thrust of his body, it felt as if her spine was being driven into the floor. She thought there was a crazed animal on top of her that had gone completely berserk. She was afraid he was going to squeeze the life right out of her. She was certain she was going to die.

Then it was over. He got off her and put his pants back on. He wiped her stomach off. He put her pajama bottoms back on and pulled her top down. The entire time, Jessica stared blankly at the ceiling. He picked her up and carried her back to her room, where he put her in bed and pulled the covers up to her neck. Then he left.

Jessica did not move a muscle. Her body stayed in the exact position it had rolled into. Although she heard him walking way, she was too terrified to turn her head to see if he had actually left. She tried breathing very slowly and very quietly. She was scared that any noise might bring him back.

After awhile, she heard footsteps coming toward her room. Her whole body tensed. She kept staring at the ceiling and breathing very quietly. Out of the corner of her eye, she saw him standing over her. He had a wild, half-crazed look in his eyes.

"I didn't mean to hurt you," he hissed. He suddenly started laughing. It was wild, crazy laughter. Then he started crying and pacing back and forth alongside her bed while he kept repeating, "I didn't mean to hurt you." He finally stopped pacing and leaned over her. He wrapped a hand very tightly around her throat.

With a threatening look, he said, "I didn't mean to hurt you. If you tell anyone, I will hurt you!"

He pressed his hand down harder on her throat and kept it there. Her head was filling with pressure. She was afraid he was not going to take his hand away in time. When he finally did, he warned her again that he would hurt her if she ever told anyone. Then he left. Laying on her back in bed in the dark and breathing very deliberately after someone had physically brutalized her gave Jessica déjà vu, that is, a strange feeling she had been through something like this before. However, she could not remember when.

Jessica continued lying perfectly still. She had no idea how much time had passed until she heard the front door open. Her mother and the boy were talking, but Jessica could not make out what they were saying. The front door then opened and closed. She could feel her body finally give way and relax a bit. She heard her mother go into the kitchen. A few minutes later, she came into Jessica's room. Jessica pretended to be asleep. Dorothy stood for a minute while she fiddled with the end of the blanket. Then she left.

For the twenty minutes it took for Jessica to relate this, she looked and sounded like a robot. The entire time, she spoke in a halting, tentative voice. There was hardly any emotion in her voice, even though she went into great detail at times. There was not even a tear. She did not sound afraid or angry at any point. I was convinced she had never told anyone else, even her mother or closest girlfriend. I was not surprised. Whatever invisible force was keeping her feelings locked in place was not going to give up its grip so easily. When she finished, she stared at me with her usual blank expression. I asked her to tell the most frightening parts again. Just retelling an event packed with so much emotion is sometimes enough for deeper feelings to surface. Even though this had yet to work with Jessica, I hoped the emotional intensity of this incident and the fact she had volunteered it would produce a breakthrough. However, when she went through the most horrifying parts again, she did not even shed a tear or sound the least bit frightened.

Because talking was not working, as usual, I suggested a role-play. We stood facing each other. I twisted my body into a caricature of Jack the Ripper, that is, a curved leg, a twisted foot, an arched back, a bent arm with a claw for a hand, and a comical, drooling face. Starting from several steps away, I very slowly hobbled over to her. When I was an arm's reach away, I clumsily scratched at her arm with my claw. My best comical rendition of "Hi! My name's Jack!" accompanied it.

My performance was good for lots of laughter. I was looking for this kind of emotional release. This kind of laughter, accompanied by warm or cold perspiration, is a healing response for embarrassment and light fear, respectively. Such a release is often a prelude to deeper feelings. I was more hopeful than ever that we would finally make some significant progress. I stood in front of her, clumsily scratched at her arm, and continued a steady stream of ridiculous-sounding phrases to keep her laughing. I also gave her words to say.

"Buzz off, jerko, you're not my type…Scram, big boy, you're just not in my class."

These statements were based on imaging her having the power and strength to act assertively during the traumatic event. All produced a steady stream of laughter.

We concentrated on this role-play over the next two months. Jessica laughed deeply every time we did it. After every significant bout of laughter, I had her tell the story again. Even though she no longer sounded like a robot and her words flowed freely, deeper feelings never emerged.

This attempt to crack the seemingly impenetrable shield surrounding the real Jessica met the same fate as my other efforts. Having no other new areas of Jessica's life to explore, I started reusing old role-plays, but, as in the past, I did not encounter anymore success.

About a month later, Jessica entered my office with an unfamiliar resolve in her step. She sat down smartly, pressed her knees together, and promptly folded her hands in her lap. When I engaged her attention, she did not have (much to my immense relief) her habitual expression of waiting for me to start the session. Her voice, instead of mine, now filled the air.

With the same self-assured posture she always exhibited on the couch in the waiting area, she locked her eyes onto mine and confidently asked, "Can we meet for four hours a day, three days a week for six weeks?"

Her tone was more of a statement of what we were going to do instead of seeking my agreement. Her hands remained folded in her lap as she continued to expectantly stare at me.

"I would like to meet at my house. It will be quieter than it is here…and more comfortable."

Obviously, she had given this intrepid request a great deal of thought. Even while my brain was quickly calculating that she was asking for an astronomical seventy-two hours of therapy in six weeks, more than someone would get in nearly a year-and-a-half at once a week, my head was instinctively nodding in spirited agreement. Even before the words had formed themselves firmly in my mind, an enthusiastic "Of course!" quickly came from my mouth. How could I possibly say no? How could I possibly dismiss such fierce determination and faith in me as her therapist when I had not been much help (hardly any, if the truth be known) in all of the time I had been seeing her. Despite some promising leads and neither one of us ever missing or even being late for a session, it only seemed I had piled one frustrating, unproductive session on top of another. Plus, for most of that time, I had been displaying my incompetence at the rate of twice a week.

The only days we could do the extended sessions were Friday, Saturday, and Sunday. We could not start until the following week, after I cleared my Friday schedule, which I purposely kept light. I did more so in the warmer and colder months. I only had morning sessions if people could not come at any other time. As much as I treasured being a therapist, it was not my entire life. I savored long weekends. In winter, I took extended cross-country skiing trips to northern

Michigan. In warmer weather, I had rock climbing adventures near Toronto. However, I was willing to forgo all that for the promise of a much different (and infinitely more rewarding) kind of adventure.

In the past year, we had done a few two-day and one three-day intensive sessions, where we met for four hours of session time in a day. We did the first one after we had been meeting for more than a year, when both of us were becoming acutely aware of the lack of progress. None of the intensives had produced any dramatic results, although she had optimistically asked for another one every several months.

Her intrepid request for four-hour sessions over six weeks immediately fired up my dormant creative energies. Longer sessions, at least twice as long (if not longer) than the standard therapy hour, are fertile ground for deep emotional release, or catharsis in official psychological lingo. The best medicine I know for the deepest psychological wounds. Despite the painfully slow progress of Jessica's therapy, it was a method I had numerous dramatic successes with, starting with my days as a student therapist. One of my first clients cried for about ten minutes, more deeply than she had ever done.

When the crying ended, she exclaimed with a vibrancy I had never seen in her eyes, "I feel like I have a new toy…and the new toy is me!"

While I ardently believed in the power of catharsis to transform people's lives, the idea of emotional release as the cure for psychological ills did not sit well with the vast majority of my colleagues. Ever since encounter groups had suffered a precipitous decline in popularity in the early 1970s, a growing number of my fellow professionals proclaimed that using catharsis is unproductive and might even be dangerous. I count myself among a small but dedicated group of die-hard therapists who have a decidedly different perspective. We agree catharsis might be dangerous, but only when it is used incorrectly. Even then, it must be used in an obviously incompetent way. However, we also believe it can produce the most profound change when allowed to operate naturally, under its own internal mechanisms. This is the opposite of forcing someone into deep unresolved feelings prematurely, which is precisely when it could be dangerous. Letting the healing process proceed naturally means allowing enough time for it to move under its own momentum. The extra time is especially necessary for deep-seated problems. I had become a therapist because I hoped psychotherapy could make a dramatic change in people's lives. I did not care if a session went beyond the standard hour. After all, what was a person's psychological health compared to time? After having worked on someone's brain for an hour, does a surgeon suddenly proclaim, "Oops, sorry. Time's up!"

My biggest worry was the emotional toll that having sessions on this intensive basis would have on me. Our last intensive, a three-day one, had totally exhausted me. At the end of the last day, I went right past my usual exit on the interstate and went directly to a movie complex. I did not even know what was playing. Whatever seemed like the most interesting movie that was going to start in the next half hour was fine with me. I plopped myself into a seat and sat like a zombie while staring at the screen. My mind was only dimly aware at first of the action. I had to be with people—the more the better—to sponge up the emotional energy floating around and replenish my own batteries. Fortunately, the movie was fascinating.

Afterward, I went home, made a meal, and went to bed. In the morning, after a restful night's sleep, I felt like myself again. Despite whatever emotional toll this six-week experience would take, I was eager to start. My ideas about what psychotherapy could accomplish were going to be tested in a way they had never been. At the time, I did not realize I was about to embark on the most profound experience of my life.

14

Breakthrough

When I awoke on Friday for the start of our first weekend, I was eager to get to Jessica's house. Her spirited proposal had indeed struck at my deepest motivation for being a therapist. Helping people recapture the parts of their basic humanness that had been—in an almost literal sense—stripped from them by fortuitous, injurious events from earlier in their lives left me feeling as if I was a midwife assisting at the emergence of a new life form.

At those times, when the power of the natural, cathartic healing process transformed a person, an instinctive urge to prostrate myself before the gods and express my gratitude a thousand times over for having the chance at being a participant in the process nearly overcame me. I often fantasized, if the only place to be a therapist was the middle of the desert, I would have set up shop even if I had to dig an irrigation ditch, string electrical wires, and pave a road.

The Page's house on the tree-lined dirt road, less than a minute's walk from Hansen's Bay, was smaller than most of the others, but a large, three-sided, screen porch added a welcome addition in warmer weather. I parked under an old, majestic, maple tree that sat like a benevolent guardian in the front lawn, casting a cooling shade over the house in the summer. The trip had taken fifty minutes. I was a few minutes early. We had agreed to start at nine and end at two. There would be an hour break in the middle.

Somewhere high in the tall trees that lined the road, the loud piping of a pair of cardinals and the melodious notes of a lone Baltimore oriole with brilliant orange wings against a shimmering black body greeted me as I stepped from my car. While winter had spent its final arctic blast more than a month ago, brown continued dominating the land. Green would not blanket this part of the earth for another month. For the last weekend in March, the temperature was expected to edge above fifty degrees, approximately the average for that indeterminate period in Michigan between the end of winter and warm spring days. Small stones crunched under my shoes as I stepped down the dirt driveway to the back door.

Jessica was waiting. She opened the door and welcomed me with the same eager look she gave when she had asked for these extended sessions. I stepped into a small utility room crammed with a washer and dryer. We went through the kitchen and small dining alcove. Two small bedrooms and bathroom were off to the side. We went into the living room. As soon as we stepped in, Jessica reached over to a small desk and handed me a check, saying it was for the total amount we agreed on. While I folded the check in half and stuck it in my back pocket, I quietly thanked her.

Since we had not discussed when she would pay me, her faith humbled me. I also breathed a sigh of relief that she had not first wanted to know if I had any new ideas.

While we stood in the living room, I was painfully aware that I did not have even a hint of one. Several times over the past week, I had set aside time to think about what I knew about Jessica and how her therapy had (or more appropriately in this case) had not progressed. I also spent time reviewing what some of my favorite thinkers had to say about psychotherapy and human nature. There was plenty of information floating around in my head, but none of it had coalesced to produce any new ideas yet. Still, from experience, I knew my mind was at its creative best when I was in the act of confronting a challenge, provided I had done lots of preparation beforehand.

The only firm decision I had made was to focus on role-plays and exercises instead of just talking. Role-plays and exercises work best when there is lots of time. In the usual therapy hour, time had to be initially spent clearing away upsets since the last session. In the remaining time, an attempt could be made to coax deeper feelings to come forward. Clients with ready access to their feelings could begin with a present upset and rather quickly connect with unresolved emotions. However, Jessica was not even close to being able to do that.

Over the three days of this first weekend, we did several role-plays. I tried some of the same ones in the morning and afternoon sessions, not because I could not think of others. Instead, I hoped that a second or even a third attempt in the same day might work. All of the role-plays worked, and practically all of them followed the same, familiar pattern. Either some laughter, tears, or light anger appeared after awhile and lasted from ten to twenty minutes. It then slowly faded away.

We spent most of the time on the sexual assault because that was the last event we had worked on in my office. Besides, it was the only one she had volunteered.

The other major area we attacked was Jessica asking for what she needed. This also had to be approached in a light way. Having her actually practice saying "I need" had never led anywhere. Her whole face just went blank, and she just repeated the words in a forced, mechanical way.

My most productive idea was asking her to picture herself in a scene from her childhood where she remembered feeling that she needed her mother. When I asked her to do this, she immediately protested that she did not have such a memory. Even though it was extremely difficult, if not impossible, to accept her statement (don't we all have at least one memory of wanting or needing a parent for something), I was not surprised. I immediately knew what would happen if I exclaimed, "Well, my gosh, when you were walking out of the hospital with your broken arm, weren't you hoping your mom was going to take you home instead of to Aunt Iris's house?" I would hear the familiar, "My mom was just doing the best she could!"

Despite Jessica's protestations, I asked her to imagine needing her mother. Jessica had definitely needed her mother. She was just unable, for whatever reason I could not fathom, to feel that. For this exercise, Jessica just picturing needing her mother, even if she had to force it, was close enough to what her actual experience must have been.

While she did her part, I did the voice part for her. In my best imitation of a high-pitched talking doll, I said, "Mama! Mama!" repeatedly. Even before the sounds of the first "Mama" had faded away, she burst into vibrant laughter. It lasted for a longer time than I had ever heard from her. However, it all eventually faded away.

We did this role-play once or twice a day all three days. It worked the same way every time. While it held a promise of me being on the right track, I was once again forced to swallow another disappointment. Even though our first weekend had not produced a breakthrough, I was eager to try again.

When I arrived the next Friday, the cardinals were piping away and the lone Baltimore oriole was still singing for a mate. The spontaneous sounds of nature restored my sense of optimism. However, nothing new happened on this Friday, Saturday, or the first hour on Sunday. It was all a repetition of reaching the same familiar impasse. With more than one hour gone on the second Sunday, there was the very scary prospect of this weekend ending the same way. She and I would have used one-third of our six weeks with absolutely nothing to show for it.

A growing panic was tearing at my basic belief in profound, psychological change. Were I and other like-minded colleagues correct about assuming that people had the ability to recover their lost humanness? If there was a way, was I smart enough to figure it out?

Besides that discouragement, I felt guilty about letting Jessica down. I was not worried so much about the fact that she had already paid for the entire six weeks. I was more worried about her innocent faith in me. Anyone who placed this much trust in another human being simply could not be let down. With a renewed sense of optimism, which, on a few occasions over the past two years, I had to talk my mind into, I suggested an old role-play. It was one we had done a number of times in the past but had not used in awhile.

Standing, we faced each other, a few steps apart. With my arms extended, my fingertips reaching for her, and a beaming smile saying she was the most precious thing I had ever seen, I proceeded to walk very slowly toward her, looking as maternal as I could. Jessica was to let me come as close as she could and then express her feelings in whatever way she wanted to.

When my extended fingertips were inches away from her cheeks, she put her hands on my shoulders and pushed me a few steps backward. I stepped right back to the spot where she had pushed me and then started to slowly move toward her, smiling. My arms were extended, and my fingertips reached for her. This time, I encouraged her to say the feeling that made her push me away.

"You can't touch me! You'll just hurt me! I've been hurt enough! I don't need you! I hate you! Stay away!" These warnings came from her mouth as I walked toward her. They were not her real feelings about me. They were from past experiences. I was simply a safe target.

After a few minutes of Jessica commanding me to stay away and I repeatedly coming back, Jessica's eyes started filling with tears. Even though I was sorely tempted, I did not ask, "What's the feeling that's bringing the tears?"

More tears—big ones—came quickly. Each one flowed freely right after the previous one. As she voiced her fears about being hurt again if I got too close to her, her voice was more vibrant than usual. This rush of stronger feelings lasted for several minutes.

When I started walking toward her again and my fingers were inches away from her face, her arms hung limply. She did not make an effort to push me away.

Some moments later, she cried out, "It's not working!"

I immediately reached out and touched her shoulders with my fingers, which I had not yet done. I hoped this would make her feel a bit more of the fear.

She immediately said, "Stay away." She then shoved me backward. This new burst of energy carried us for awhile longer.

I kept coming back and touching her shoulders. Every time, she smartly shoved me and cried out, "Stay away!" More tears flowed. I continued a constant stream of encouragement. I sometimes had to nudge her arms up before her own energy took over.

As the end of the morning's session drew near, Jessica's tears began slowing down. Her pushes became weaker. When I let her arms go after nudging them up a little, they flopped back down. I waited a few minutes to see if the feeling would come back, but it didn't. Jessica's head hung down like a rag doll, and she stared at the floor.

Neither one of us had to acknowledge that we had reached the same impasse again. This was the most emotion, both in terms of vibrant anger and bigger tears, than I had ever seen from her. My hopes had been high.

It was time for our scheduled lunch break. Jessica continued staring at the floor. I try to never end a session with a client upset. If necessary, I go overtime so the person can leave feeling better. At this time, I did not know what to do. I quietly turned around and told her I would be back in an hour. She did not respond. Just before stepping into the kitchen on my way to the back door, I turned around. She had not moved. She looked like she was about to collapse into a bundle of utter despair. I kept going toward the door. Undoubtedly, I was leaving solely for my benefit.

During lunch, I could not shake a sense of dread about the afternoon session. I was very afraid that, if we did not see a significant breakthrough on this second weekend, Jessica's spirit would be completely broken.

The prospect of actually seeing this happen was bad enough. Equally frightening was doing battle with my own feelings. Perhaps my ideas and those of some of my colleagues about recovery from deep psychological wounds were only effective to a point. If that was true, could I continue being a therapist? Could I tell people who had lost significant parts of their humanness that recovery was possible?

While I picked at my food in the restaurant, the creative part of my mind, seemingly unaffected by my feeling of discouragement, was staying busy. When we resumed, we would return to Jessica pushing me away. It had nearly worked. Trying again seemed like a good idea. In case it didn't, my mind produced a backup idea, one I had never tried before. As soon as an image of it flashed in my mind, I could not understand why I had never thought of it.

With an equal mixture of fear of failure and hope for success, I let myself in Jessica's house. She was sitting on the living room floor in the exact spot where I had left her standing. Her body was slumped over. I did not ask if she had been there the whole time. She mechanically stood up.

We immediately started the pushing away role-play. Jessica put her body through the motions. Some tears came, but they quickly went away. Her wimpy-sounding anger would not have frightened a mouse. I could sense her unspoken fear. This exercise was not going to work, and nothing else was going to work either!

Nonetheless, I encouraged her to persist. She did so, obediently. However, after several minutes, I did not have the heart to continue. I quickly said, "Okay, I guess we can't pick up where we left off." With as much enthusiasm as I could muster, I announced, "I thought of a new idea at lunch!" A blank look appeared on Jessica's face because she had heard many new ideas from me over the past thirty-four months and none had worked yet.

I told her to grab my shirt collar with both hands, shake me vigorously, and plead, as desperately possible, "I need you! I need you!"

This idea excited me because it seemed to deeply strike at what I believed was her basic fear, the one that had been smirking at us ever since she had first stepped into my office. Despite how dejected Jessica looked, she immediately perked up and gave an excellent performance. She shed some tears and laughed a lot. I kept modeling an increasing desperate tone of voice. Every time she mimicked me perfectly. Every time she did so, bigger tears rolled out.

The tears lasted as long as they did in the pushing away exercise from the morning. They eventually dried as well. There was no more laughter either, and her "I need you" became increasingly weaker. She stopped the exercise herself. I did not attempt to encourage her to keep going. Her shoulders sagged, and her head drooped. Dejection spilled from every pore in her body. I did not have the heart to ask, "How are you feeling?" or "What are you thinking?"

My brain had shifted to turbocharger mode though. Images of every piece of information I had ever learned about psychological change and all the challenging questions I had ever asked myself about why psychotherapy was not more effective flashed through my mind. No bulbs lit up in there. However, my brain continued running through all of its memory banks.

Jessica continued staring at the floor. She had not said a word since she had stopped the exercise. Perhaps her look of utter dejection was the trigger. My instincts just took over. A very clear picture of what to do suddenly appeared in my mind's eye.

I did not waste any time thinking about it or even worrying if it was going to work. With instinctive certainty, along with a great deal of empathy, I tugged at her arm and motioned her to the couch. She did not offer any resistance. I sat down on one end and told her to stretch out and place her head in my lap. Without a moment's hesitation, she did so. Her face turned away from mine and faced out into the room.

I then completed the image from a few moments ago. With my fingertips, I began lightly stroking her forehead. She did not say a word or move a muscle. A minute later, she closed her eyes. I continued caressing her forehead. No words were spoken. I did not have any, and I did not ask if she had any.

Five minutes passed…then ten. All of my attention was on stroking her face. Her eyes stayed closed. My mind stopped searching for a new idea.

The very top of Jessica's back was pressed against my left thigh. For a second, I felt—or thought I had felt—a slight twitch emanating from that part of her body. I was not sure because it had happened so fast and was so faint. I waited.

Jessica did not respond. Her eyes remained closed while I continued lightly running my fingers over her forehead. A minute later, there was another momentary twitch, nearly as imperceptible as the first.

In a minute, there was another tiny twitch, just like the first two. Everything else remained as it was. Another twitch came a minute later. Several more were all about thirty seconds apart. Then the twitches, still very slight, were fifteen to twenty seconds apart.

The nearly dead flame of hope inside of me flickered the tiniest bit brighter. If a part of my body had not been in contact with hers, I would have never noticed the faint twitches. Almost certainly, I would have stopped touching her and changed our position. Instead, it felt as if all of the nerve endings in my body migrated to the upper part of my left leg. She remained motionless. I continued caressing her forehead.

The urge to jump, shout, and bounce around the room was nearly irresistible, but I did not dare move the tiniest muscle or even interrupt the steady rhythm of my breathing. Any force in the world could not make me break the magic spell.

Her eyes had been closed ever since I had started stroking her forehead. She now turned her face and peered at me with a quizzical look.

"What's happening?" She sounded genuinely intrigued by the strange reaction her body was having. Intuitively, she seemed to know that something profound was happening.

With a beaming smile, I eagerly announced, "You're starting to shake!" Jessica's body was starting to rid itself of the ill effects of some long ago, terribly frightening experience.

Shaking is how the human psyche cures itself of a particular kind of frightening event. It is when a person has been threatened with or actually experienced serious physical injury or an assault to one's basic psychological integrity and the person was helpless in being able to defend against or ward off the threat. The release of heavy fear is experienced as spasms running along the spine, ranging from imperceptible to pulsating vibrations. The latter can cause the whole body to shake rapidly. The person's skin becomes moist and clammy. In the most intense reaction, one can hear teeth chattering uncontrollably. A common feeling for most people upon first experiencing this least known, even among my fellow professionals, form of cathartic release is that their body is falling apart.

I had learned about shaking a year or so after obtaining my graduate degree. One of my female friends, whose only interest in psychology was for her own personal reasons, told me of a therapist she had learned about from a friend who knew this fellow personally. He had accidentally happened upon shaking in 1950. When his best friend, an owner of a small painting business, asked him to at least try helping one of his employees, a rather pleasant fellow in his early twenties who was quite depressed, he reluctantly agreed. Although he had attended college for several years, his formal knowledge of psychology then amounted to having browsed through one of his wife's textbooks on counseling. After helping the young man cry deeply and shake vigorously and even experiencing shaking himself over a traumatic incident in his own life when he and his friend exchanged the roles of counselor and client with each other, he was impressed enough with the results to quit his job and open an office. Over time, he made a few other discoveries about how the human psyche cures itself of injurious experiences. When I learned of him twenty-five years after his initial discovery, he was leading workshops throughout the country. I attended one and learned about laughter and shaking.

A few minutes after I gleefully announced to Jessica that she was beginning to shake, the twitches, now more pronounced, were a few seconds apart. With her body releasing heavy fear under its own momentum, I slid off the couch, kneeled on the floor, rested my upper body on top of hers, and had her grip my back. I slid my arms under her back and held her securely. For the release of heavy fear, physical contact makes the person feel safer and allows the shaking to proceed more vibrantly and efficiently.

Jessica's body shook, with a few very short breaks, for more than an hour. The spasms running along her spine made my fingers feel as if they were resting on a fire hose that had bursts of water blasting through it every moment or two. I did not know what terrifying experience her body was curing itself of, and Jessica did not have any thoughts either. At this point, that was not important. We would know when enough fear had been released. She hardly said a word the whole time. She only gave an occasional comment of amazement over what her body was doing and for reassurance that all was okay.

Toward the end of the session, her shaking began slowing down. When I left for the day, her appearance was the exact opposite of what it had been when I had left for lunch. She looked vibrant and alert, much more so than I had ever seen her. Outside, the piping notes of the cardinals kept tempo with my buoyant steps on the way to my car.

For the next several days, time seemed to crawl by. After months and months of dashed hopes, real therapeutic progress seemed on the verge of happening. Friday could not come fast enough. On Wednesday, I called to see how she was doing. She had lost most of the emotional high from Sunday, but that was not a surprise. More emotional release was necessary for a longer, lasting change. She was not discouraged, but she hoped the feeling of well-being returned.

When I arrived on Friday, Jessica was eager to start. We went right to the couch, and she immediately lay down. I knelt on the carpet beside her and rested the upper part of my body on hers. The instant her fingers gripped my back, vibrations radiated from her spine. Like a perfectly calm pool of water suddenly erupting into a geyser, Jessica's body transformed itself into a shaking dynamo while she dug her fingertips into my back. The start of this session was in such stark contrast to how all our past sessions had started. I reminded myself this was the same person I had laboriously struggled with for so long.

For the start of our third weekend, shaking was the order of the day. There were several thirty- to forty-minute bouts. Jessica did not have any idea yet what the fear was about. At the end of the day, she looked as alert and as refreshed as she had at the end of the previous week's session.

When I arrived the next day, she let me in. Without a word, she hurried to the living room, leaving me to follow her. As soon as I stepped in, I spotted her on the other side, standing in front of the couch. The instant she saw me, she jumped backward a bit, almost falling onto the couch. Her face seemed to be frozen in terror. I stayed where I was, continued smiling, and waited. The fear stayed in her eyes.

Keeping my distance, I cautiously asked, "What are you feeling?" This time, I asked it with the anticipation of knowing I would get a real answer.

She immediately responded, "You're a man. You scare me." She took another step backward and bumped into the couch.

The instant I heard her words, I knew. The sexual assault.

When I mentioned this, she slightly nodded her head, but the fear remained in her eyes. I proceeded to move toward her with excruciatingly small steps, waiting a minute after each tiny step to gauge her reaction. About twenty minutes later, I was standing in front of her in my Jack the Ripper caricature. Now, when I clumsily clawed at the air in front of her, she stood in place. Her body shook as vibrantly as it had on the couch. When the shaking died down, I moved a tiny step closer and lightly rested my claw on her shoulder. When this position did not produce any shaking after ten minutes, it was time for a closer approximation.

I had her lay down on her back on the carpet. She had the choice of where and how far from me. She moved a few steps away. When she indicated she was ready, I started to move very slowly toward her.

Over the next half hour, during which her body shook continuously, my slow movements brought me to a standing position over her. My act of looking directly down at her agitated a deeper level of the fear. With a terror-filled voice and her body shaking rapidly, she described the boy returning to her room, laughing eerily, and placing his hands around her throat while threatening to choke her to death if she ever told.

Jessica's body shook for close to an hour as she went over these details many times. Then we broke for lunch. After eating at the local restaurant a few miles from her house, I went to a nearby park and walked along the water. I watched the gulls and terns flying gracefully in the air. When I returned to Jessica's house, we were able to pick up right where we had left off as I stood over her.

Jessica's body did not respond, and she did not have anything to say. I did not know if she was finished shaking or not. To check, I described my next approximation. This time, her body shook just upon my description. When the shaking began lessening, I very slowly started to lower myself to my hands and knees as her body shook the whole time. We progressed through the motions. I kneeled alongside of her, placed one hand and the other on the floor on either side of her body, and then lowered myself on top of her, just as we had done on the couch. While she gripped my back, her body shook more vigorously than it had done before and let loose with the scariest part of the experience. In the space of two days, with several hours of actual shaking, Jessica seemed finally free from the traumatic effects of having been brutally assaulted at the age of six.

When I left for the day, she insisted I give her a hug. There was a calm about her that I had never seen. What a contrast to how she had reacted to me when we had started two days ago.

During my fifty-minute drive home, I basked in the glow of a job well done, but frustration tinged it because we had to wait so long. On a deeper level, I felt a profound respect, even awe, for how the natural healing process was operating. The human psyche does not operate randomly. It works very logically, which often takes hindsight to fully appreciate. Jessica's psyche had brought up the sexual assault for a specific reason. If the healing process was going to continue to work, now that the block to her expressing any upsetting feeling had been resolved, she had to feel as safe as she could with me, a male.

15

Second Daring Proposal

Several times on the drive home from Jessica's house, an urge to spin the car around and start the next weekend nearly overcame me. I wanted to jump into a time machine and be transported four days into the future. Throughout the week, I continued fantasizing how I was going to respond when Jessica told me the good news of staying home at night. I could not imagine what else could have made her feel so terrified of being alone at night than having a strange male at least twice her height and several times her weight attack her in the darkest hours of the night. Given our perseverance for the past three years, it seemed only fair that fate was finally on our side.

Friday finally came. A warm spring breeze was in the air. I drove a bit faster than usual on the interstates and made the trip in just over forty-five minutes. I parked under the maple tree and hurried down the driveway. Instead of knocking, I pushed the door open a tiny bit and announced myself. Footsteps on the linoleum floor in the kitchen were the only sounds that greeted me. In my mind, I imagined a face breaking into a wide grin and a voice getting ready to exclaim, "Guess where I spent the last few nights?"

After a step into the utility room, I finally spotted her. She caught my eyes for an instant. She then dropped her head and reached for the damp cloth lying on the counter. For a few minutes, she busied herself with wiping all the countertops in the kitchen. I stood where I was and watched, perplexed. The entire time, she did not look at me or say a word. When she finished, she folded the cloth neatly and hung it on a rack. Then she turned around without looking at me, headed straight for the living room, and sat down on the couch. I pulled up the wooden-framed armchair and sat down opposite her. She continued to avoid my eyes.

"Well, how are you doing?" I finally asked.

"So-so," she quietly replied.

After only a few seconds had passed, I could not restrain myself any longer. "Did you notice any results from all of the shaking last week?"

She immediately replied, "I don't feel afraid of you as a man." After a brief pause, she added, "I'm not afraid of Roger anymore." I noted there was not any excitement on her face.

Obviously, Jessica not feeling afraid of men was a major sign of improvement. However, when more time passed with a blank look on her face, I asked, "What about spending nights at your mother's house?"

She responded immediately. "I can't stay home yet. That problem hasn't changed." She stopped talking abruptly and sounded defensive, as if I was blaming her for not being over this problem yet.

The fact that all of the shaking from last weekend had resolved one fear and not the other meant the unresolved one was a deeper fear. It had to be from another experience, one she probably had not remembered yet, although what it could possibly be totally mystified me. Our only course of action was to forge ahead with what was, thankfully, now working. When her psyche decided the time was right, as it had done with the sexual assault, the buried experience would emerge.

As she sat across from me, Jessica looked as if she did not even have the energy to get out of the way of a steamroller bearing down on her. Because there was not any sign that anything had emerged from the depths of her psyche, I was forced to ask very basic questions.

I began with the most obvious. "What's happened since last Sunday?"

Subdued, she could only say, "Not much."

I asked if anyone had upset her, but she provided an unemotional, "No."

In the past, I did not have a choice except bombarding her with questions, hoping to trigger some kind of emotional response. Now, much to my immense relief, I had another option. We had access to the natural healing process. Perhaps we could plug into it by using the role-play that had cracked open her fear of expressing feelings.

As soon as I told her to grip my shirt and plead, "I need you!" her eyes sparked up.

This time, as soon as she said the magic words, her body started shaking. After a few minutes of shaking, she suddenly exclaimed, "I can't need you! I'll be too much of a burden!" A feeling of immense relief washed over me.

Her words announced a new, unresolved feeling had emerged. I focused my attention on the keyword, burden. An idea quickly popped in my mind. Without a word of explanation, I stood and asked her to stand behind me and lock her arms around my neck. She did so without hesitation. With a slight dip of my knees, we were the same height. I started to very slowly bend forward. I wanted to lean over far enough to lift her completely off the ground. If this did not make her feel like a burden, I did not know what would. I knew her fear was of being a psychological burden, but I hoped that feeling like a physical burden would be a close enough approximation.

I only said, "Hang on tightly!"

As soon as she began feeling the first hint of my body supporting her body, she started laughing very spontaneously. The more I bent forward and the more she was lifted onto my back, the deeper she laughed. By the time her big toe had left contact with the rug and my body was completely supporting hers, she was so overcome with laughter that she seemed as helpless as a tub of jelly in an earthquake.

We did this exercise for most of the morning, for about ten to fifteen minutes at a time. That was the limit for my body being able to support her full weight.

After lunch, it worked just as well as it had in the morning. During a break, Jessica said she wanted to lie on the floor. When we took a break, we usually sat down on the couch or went to the kitchen for a drink. This request was different enough for me to wonder if her psyche was directing all of this. She stretched out on her back. I sat on the floor near her. For a few minutes, neither one of us said a word. She then glanced at me with a penetrating stare. A mass of blood suddenly rushed to her face, making her look as if she had just stepped from a sauna. She covered her eyes with her hands.

"I can't look at you!" she exclaimed. I leaned my head directly over her.

After a few moments, with her hands still completely covering her eyes, she repeated, "I can't look at you!"

Despite the apparent intensity of her feeling, there was not any laughter or shaking. I waited a bit, but she kept her hands over her eyes and did not say anything.

After saying what I was going to do, I reached over and very slowly started to lift one of her middle fingers that covered the center of her eye. There was no resistance. My head loomed directly above hers. My eyes stared intently, but lovingly, at her eye. The instant her eye was exposed for her gaze to meet mine, her eye snapped shut. She then dissolved into deep laughter. When the laughter began diminishing after a minute or two, her eye flipped back open. The instant she caught a glimpse of my beaming face, she once again dissolved in laughter. We repeated this for most of the hour.

Although Jessica was releasing a lighter feeling instead of a deeper one, as with shaking or crying, I was elated. We were back on track. Whenever her eye met mine, it seemed like a window to the real Jessica. Reaching the real Jessica had been my goal since our very first session. For now, laughter would do very nicely. I hoped deeper emotional release would automatically follow.

It happened while we were doing the hands over eyes exercise. Without any warning and in the midst of very deep laughter, she suddenly stared at me with her mouth hanging wide open, as if it was permanently stuck in that position. When she started frantically waving her arms, I realized she was not breathing. Although her eyes pleaded for help, I knew the worst that could possibly happen was that she would pass out and resume breathing on her own. I hurriedly mentioned it to her, hoping it would alleviate some of her fright. But she kept fanning the air.

After a few panic-filled seconds, I heard a sharp intake of breath. She exclaimed, "I couldn't breathe! What happened?"

I did not know exactly. My best guess was that, sometime very early in her life, she had had trouble breathing and it had frightened her. Her psyche had tapped into that experience. These bouts of breathlessness occurred every fifteen minutes for the rest of the day, and they only occurred when she was laughing deeply. She never passed out.

However, as this weekend progressed, a familiar feeling slowly crept into our work. Regardless of what exercise we did, Jessica's laughter lasted for shorter periods. At the start of any exercise, it was quite intense. However, it quickly lessened. Almost immediately, Jessica would exclaim, "I feel confused." All emotional release would cease. Then I would switch to another exercise, hoping the feeling of confusion would go away. It did initially, but it kept returning. All exercises came to the same quick demise as Jessica said, "I'm confused."

Neither one of us had any idea what was causing the confusion. The only thing I could think of was to not try anything and wait. Maybe something was coming up, and we were only interfering with it. If we waited, maybe we would see a clue. Jessica stretched out on the floor. I remained on the couch.

A few minutes later, she peered at me and said, "I feel like my face needs to be touched."

I scooted over to where she was on the floor, placed my fingertips on either side of her face, and ran my fingertips up her cheeks very slowly and very lightly. Every time I did, her body erupted into deep laughter.

We did this exercise for about an hour. Jessica's laughter lasted a few minutes each time. Bouts of breathlessness happened about every ten minutes. By this time, Jessica was no longer frightened. She seemed curious to see what her psyche was doing.

Then it happened again. The laughing stopped abruptly as Jessica exclaimed, "I'm confused!" I ran my fingertips over her face a few times, but nothing happened. There was not anything else to do but wait.

Jessica remained on the floor, staring at the ceiling and not saying a word. Every few minutes, I asked if she was having any thoughts or feelings.

Subdued, she only said, "No."

A growing panic began tearing at my spirit. Had we reached another impasse? Was Jessica's psyche playing tricks with us? Was it going to shut the window to the real Jessica again? We both searched each other's face. Our unspoken fear was mirrored in each other's eyes.

Now, I knew how a prescientific people must have felt in trying to understand an unpredictable natural force like a volcano. I had an acute appreciation for them doing whatever they thought would appease the appropriate deity.

After fifteen silent minutes had passed, I decided I could not just sit by idly and wait. My only thought was to try the same technique that had ignited the healing process.

With as much enthusiasm as I could muster, I said, "We've been here before. Maybe the same thing will work again."

I sat down on one end of the couch. Jessica stretched out and put her head in my lap, just like a few weeks ago. I slowly caressed her forehead, and she closed her eyes. There were no twitches. There was no sign of anything, except her deep, relaxed breathing.

About ten minutes later, after I stroked her face the whole time, her eyes suddenly popped open. She turned her head to look at me and asked, "Can you remember your birth?" She spoke somewhat hesitantly, as if she would not be upset if I said, "No, not really."

Without a moment's hesitation, I confidently said, "Sure!"

That was a bit of a lie because I did not know if remembering one's birth was possible. In the past few years, I had heard scattered reports from a few people that it was possible, but I did not have any firsthand experience of actually watching someone having that kind of a memory. I certainly had not done so myself. In fact, my earliest memory went back to maybe three years of age. If Jessica thought she had remembered her birth, that was good enough for me.

For the past hour, she said she had been getting split-second flashbacks, especially when I was running my fingers up her cheeks.

"I was afraid to tell you," she said. "I wasn't sure if you'd believe me."

My immediate impulse was to lovingly scold her for thinking that. After all we had been through, how could she still have any doubt about my believing anything she said? This, of course, was not the time to discuss that. As for her latest question, we had never talked about remembering one's birth or anything about birth. It had never dawned on me that we had any reason to do so.

Before I could say anything else, she added, "At first I didn't know if I was dreaming or maybe imagining it. But now I'm certain." She sat up smartly and started talking slowly in measured tones. Her voice had a twinge of awe.

"I was floating in water and hearing it flutter in my ear. I heard a steady heart-beat. I was stretching and yawning, calm and peaceful. My only concern was growing. All that was happening seemed to be in preparation for a different dimension in my life.

"During labor, I felt squeezed. I wasn't frightened. I was going along with the process of being born. I was starting to get out when someone pushed me back in. I was pushed, pulled, and turned. I was not in charge of my birth anymore. I was very frightened and confused. I could not breathe. I thought I was going to die before I could get out.

"My mom hurt. The medical team was in a panic, and everyone was yelling. There was a lot of confusion. The lights were bright, and the room was noisy. Two nurses took me and washed me roughly. They were laughing and talking with each other, and they were unaware of how they were treating me or how I felt."

In Jessica's first telling, she paused often, as if she could not believe she was actually remembering her birth. I asked her to tell the details a few more times. With each telling, more of the feeling of awe went away. She cried more, always over the same feeling, confusion. During the seventh or eighth telling, there was a very intense, but brief, burst of tears. Jessica suddenly exclaimed, "My head feels very clear! I've always had this chronic feeling of low-grade confusion in my head. Now it's gone!"

After we took a break, I had her tell her memory of her birth again, just to be sure she was finished. She willingly jumped to the task. She quickly began experiencing other feelings about her birth. Breathlessness grabbed at her when she spoke of not being able to breathe. It disappeared after several more accounts and never occurred again. There were short, but very intense, bursts of indignation over not being completely in charge of her birth. The doctor's manipulation of her body may have been medically necessary, but, for Jessica, it was an unwanted and unwelcomed intrusion. Starting with her grand entrance into the world, she was already being told what she could—and could not do—under her own power.

A part of her recall was a detailed description of how some of the people looked, particularly the doctor.

"Not surprising," I thought, "because she probably had the closest look at him."

A few days later, Jessica related all of the details she had remembered to her mother, who was completely shocked. Dorothy claimed she had never discussed Jessica's birth with her, but she confirmed every detail, even down to what the doctor looked like.

Jessica's recall of her birth was a new, awe-inspiring experience for me as a therapist. I was convinced it had happened just as she had explained it.

The last day of our sixth weekend, the last according to our agreement, was ending. I was very pleased, even honored, that Jessica had asked me to do them. She had certainly placed her future, her future psychological health, in my hands. I had learned more about deep emotional release in these six weeks than I had in my previous twelve years as a therapist. I did not think she was finished with her therapy. However, without a doubt, we had achieved the breakthrough both of us had been waiting for. Moreover, we had made very definite progress beyond that as well. I was fully expecting her to say she was ready to return to meeting in my office.

We were sitting on opposite ends of the couch. She suddenly looked at me with the same resolute expression I had seen seven weeks ago. In the same confident voice she used then, she asked, "Can we continue to meet like this?"

Before I had a chance to say, "Of course!" she spoke again. "Before you answer, you need to know that I can't pay you until we get our income tax back." That was about eight months away.

"That's okay," I said. If future sessions were as exciting as these, any wait would be just fine.

However, my "okay" about the money had not taken away the serious look on her face. Without waiting more than a moment or two, she asked, "Can we meet four days a week, Friday through Monday?"

"Sure," I said, again on impulse. This time, a humbling certainty that Jessica knew what she needed better than I did backed my statement. Four days a week had to produce more results than three days a week.

Besides, I had not found the weekends as exhausting as I had originally feared. Perhaps I was doing them more efficiently, although, after each day, I did not know if I was ready for another one until I awoke the next morning. When I did, I was always eager to try again.

With this last request from Jessica, I assumed this last session of our six-week agreement was over. I grasped the arm of the couch and started leaning forward.

Before I was interrupted, I could only say, "Well…"

"I have one more condition," she said. She hesitated. Before any words came, I was already nodding in agreement. I could not imagine any condition I would not agree to. I thought she was thinking of a time limit, but that did not worry me. How long would we have to meet for four days a week? She had recovered from the sexual assault. There had been good work on her feeling like a burden. She had even recalled her birth. My only worry was that her crying was not as deep as her laughing or shaking. Crying resolved the deepest assaults to our basic humanness. Maybe that was what she wanted to accomplish before stopping our meeting this way. Even with my consenting nod, she hesitated just a bit before speaking,

"The decision to stop meeting this way has to be mine."

Without even thinking about why she might be asking, I quickly said, "Sure."

Jessica never said for how long she thought the four-day weekends would last, and I did not ask. I guessed we would do them for a few months. In case we ran into unexpected problems (which I could not imagine), I thought five or six months at the very most. Surely we would be done in December, the start of the cross-country skiing season. By then, I would have solid evidence for my belief about profound psychological changes, and I would have heartwarming memories to reminisce about for the rest of my life.

16

Recall of Battle of Wills

When I arrived the next Friday, Jessica was waiting at the back door, holding it open. With an inviting look indicating for me to follow, she made a beeline for the living room. As soon as I was settled in the armchair across from her, she exclaimed, "After you left last Sunday, I felt good for about three seconds." She then abruptly stopped talking. Almost immediately, her eyelids began drooping, and her head drifted slowly backward. In a few moments, her head came to rest against the wooden frame that protruded a few inches above the top of the cushions. A silent minute or two elapsed with her eyes remaining closed.

"What's going on?" I finally asked.

Without opening her eyes or moving her head, she continued from where she had left off a minute ago. "I remembered another experience from when I was a newborn..." After a slight hesitation, she added, "I was about two weeks old."

I had to literally bite my tongue to keep from saying, "How do you know you were about two weeks old?" When she had startled me last week with her remembrance of her birth, I had been comforted by reports from a few of my friends that such a recall was not as strange as it sounded. If any event from infancy was significant, it had to be being born. Wasn't that our grand entrance into the world? However, I had never heard any reports of the recall of events after birth. All I could do was take Jessica's word for it.

After her last words, her eyes stayed closed for a bit. She then opened them and slowly lifted her head off the back of the couch. She started slowly talking, with little emotion, in small groups of words. She paused between them as if she had to briefly reflect on them before saying more. The entire time, her eyes remained transfixed on something over my shoulder.

"I woke up crying because I was hungry, cold, and wet. I kept crying, and nobody came. I felt vulnerable and alone. I started remembering how my mother had treated me in the past, how hard it was for her to care for me. She was always upset and seemed to resent having to do anything for me.

"I feared she would not come to get me and I would starve, freeze, or die of loneliness. I decided, when she came, I would watch her closely to see if what I was feeling about her was true.

"When she came, she was very angry. I must have interrupted her sleep. She changed and fed me as quickly as she could before laying me down. I wanted her to hold me, so I started to cry. She picked me up again, and I stopped crying. She put me down, and I cried again. This happened a few more times.

"She told me I was spoiled and I had to understand that she could not hold me anytime I wanted. She had another small child and a husband to take care of, and there wasn't enough time for her to just hold me.

"She was angry. It frightened me and made me cry more. The more I cried, the more upset she became. She started to yell and covered my mouth with her hand. She picked me up, shook me, screamed I was bad, and said she'd hurt me if I didn't stop crying. She said she never had these problems with my sister and something was wrong with me. I could tell she was out of it. I was terrified she would kill me. She finally threw me down and left."

When Jessica finished her halting, unemotional account, her head slowly drifted backward and eventually came to rest against the wood on the back of the couch. Even her words about feeling terrified over being killed came out with as much emotion as an automated computer voice. In a few seconds, her eyes closed, and her breathing deepened.

While I waited for a signal from her to see if, or how, she was going to continue, I was silently clucking to myself. This is it! The answer to the question that had perplexed me for months: Why had she been so terrified of revealing any upsetting feelings, especially by crying? I could now look back in amusement at one of our early sessions when I said, "What's making you cry?" She had then shot back, "I'm not crying!"

I now understood why Jessica gripping my shirt and pleading "I need you" on the last day of our second weekend had caused her vibrant shaking. The first therapeutic breakthrough had to be the release of her very deep fear about expressing a need. It was a fear so terrifying that she was convinced that expressing a need was to invite her own death.

A few minutes passed without any signal from her that she was about to continue. This was very puzzling. The last session had obviously generated the memory. It had been sitting in her mind since then. It had to be next in line.

"Any thoughts or feelings?" I finally asked.

"No," she said quietly. Though her head was resting on the back of the couch and her eyes were closed, she seemed to have all of her senses about her.

"Think you can tell the story again?" I tentatively asked.

A moment or two later, Jessica opened her eyes and slowly brought her head forward. I scrutinized her very closely for even the slightest sign that I was forcing her to continue.

She started talking immediately. This time, she said a sentence or two at a time instead of a small group of words before stopping. She spoke in the same unemotional tone. The lack of emotion worried me more then anything else. With even a little bit of it, I would have felt more certain that I was not forcing her to continue.

When she finished with this second telling, she slowly closed her eyes, and her head tilted backward against the wooden frame. She remained silent and motionless for about a minute. Her body was so still and her breathing was so slow that she seemed to have fallen asleep. A few moments later, her eyes opened, and her head snapped forward. She seemed alert, so I asked her to tell the story again.

On this day, she told the story many times. She could never keep her eyes open for more than a sentence or two at a time and never dozed off for more than a few moments. When her eyes popped open, she always said, "Where was I?" She sounded very alert every time. After I repeated her last few words, she always agreed, with a nod of her head, that was where she had left off. She continued from that point. Tears came in a steady trickle, though randomly. It was the only thing keeping us going.

When I arrived the next day, Jessica seemed alert, but she was not sure where she wanted to start. I was bursting with curiosity about yesterday, but she had to choose. After a few minutes, she decided to pick up where she had left off.

As with yesterday, Jessica said a sentence or two at a time before her head tilted backward and her eyes closed. Then, after five or ten seconds, she would snap awake and say, "Where was I?" With each telling of the story, there were tears at only one point, almost always on the next sentence or two after the ones she had cried on during the previous telling or, rarely, the same words as in the previous one. There was never an exception. Her tears never went backward in the chronology, and her psyche never leaped ahead. It was as if all her psyche could handle was to focus on a particular point at a time. By the end of the day, she was tearing a bit more than at the start, but not actually crying.

In my twelve years as a therapist, I had never seen anything so mystifying. I was ready to bow down to the deity in charge and say, "Take over!" There had to be an orderly process at work, but I was equally convinced that I had very limited control, if any, over it. I could only arrange the right conditions and wait for this mysterious process that operated under its own mechanisms. Since these weekends had started, my role was becoming more of a midwife. That is, I was some-one whose main goal was not to do anything that interfered with this natural process.

On the third day of the weekend, Jessica continued with the battle of wills. With a vibrant tone of voice, she started on the first sentence and gave particular emphasis to the last word, wet. She said it nearly gleefully. When she did, she laughed deeply. She repeated this sentence many times, always building up to the last word and then exploding in laughter.

When the laughter began subsiding, she proceeded with the rest of the story. Anger, crying, or shaking appeared at various points. On this day, she did not doze off.

On the next day, the last for the weekend, Jessica continued from where she had left off the day before. She told the story with great emotion, sounding like someone rehearsing for a performance. After a few accounts of the event, the last one with some tears while repeating in a quiet, but anguished voice, "She threw me down."

When she seemed ready to say it again, a woeful sound came out instead. With it, the tears came quicker, running in a steady stream down her face.

She then gave an agonized cry. "I just remembered what happened after that!"

With that, Jessica whirled her body toward mine. She gripped my shirt collar and buried her face in my neck, as if she was diving into a foxhole to save her life. In grief-filled staccato bursts, she related the rest of the battle of wills.

"When she threw me down, I was afraid to move. I realized I was right. She hated caring for me. I had destroyed her life when I was born. I was a terrible, awful person and responsible for making her life so unhappy. I felt I was so unim-portant that no one could love me."

These were the most heartbreaking words I had ever heard from another human being. I could only imagine what it must have been like for her as an infant. If I had acted purely on what I was feeling, I would have ripped out my heart and given it to her. However, while she gripped my collar with both hands, I could only wrap one arm tightly around a shoulder, cover one side of her face with my other hand, and encourage her to sob it all out.

We stayed glued to each other for about twenty minutes as Jessica's crying gradually decreased. When it finally stopped, she nestled against me for a few minutes. Then she pulled her head out of my neck.

When she spoke, she continued from where she had left off. "I knew I could never trust her again. She would never be there when I needed her. I stopped expecting anything from anyone."

No wonder she couldn't say what she needed! Despite the desperate tone of her words, her voice was definitely lighter, as if a huge burden had been lifted. She was silent for a few minutes, staring into space the entire time.

Then she continued. "I couldn't handle all those feelings. I stopped feeling everything. I knew I was all alone. I saw no hope that anything would ever be right. I decided not to live."

When Jessica was born, she needed to feel at least one person in the world was going to love her. At the time of the battle of wills, she was still waiting. In the middle of this night, she desperately wanted the most important person in her life to love her and tried to let her know that in the only way she knew, by crying.

While she lay in her crib, terrified over whether she was going to live or not, her survival instincts took control. They occupied all the necessary command positions, marshaled all the resources, and sounded the alarm.

"If this brand-new baby girl is going to live, she can't be a real human being. These are emergency measures. But at least she'll be alive!"

For several minutes, Jessica had been leaning against me, not pressing her body into mine, just like when the memory had first come back. Her fingers loosely held the front of my shirt. Without warning, her fingers suddenly tightened their grip. Her body pressed into mine. An agonized cry erupted.

"Tell me it wasn't me! Tell me it wasn't me!" Her grip tightened so much that I thought her hands had turned into a vise. My shirt collar dug deeply into the back of my neck. Her body found every corner of my body to press into. It seemed, if she lost physical contact with me, she would shrivel up and die.

While she gripped my shirt even tighter and the collar dug deeper into my neck, the stark terror flew from her mouth. The disbelief, the overwhelming urge to deny it all, streamed out as if a dam had burst.

"Oh, tell me it wasn't me! Tell me it wasn't me. I wasn't that baby who was thrown down! I wasn't! I wasn't!"

My heart was broken. Like a terrified animal trying to dig into the ground to save its life, Jessica tried burrowing into my body. As frightening as this seemed to her now, she had already survived the hardest part, that is, trying to survive it all at the time with the meager resources available to her.

This outburst of disbelief over the realization she was the infant who had been thrown down eventually ran its course. When it was over, she remained snuggled against me. Her breathing was very relaxed. I let her stay where she was. She deserved a rest.

After several minutes, she said, "I'm getting this strange sensation." She quickly added, "It's something I've never felt before…at least I don't remember feeling it."

A few seconds later, her body jerked away from mine. She sat rigidly straight, staring at me with a look of utter bewilderment. For a few brief moments, her mouth hung open. Her eyes grew bigger, and her face was a giant question mark. She dove for my body. Instinctively, I put both of my arms around her.

She cried out, "I don't feel a thing. I don't feel a thing!"

At first, I was bewildered. With tears running in channels down her face and soaking my shirt, how could she not be feeling anything? But she kept insisting she did not feel anything and continued squeezing my body.

Jessica ended her original description of the battle of wills with, "I couldn't handle all those feelings. I stopped feeling everything." At the time, that had not been a conscious decision. Her psyche had taken over to save her life. She was now refeeling that part of the experience. An infant is not equipped physiologically to handle the incredible strain such intense feelings put on vital, vulnerable organs of the body. When her psyche took over, Jessica felt the experience of not feeling.

About twenty minutes later, this rush of intense feeling over not feeling had lessened. I explained my thinking to her. She listened, but she could only say, "I don't feel a thing!" After she cried it out a few more times, she asked me to explain it again. When I finished, she grabbed my shirt and stared at me as if she was pleading for understanding.

"Are you sure? Are you sure nothing's broken?"

Every time I reassured her, she pleaded for more reassurance.

"How can it be that I can't feel a thing after the terror I just felt over being thrown down?"

It seemed bewildering to me as well. I had never seen anyone go from such an intense fear to a feeling of no feeling in such dramatic fashion. All of it happened within twenty minutes. I could only tell her that we were learning how the infant psyche handled traumas.

I was ecstatic about this session. The great fear I had been locked in combat with ever since my first question to her was now exposed. Completely resolving the fear could not be far away. After tying up loose ends, we could be finished in a few months. Maybe in September and early October I could get in a few weekends of rock climbing.

17

"It's Me! It's Me!"

For close to three years, every session of Jessica's therapy had been a struggle because of the invisible forces imprisoning her. That barrier cracked wide open when she grabbed my shirt collar and pleaded, "I need you! I need you!" Since then, sessions had been radically different. For about two months, from her initial shaking to the battle of the wills, the healing process had been working automatically. Regardless of what I did (imitate Jack the Ripper or her mother or just listen attentively), it worked.

When Jessica recovered from the terrible fright over not feeling from the battle of wills, she suddenly lost this easy access to her feelings. Now, when I asked, "How are you doing?" at the start of sessions, this only caused her to stare over my shoulder. She did not even ask, "Well, what would you like me to talk about?" Even though that question had caused immense frustration in the past, it would have now been a welcome invitation.

When I asked, "Tell me what you've been doing since I last saw you?" even if we had just seen each other the day before, all I heard, after time seemed to drag interminably, was a subdued, "Nothing."

I immediately wanted to exclaim, "What do you mean you've been doing nothing? You have a husband and a daughter. You stay overnight at your mother's house. You have sisters, brothers, friends, and neighbors. You do child-care four days a week." It was impossible for her to have been doing nothing!

Because Jessica was as distant from her feelings as the North Pole was to suddenly becoming a desert oasis and I was unable to think of an exercise to get her going, there was no chance of the healing process moving forward. My only choice was to keep asking questions. Once she was engaged in talking about the details of an incident, feelings usually eventually trickled out.

I started with the person Jessica was usually the most upset with. "Did you talk with your mother yesterday?"

Slowly resigned, she said, "Yes."

"What happened?"

Quietly, she said, "Nothing." More silent moments followed.

"Did you talk with her this morning?"

After some moments of staring over my shoulder, she quietly said, "No."

"Did she talk to you?"

Jessica just nodded her head.

"What happened?"

"I stayed to help her can tomatoes," she offered after only a few seconds. Then she did not say more.

"How did it go?"

"Okay."

I immediately realized my last question had not been specific enough. "Did she say anything that upset you?"

"No, not really." The qualifier had to be checked out.

"What did your mother say?"

"Nothing really."

"Tell me what she said?" I urged.

"It was nothing really."

"Did she criticize you?"

"Well, no. I wouldn't call it that."

"Tell me what she said," I urged again.

"Really, it was nothing. Can't we talk about something else?" I now heard an edge in her voice.

"Did she tell you that you were complaining and say, 'If you're not happy, there isn't anything I can do about it?'"

"Listen!" Jessica immediately shot back. "I didn't complain about anything. My mother did not get me upset. Now let's move onto something more important. I need to get to deeper issues. You said so yourself."

I was uncertain if Dorothy had accused Jessica of complaining or had just made her feel that way. So far, that word was my only clue.

"Did she complain about something you were doing?"

"Listen! Whatever she said was no big deal. I'm okay now. It was a little upsetting at the time, but I'm all calmed down now. Can't we work on something important, like being thrown down?"

Obviously, Jessica was not all calmed down. Even so, her invitation was very tempting. Resolving earlier events usually leads to bigger changes. Yet, when I asked her what she wanted to say about being thrown down, she had a one-word answer. "Nothing."

I returned to my only clue. "What did your mom complain about?"

"Look! I've already told you. It wasn't anything to get upset over or cry about." With that, some tears trickled out. Some moments later, the trickle became a flood.

She could no longer hold it in. "My mom can't understand why I can't stay home when Roger works at night. She can't imagine what I can be so afraid of."

Even after a little more than three years of therapy, most of it at twice a week and even more intensely for the past few months, I could not imagine what Jessica could fear either. But I didn't say so.

While tears ran down her face, she talked about some childhood experiences for which her mother had blamed her, unjustly in Jessica's opinion, but she did not say a word about why she could not stay home at night.

For about a month, every session started just like this one. I had to ask very specific questions, and Jessica denied she was upset about anything. After some time, tears would appear, and an upsetting feeling would come bursting out.

Most of the time, this process took at least an hour. Occasionally, it took close to two. Our having to do this every session never ceased to amaze me. It did not matter how wide a channel Jessica had to her feelings on the previous day. When we began, it was as if none of that had ever happened. It was extremely frustrating. I just could not understand why we had to go through this tortuous beginning every session, even though she always, except for one time, eventually cried.

My frustration over these laborious beginning phases became my own personal demon. The same pulsating thought reverberated in my head as I drove away from her house at the end of each day.

"I'm never doing this again! Never! Never!"

For the first five or ten minutes of my drive home, I was convinced I was never going back. After another five or ten, there was a slight possibility of it. As the miles sped by and my frustration continued subsiding, I was ready for another session by the time I arrived home.

Was Jessica being stubborn? Was she willfully not doing what was best for her? Was she sabotaging her therapy? Was she stunting her psychological growth? Should I have lectured her and threatened to stop her therapy even though I agreed that decision was hers? Should I make her toe the line? There was a two-part explanation for all this: endorphins and repression, at least the understanding of how repression operated I shared with a few of my more innovative-thinking colleagues.

First discovered in the late 1970s, endorphins are chemicals produced by the human body. Extremely powerful, they are the body's natural painkillers. The most powerful endorphin is 1,000 times more powerful than an equivalent amount of morphine, the most powerful artificial painkiller. Another is 700 times more powerful. Others are 300 to 400 times so.

Endorphins literally save our lives. They are the major factor in regulating the amount of pain, physical or psychological, we feel in a traumatic situation. They do this by preventing the pain-regulating system in our body from overloading. Physiologically, our bodies can process only so much pain at one time. Too much pain overloads our body's ability to handle it. If this happens, the pulse rate could increase to 300 to 400 beats a minute. The heart or other vital organs could rupture.

The tremendous power of endorphins helps to explain why recovery from very early experiences takes so much longer than for events that occur later in life. Because infants and very young children lack the physiological resources to process deep assaults to their basic humanness, endorphins make them numb to most of it, until later when their nervous systems have matured. Even then, if a big reservoir of upsetting feelings has built up, the buried stuff comes out in bits and pieces. When the session is over, the wide-open channel to upsetting feelings that had existed slams shut. The endorphins reassert themselves, though minus a bit of their previous strength.

Endorphins are a part of the process of repression, but repression itself is a more complex matter. Repression operates in one time frame only, the original experience. From repression's perspective, the past is always threatening to erupt. The protective mechanisms involved do not recognize any difference between the past and present. They constantly scan the horizon, looking for any experience that is too similar to a past traumatic one. They do this so a present event will not trigger the emotions our psyches could not handle at the time.

While repression helps save our sanity early in our lives, it becomes our greatest enemy when we later try recovering from these fateful early events. Whenever our psyche senses an impending danger, it reacts instinctively. When that happens, the sympathetic part of the autonomic nervous system, known since the 1930s as the fight-or-flight response, is activated Our bodies prepare for the emergency. Our pulse quickens, and our breathing accelerates. Adrenaline pumps and other physiological functions increase so we can face the emergency more effectively.

Jessica always began her session with a present event because the repressive mechanisms are on as long as the past trauma remains unresolved. Because her psyche saw the present events as threats, they triggered the overwhelming fears from earlier events. The autonomic nervous system took over and primed her body for an emergency, causing her, for example, to pace back and forth and plead, "I can't do this! It's too scary!" while I was only smiling and looking at her.

After awhile, after her psyche "realized" the situation was not actually threatening, the safety I represented became more real to her. The imprints from earlier in her life lost their grip. The rush of anxiety faded away, and she could deal with the earlier trauma more productively.

My feeling of frustration also began dissipating as I learned more about what had happened to Jessica as an infant. Then I could truly appreciate her struggle. That part of my brain that seemed to keep yelling, "I can't understand this!" (probably from some very early experience of mine) finally had to surrender to what it was seeing day after day. Jessica's infant traumas, especially the battle of wills, were far more embedded in the depths of her psyche than I had ever imagined or wanted to believe. I consoled myself with the most basic facts. I was trying to be the best therapist I knew how to be, and she was working as best she could.

"Just be patient," I kept reminding myself. "It will all work out."

I never blamed Jessica for how our sessions were going during this period when she lost easy access to her feelings. I tried my very best to keep from even hinting at such, except for the one time when she did not cry at all. On that day, when I helped her get in touch with her feelings, it went slower than usual. More questions were necessary. Her responses were shorter than usual, and there was more silence between them. After more than an hour, I did not have a clue about what had upset her.

My frustration must have caused me to glance away for a bit. Before I realized my own feelings were taking up my attention, I suddenly heard her cry out, "I can't do this!" With that, she jumped up from the couch and hurried past me, heading for the doorway.

The sight of her walking away unhinged me. What right did she have to act like that? Wasn't I giving her sixteen hours of therapy a week? Didn't I agree to postpone payment for months? Wasn't the fee rock-bottom? How could she be so ungrateful? Even while these thoughts ran through my head, I knew my frustration was getting the best of me. I was not able to get control of it fast enough.

The words "I can't do this!" echoed in my head. Before she reached the kitchen, I swiveled around in the chair and commanded, "You will, or we won't do this!"

As soon as the last word left my mouth, I silently castigated myself for violating one of my cardinal beliefs about therapy. Never blame the client. Jessica stopped abruptly and slowly turned around. Her head drooped, and she stood in place for a few seconds while some tears trickled out.

Underneath my frustration, which was rapidly dissipating, I realized I had exploded at her because I truly cared about her. My outburst was my way of saying, "How can I help you if you don't stay here?"

Jessica, of course, could not hear my real concern. She could only hear that I was telling her she was doing something wrong. She returned to her seat and did her best to be a good client, but it was forced and mechanical. Nothing was accomplished for the rest of the day.

About two weeks after I exploded at her, the same incident happened again. During the slow, beginning phase, she suddenly jumped up, without any warning that I could see, and exclaimed, "I can't do this!" As she hurried out of the room, I kept my mouth shut.

Within moments, her footsteps stopped in the kitchen. I rushed to the doorway. She was on the opposite side, standing with her back wedged into a corner. She stared at the floor. Her shoulders drooped, and her arms hung limply from her sides. Tears streamed down her face. I started to slowly walk toward her, smiling. When I was just a step or two away, her head suddenly snapped up. Her eyes were on fire.

"Go home!" she commanded.

Without a doubt, that was the worst possible thing I could do. I had no idea what was frightening her so. I had only been trying to get her to talk, trying to get through the usual, slow going opening phase. It was something we had been through many times in the past. I stood in place, continued smiling, and waited.

While she stared at me, some tightness drained from her face. Her eyes softened a bit. I heard another "Go home!" which was weaker than the first one. A great burst of tears followed. She then pleaded, "I can't do this!"

She stared at the floor. The flow of tears slowed. For a minute or two, she did not say anything. At that point, I took a very slow, very tiny step toward her.

Her head suddenly snapped up, and she exclaimed, "Do you know who you're talking to?" An intense burst of tears followed. After a minute or two, they dried up. When she did not say anything for another minute, I took another tiny step toward her. With one more, I only had to lean forward to touch her with my fingertips. Before I could move any closer, she hurled her question at me again with an added emphasis.

"Do you know who I am? It's me! It's me!" With these last cries of despair, she buried her face in her hands. Muffled cries of "It's me!" escaped through her fingers.

My immediate wish was for magical powers so I could cast a spell and make all of this turmoil and agony disappear for her. Despite how distressed she appeared, I knew Jessica was experiencing a tremendous feeling of relief. From the earliest days of her life, her psyche had been patiently waiting for the right set of conditions to start the healing process. It had been a very long wait.

The muffled cries of "It's me!" gradually ended. She slowly lowered her hands and stared at me with sad eyes, inviting me forward. I inched forward and slowly reached for her. When my fingers were about to touch her shoulders, her body suddenly jerked backward, her hands flew against her chest in protective fists, and she cried out, "No! No! Look! It's me! It's me!"

She had an incredulous look on her face, as if she could not comprehend how I could persist in being so dumb and not see who "me" was. I could only beam my biggest smile at her and, with my outstretched hands, urge her to tumble into my arms. That only prompted more outbursts from her.

"Don't you see? Look! Don't you see?"

I leaned forward a bit, as if I was about to hug her, but I refrained from actually touching her, fearing she might shrink backward again. She immediately reacted. She unlocked one fist and jabbed a pointed finger into her chest. With that, she cried out again, "Listen! It's me!" She was pleading with me to see what was so frightening and terrifying to her. I only saw a person I deeply cared about, a good person. I continued smiling and reaching for her.

Over the next thirty seconds, she pleaded several more times, "Listen, it's me!" while I remained riveted to the spot, smiling and reaching for her. Immediately, with the last "It's me!" both of her arms flopped helplessly to her sides. In a voice saturated with resignation that she could no longer hold back what she so intensely feared, she exclaimed, "Listen! Let me tell you! I'm the one who was thrown down! I'm the one she didn't want! I'm the one she couldn't love! It's me! It's me!" Her voice quivered. Her arms waved frantically in the air, and her legs shot up and down like pistons. Her body seemed be dancing in midair.

When her cries of "It's me!" finally ended, she buried her face in her hands. Tears ran threw her fingers and trickled onto the floor. I could only nudge her shoulders with my fingertips in order for her to tumble into my arms. She cried for a long time, deep, soothing crying.

Jessica's words that followed her exclaiming "Let me tell you!" had greatly surprised me. I had assumed (wrongly again) that she did feel and know with absolute certainty that she was the person, the infant, who had been so terrified during the battle of wills. When she had remembered that event, taking a whole weekend to do so and experiencing a great variety of emotions throughout, she did not seem to have any doubt that she was that person. To know it intellectually was one thing. Actually feeling the full psychological impact of it was an entirely different experience. This episode of crying in the corner had not actually drained all of the emotion.

A few sessions later, during the usual, slow beginning phase, Jessica suddenly jumped up and ran out of the room. Cries of "I can't do this!" trailed behind her.

I waited to see if she was going to stop in the kitchen, but I lost the sound of her steps somewhere on the other side of the house. The rattle of a coat hanger catapulted me out of my chair and sent me hurrying through the kitchen to the small utility room. Jessica had her shoes on. She was holding a light jacket in her hand.

I jumped past her and stood with my back against the outer door. The room was so small that I could easily reach out and touch her with one step. Her coat hung limply from her hand. Tears were beginning to trickle out of her eyes. I raised my arms for her to tumble forward, but she stood in place.

"Listen! Please! I can't do this!" A few moments passed as I smiled at her, hoping she was receiving the warm vibes I was silently sending her way. Her coat fell to the floor. Then her hands slowly transformed themselves into tight fists, and she pressed them against the sides of her head. Fresh words came.

"I couldn't make anyone love me! Not even my own mom!" Big tears ran down her face, and her body suddenly arched backward. She exclaimed, "If you can't make your own mom love you...Ow! Ow!" She grasped her head in her hands and finished her agonized cry, "What kind of a person are you?"

Instinctively, I nudged her shoulders with my fingers. She collapsed in my arms.

These emotional upheavals over who she feared she was happened once or twice a week for a month, each time diminishing in intensity. It took only a few of these sessions for Jessica to hear from other people that she was behaving differently. She had attended a barbecue and knew some of the people quite well. All of the comments had the same message. She looked more real. One person actually said, "You look like a wanting person!"

Jessica had maneuvered her way through life by doing what was expected of her. Everyone who knew her thought she was quite responsible. How could they not? That was not the real Jessica though. That was wooden behavior with no inner self, despite how she appeared to others. People were now becoming aware of the Jessica who had always been protectively hidden away. None had been aware of the emotional storms brewing inside. They only came out when I was around. I never stopped being amazed, even though I could explain it quite rationally at how calm she could appear to others and be just the opposite with me.

There was another aspect to the social gathering Jessica attended that reminded me of how insidious the ill effects of hurtful experiences could be. Throughout the evening, she tried enjoying herself. She chatted with many people, some she had never met. However, her conscious attempt to engage spontaneously with others had triggered another layer of her unresolved feelings. As she was telling me about how she tried sharing more of herself with others, she suddenly became very frightened and said, "I feel like I did something I wasn't supposed to do."

"What was that?" I quickly asked, having not a clue about what she meant.

"Have a good time!" she answered and cried a little. The fact she could state exactly what she was feeling, cry about it, and then carry on impressed me. She was looking forward to her next social event.

While Jessica honestly believed these comments about how she was appearing, she was far more concerned about feeling better, which was not happening yet. It is a strange, disquieting mystery in recovery from early assaults to our humanness that behaviors change before feelings. Unfortunately, this is the exact opposite of what most people hope for. In the first several months of the weekends, Jessica would often exclaim, after a long burst of crying, "I don't feel any different!" I knew she was disappointed, but I was not surprised. I could only comfort her with the knowledge that it is just the way we're built. With enough deep crying, I was convinced she would eventually feel better. Now that she was feeling she was the infant who had been thrown down and who was not able to make her own mother love her, I hoped the change she most yearned for was very close.

I believed that would happen because that was the only thing I could believe. Based on what I knew about deep psychological change, those were the only ideas I could come up with. What actually happened shattered those ideas to useless bits.

18

False Hope

I did not have to wait more than a few sessions for the first sign that my silent prediction was way off. There was a double-barreled explosion on two consecutive days.

On the first day, after exchanging "hello" when Jessica let me in, she said she had to finish wiping the kitchen counter, so I continued into the living room. I slid the armchair I usually sat in around to face the couch. My back was to the doorway on the opposite side of the room that led to the kitchen. A minute later, I heard her walking from the other end of the kitchen, where I had left her, into the dining alcove, where she had backed herself into a corner in recent sessions. When thirty seconds elapsed and she did not appear in front of me, I turned around. Just inside the living room, sitting yoga-style on the rug with a tense, forward lean, was a fire-breathing ball of anger.

For several minutes, she sat as immobile and as silent as a marble statue. For the longest time, her eyes did not blink. I felt a great temptation to ask what she was feeling, but I was certain she would deny she was feeling anything. Even if she did happen to state a feeling, I was also equally certain that it would be a surface feeling, not the deep fear that had suddenly seized control of her behavior.

After turning the rest of my body in her direction and maintaining inviting eye contact with her the entire time, I very slowly started raising my body from the chair. Before I could even get it into the air, I was blasted.

"Go home!"

Unlike her desperate plea of "I can't do this!" from a few weeks ago, this was a command for me to immediately vacate the premises. She remained anchored to her chosen spot and continued glaring at me. We stared at each other for few minutes, and neither moved a muscle. Instead of trying to stand, I began inching my way off of the chair, hoping that being physically closer to her level might take the sharp edge off of her fear. When I was about to slide off onto my hands and knees, I was blasted again, just as forcefully as the first time. While perched on the edge of my chair, I stayed very still. Her fear was stronger than I had originally thought. I had to wait for a clearer sign that it was safe enough before I could start bridging the distance.

"Go home!"

Thirty seconds later, she yelled, "Go home, or I'll call the police!" Although this command and its attending threat did not pulse the air with quite the same decibel level, it was uttered with the same fierce determination.

Even so, she did not make a move toward the phone, which was only an arm's reach away. I did not know what I was going to do if she actually called the police. Leaving was out of the question. If I asked her not to call anyone to save both of us from the embarrassment, it would probably interfere with whatever her psyche was playing out. If she actually reached for the phone, I could only hope that the act of dialing or even hearing a voice from out there would snap her into her public mode. I feared her verbal blasts would cause a neighbor to call the police, even though the windows were closed.

Over the next several minutes, she threatened to call the police a few more times, but she never made any move to do so. From when I had turned around to see where she was, about twenty minutes ago, she had yet to take her eyes off me.

"Go home! You only come here to hurt me!"

A tear fell from her eye and ran down her face.

About every thirty seconds for the next several minutes, Jessica repeated this command. The entire time, I stayed perfectly still.

"Don't come near me!" With that, a few tears trickled out.

In this last command, her voice was not as loud or harsh. I decided it was time to move closer. Very slowly, I lowered myself to the floor and started moving toward her on my hands and knees, watching closely for any adverse reaction.

Before I had moved more than a hand and a knee, she spoke again. "Don't! You just want to hit me!" Tears flowed freely.

For the next ten minutes, I continued moving ever closer, a hand or a knee at a time. I waited about a minute after each "You just want to hit me" for her fear to diminish a little more. I did not say a word the whole time. I just kept smiling until I was alongside her. I was then able to hold her while her body shook for a long time over the teenaged male babysitter who had hit her to make her stop struggling.

Once again, surprise overtook me. Hadn't the sexual assault been laid to rest a few months ago? It was a sharp reminder to never assume that any client was finished with any experience, regardless of how much emotional release had happened.

When I came the next day, we exchanged "hello" when she let me in. I went into the living room to wait for her. I hoped yesterday's travails were finished. I was not looking forward to going through that experience again. The various twists and turns Jessica's psyche brought forward were quite enough to engage my full attention, and I did not need additional worries about neighbors or the police.

A minute later, I heard her step into the living room. When she did not quickly appear near me, I turned around. She was sitting in the exact spot as yesterday, looking exactly the same way.

"Go home!"

Her command was not quite as loud or as forceful as yesterday.

Back-to-back sessions starting in this strange way were not a fluke. Her psyche must have been orchestrating this. After waiting about a minute to see if she was going to say anything else, I lowered myself to my hands and knees.

Over the next half hour, she yelled at me to go home every few minutes and voiced her fear that I was going to hit her. This time, she did not threaten to call the police though. Her reactions were not quite as intense as the day before, and they did not last as long. In about half the time it had taken the day before, I was holding her while she shook and cried about her mother hitting her—or trying to—with any object that was within reach. It was usually about chores that were not done to her liking.

For the next few weeks, Jessica's psyche seemed content to finish with the unresolved parts of all that she had remembered since we had started the weekends. There were not any new memories. Her jumping up and exclaiming, "I can't do this," had apparently ended. One day, we focused on her fear of needing. While we stood a step or two apart, I had her very slowly extend her arms, as I usually did, and reach for me. When her fingertips were a about a foot away, her body started shaking. A few minutes later, when the shaking lessened, I had her reach a little closer. When that bout of shaking was finished, I had her extend one finger and just barely touch the back of my wrist with a fingertip. The instant she made contact with my skin, she immediately drew her finger back, as if she were touching a flame. Then her body went into deep vibrations.

She had been silent through the whole exercise. At this point, she exclaimed, "I'm terrified of what might happen if I let anyone know what I need!" In more than three years, this was the first time I had actually heard her use the word *need* in reference to herself.

The shaking triggered other comments. "All of my life, I've never wanted anyone to touch me. Every time someone does, I must bite my lip. I don't like Melissa to touch me either, but, knowing she needs it, I make myself do it. It's all from my mom not really touching me as an infant. It left me feeling like I wasn't any good to touch."

At the end of this exercise, which lasted nearly an hour, Jessica wanted to change our customary sitting arrangement. She had me sit on the floor with my back against the couch. She sat alongside me, stretched one leg out in the space behind my back, stuck the other one straight out parallel to mine, wrapped her arms around my neck and shoulders, and rested her forehead against the top of my arm. She said she had always wanted to sit like this because of the physical reassurance, but she had been too afraid to ask.

There were many other unmistakable signs of improvement. Now, in addition to crying and shaking, she was also expressing vibrant indignation over how she had been treated. Indignation has a much more optimistic quality to it than crying and shaking. In those kinds of release, the person is letting the world know how heartbreaking or frightening an experience was. With indignation, the person is responding much more powerfully. The person is saying, "I'm too important for you to treat me like that!"

In the middle of a session, during an exercise when we were standing opposite each other and I was encouraging her to push me, she suddenly grabbed me by the shoulders and started shaking me.

"I'm a human being! How could you let them treat me like that?" She was saying this to all of the people who, from an infant's or small child's perspective, should have intervened and not let her be hurt. I just happened to be the handiest, safest target.

She let go of my shoulders and stretched out, full-length, on the floor on her back. Looking just like a small child throwing a tantrum, she beat the carpet with her hands and feet. In a richly indignant tone of voice, she let the world know what she was raging about.

"They didn't touch me! Grrr! They didn't hold me! Grrr! They threw me down! Grrr!"

After two or three minutes, she sat up and exclaimed in a vibrant tone, "If I were a big person, I would love me. I would hold me. I would tell me I was precious!"

A few tears came to my eyes. What a contrast to her running to another room and screaming at me about why she could not do this or commanding I go home.

Besides these changes I was seeing right before me, there were also other long-awaited ones. In one session, she told me she had spent the last few nights at home with her daughter. She had been hesitant to tell me after the first night because she was not sure if it would continue. By now, she felt confident about being home at night though, but it was not easy. She still felt frightened. She slept on sofa cushions on the living room floor. Whenever she started feeling too afraid, she would shake. The fear would decrease enough for her to go back to sleep. However, she did not tell me what she feared, and I did not ask.

Another big change was Jessica driving by herself, just back and forth between her and her mother's house, from one side of Bayport to the other. One day, she just decided to follow me. Before driving off at the end of the day, I usually spent a minute or two jotting down a few brief notes that I would expand on at home in the log I kept there. When I was at the stop sign at the end of her block, waiting to turn onto the blacktop road that bordered Hansen's Bay, she was pulling out of her driveway. While I had been making my notes, she had gone out the back door and into her car. All of which I could not see from the front of the house. When I turned at the end of her street, she pulled from her driveway. She stayed a good distance behind me, even allowing a car or two to get between us. As long as she could see my car, she felt confident enough about driving. When I went past the road Dorothy lived on, where Jessica had lived as a teenager, just before the interstate, she simply turned off.

It was now the end of November. It was our eighth month of weekends, and it was too cold for rock climbing. Our only interruption had been my two-week backpacking trip to Colorado during July. It had been my first vacation in three years. Given my commitment to Jessica, it was my shortest trip ever out to the West. I did not regret my agreement to Jessica's conditions. Our work together had been the most exciting, profound experience of my life. With her therapy moving forward as quickly it was, I was looking forward to cross-country skiing trips in December.

On the last day of our last weekend in November, my predictions about her therapy for once seemed to be coming true. Throughout this weekend, Jessica had been crying, though not too deeply, about no one loving her, especially when she so desperately needed it as an infant. In sharp contrast to past sessions, she was not blaming herself for not being the right kind of person. Plus, she was not running to another room.

With about twenty minutes to go on Monday, I was content to let the crying diminish by itself. We were sitting on the floor, facing each other, where we had been for the past half hour. After a few more tears trickled out, she sat quietly for a few minutes and stared at the floor. While my eyes were giving her undivided attention, another part of my mind started daydreaming about the extra time I would have once the weekends stopped. I started becoming lost in my own thoughts. However she wanted to spend the rest of this session was up to her.

Then I heard a woeful cry. "I just wanted someone to love me!"

The plaintive sound snapped my attention back to the present. My first awareness of Jessica was seeing her hand resting gently over her heart, as if she was cradling the spot on her body that had been hurt. Before the sound of her words had faded away, her body erupted into a deep, cleansing cry, which gradually tapered off and ended a few minutes later. When it did, her arm stayed pressed against her chest, but her hand, like that of a broken rag doll, flopped backward at the wrist and hung limply away from her body.

The mournful cry came quickly again. "I just wanted somebody to love me!"

Simultaneous with the words, her hand snapped back over her heart. Deep crying followed for another minute. When it ended, her hand flopped helplessly backward again.

These few words and the way they were said seemed to sum up all the years of unfulfilled hope for someone to see her as a real human being, not as an infant who just needed to be fed, changed, and kept warm or as a child who seemed to enjoy long hours of hard work and never complain.

Some people in Jessica's life had tried loving her as best they could. However, no one had ever done it with enough persistence to get past her fear that she was the kind of a person that no one could love.

For the next three hours, my only task was to not say a word, look attentive, watch her place her hand over her chest, and listen to her say, "I just wanted someone to love me." The intensity of the crying gradually softened, the length of time she cried became shorter, and the periods between her crying and voicing the trigger words grew longer.

After the last sprinkle of tears, as the winter sun was low on the horizon, Jessica looked very alert, more so than I had ever seen her. Without a doubt, she would finally begin to feel better, permanently. After eight months of weekends, two more than my original forecast when we had started four days a week, it was about time.

19

The Haunting Secret

For several days after Jessica's three-hour cry, I felt as if I was floating in a time warp. Friday could not come fast enough. In my mind's eye, there was an image of a face radiating excitement and a voice sounding exclamations of delight over new, wonderfully exciting feelings.

One Friday morning, cold with a brilliant, blue sky and the ground covered in frost, my impatience to arrive was tempered by slick roads off the interstate. When I finally pulled up in front of Jessica's house, I hopped out of my car and hurried down the driveway. The frost-covered ground crunched beneath my feet. I gave the back door a quick knock, and Jessica let me in. By the time I stepped in, she had backed into the kitchen. I peeked in from the laundry room while wiping my shoes and gave a cheery "Hello!" Her eyes met mine momentarily, just long enough for me to see that hers were glazed over. Her head immediately drooped. She turned away and stood where she was, staring at her feet.

I quickly hung my coat in the laundry room and hurried over to her. She continued staring at the floor. This was not the reaction I was expecting, but I could not think of any appropriate words. I just patted her on the arm and said softly, "Come on." She trailed after me as I headed for the living room. I sat down on the floor in front of the couch. She sat down opposite me and stared at the floor.

During the first hour, Jessica did not have much to say. She gave her usual, short, unemotional answers to any question I asked. A few tears trickled out about a feeling that was similar to the "I just wanted somebody to love me" from last Monday. Today, her words were, "I just wanted one person in this whole big world to make me feel that I matter, that I'm enough." There were sometimes shorter versions, "I didn't matter to anyone" and "No one thought I was enough." A short burst of light tearing followed each, though none for more than a minute.

Throughout the morning, the release of feelings occurred very erratically, like a balky engine trying to get started on a cold day. Regardless of what I encouraged her to talk about, she somehow always ended on the same emotional note, briefly repeating she wasn't enough or she didn't matter. About a minute of light tearing followed. There was not any transition from the slow going, opening phase to the free-flowing release of feelings.

It did not take me very long to realize that, ever since the previous Monday, I had been living in a fantasy. I had barely managed to accept the reality of this latest twist in her therapy when, seemingly unrelated to anything she had said so far on this day, she suddenly exclaimed, with a few tears running down her face, "I want to give up and die because I feel no good."

Give up and die! I had to literally hold my tongue to keep from shouting, "What do you mean give up and die?" I had never heard such talk from her.

After she repeated this shocking revelation a few more times, I suddenly realized her last session had indeed changed something, even if it was not what I hoped for. The words "Give up and die" were an announcement from her psyche that something new was on its way up. I had no idea what that might be. I could not imagine anything more devastating than the battle of wills.

At home that evening after dinner, as my body sunk deep into the cushions of my favorite lounging chair, the lilting tones of Bach's first clarinet concerto, my favorite piece of classical music, helped soften the sound of the whistling winter winds. My mind drifted slowly into a meditative state. For most of my life, I had been listening to my inner voices, my intuitions. After awhile, an impression that had been emerging from the depths of my subconscious solidified itself in my mind. The message was very clear: bring your cassette recorder. Until now, I had been making notes after each of Jessica's sessions, starting after about two months of weekends when the twists and turns to her sessions were beyond my capacity to retain in my memory.

When I walked into Jessica's house the next day with my recorder, I said, "I'd like to begin taping."

Jessica quietly said, "Okay." She asked, "Why?"

"I'm not sure," I said with a hesitant shrug of my shoulders. "I just want to."

In the living room, I plugged in the recorder and set the remote microphone. I was not going to push the record button until we reached something that was worth saving.

This morning, she seemed more alert. Soon, she started asking if I thought she would ever feel good. "You won't have to tell me. Right?"

I immediately felt great relief. Jessica asking me seemed like a vast improvement over her devastating remark from the day before of declaring she wanted to give up and die because she felt no good.

Every time she asked if she would ever feel good, I quietly, confidently said, "Right."

It seemed Jessica's only memory of ever having felt good was anticipating being born. For all of her life, she had harbored a secret hope of feeling better since then. Even the battle of wills had not extinguished that hope. It only kept her from letting anyone know it was her most ardent desire.

She had great difficulty in believing my reassurances that she would eventually feel good and quickly let me know how absurd the whole thing sounded to her.

"There isn't any good! Can't you see? I've looked real deep...everywhere...in every corner. I can't find it! Argh!" She hurled her last words at me and dove for my body. She wrapped her arms around my shoulders and buried her face deep in my neck.

A few minutes later, Jessica pulled her face away from my neck, but she stayed snuggled against me. The rush of emotion from when she cried out, "I can't find it!" had lessened. She began thinking aloud. "Is that why I can't find good things about me? Because there aren't any? I can't seem to get that through my head. I've looked so hard and so deep, and I don't see any good."

Now that Jessica was not in the grip of strong emotion, maybe some words of encouragement and true words would give her some hope. I said, "The good is in there. It's just been hidden."

"Forever?" she replied immediately. "It's been hidden for my whole life?" she asked incredulously. "I'm telling you, I can't find it. There isn't any good. No one's looked harder than I have!"

A pleading, desperate look came over her. "I have to count on someone else to see it because I can't! There isn't anybody else who's going to straighten this out. You'd better get in gear. It doesn't matter to anybody but you. You have to make sure I do this because it doesn't matter to me."

I certainly did not have any problem about feeling in gear, and I could certainly understand why she did not feel motivated to straighten it out. Fortunately, I did not need to rely on how she felt or try to talk her into being motivated. I only had to arrange the right conditions for the natural healing process to operate.

On Sunday, we had to struggle through the usual, slow beginning before I pushed the record button. When the healing process finally started operating, feelings came out in brief staccato bursts, as they had the past two days. On this day, they were more intense. After awhile, Jessica was too agitated to sit alongside of me. She scooted to the middle of the room. It seemed it was her favorite place when she felt she needed breathing space. She sat facing toward me.

For a minute or two, she stared over my shoulder. Suddenly, she cried, "I don't even care if you know!" She then seemed to freeze in place, as if she could not believe she had even said these words. They expressed the same unspoken anguish she had shocked her mother and herself with after the drive-in theater. Dorothy had said, "I can't believe there's something wrong with you." Jessica had shot back with, "There is! I've been trying to tell you that all of my life!" Jessica looked as horrified as she must have felt then.

Given the explosive way these latest words had forced themselves out of her, I was certain that Jessica was about to express yet another feeling she had always been terrified of. It was a feeling that had been sitting in the depths of her psyche for all of these years, as if it had been daring her to try to recapture what was rightfully hers, her basic humanness, because it was certain Jessica would not win.

After quickly regaining her composure, the words revealing exactly what it was she did not even care I knew about came out in explosive bursts. In what looked like a series of mini convulsions, she spat out each of the psychological poisons that had been, ever so slowly, draining the life out of her and making her feel she was nothing more than an empty space encapsulated by skin and bones.

The first to be jettisoned was, "I'm terrible." "Awful...mean...ugly" followed in quick succession. These toxic emotional daggers had been driven deep into her spirit from the earliest days of her life. When left to ferment in her psyche all these years, their combined effect had left her feeling that no one could "love her" or "want her" and she "hurt people" just because she "was alive." When she was finished expelling these toxins from her psyche, she returned to the words she had started with. This time, she hastily added, "Because I can't change it!" While my face was radiating deep empathy for her struggle over her inability to make herself feel different, I was smiling to myself. True, Jessica had not been able to change any of it by herself. No one could have done it alone. But that didn't matter. Now that she had assistance, the magic was happening. The healing process was ready to roll.

With her last agonizing words, she grasped the sides of her head. The force of the long-buried feelings emerging in her caused her body to snap backward. She ended up flat on her back, grasping the sides of her head. More words came rushing out.

"Everybody always thought I was no good! Just ask my mom! She'll tell you! My mom told me I'm no good!"

Then Jessica sat up and started rocking back and forth. Her hands still gripped the sides of her head. The words came in sporadic bursts.

"I really didn't want to hurt her!" she cried out.

A tear or two ran down my cheek. A picture flashed in my mind of Jessica in the battle of wills, completely dependent on her mother, desperately wanting to be loved, and expecting her mother to be gentle and caring. What did she get? A raging monster. Jessica was now anguished over believing, as an infant, she had made her mother's life miserable.

"I'm just like everybody always said. I'm awful and terrible, and I just hurt people." Her body jerked back and forth. "I can't pretend anymore! I don't care if I hurt anybody. If I cared, I'd die!"

With that, Jessica tightened her grip on her head, as if she feared it would spin right off if she didn't hold on to it securely enough. She was on her back. Her body jerked from side to side as her back arched. A force greater than herself appeared to possess her. Sharp, desperate cries came from deep inside her. A few more tears rolled down my face. A strong feeling was building in my chest. A few, high-pitched "Ows!" came from Jessica.

"If I was good, I would have died!"

In my mind, a tiny, helpless infant who had been born wanting to add good to the world was feeling she had destroyed the life of the person who had given her life. A few more "Ows!" resounded from the floor.

"If I was good and cared about her, I would have died! I wouldn't live and hurt anybody!"

The pressure in my chest erupted. The sounds of muffled sobs escaped from deep inside my chest. Tears streamed down my face as I thought of an infant believing the only way to be a good baby and make her mother happy was through death.

A few moments later Jessica spoke again. "Wait!" she exploded. "I can't handle that! How can I live with this?"

Her words described exactly what I was wondering. She had to feel all of this on her own as an infant and without help. How had she lived with this? Without me asking, Jessica answered her own question. "Make me not real! Please! Make sure I don't hurt anybody. Please! That's the only way I can live."

That was how her psyche had handled these life-threatening feelings. After the battle of wills, Jessica's survival depended on her being an unreal person, not needing or wanting anything from anybody. It was now clear that being an unreal person also meant not feeling that she was responsible for destroying her mother's life. Jessica had not really wrecked her mother's life, but she was viewing this from the limited perspective of an infant's mind. At the time, her psyche came to the only logical conclusion it could.

For years, this lifesaving defense had remained as intact as the most hardened cast-iron vault. All who had known her, including myself for the first three years of her therapy, had been oblivious to these powerful forces controlling her life. They operated so efficiently behind the scenes, like a spy with the perfect cover, that the rest of us only saw a responsible, hardworking person who seemed so naturally concerned about how other people felt. Now, in a safe environment, she was finally able to experience these primordial feelings and begin the healing process that had been held in check for so many years.

When I came to Jessica's house the next day, she was in the same mood I usually found her in since we had started the weekends eight months ago. She did not smile or give a bright-eyed look. She was waiting for me to fill the air with questions. After close to an hour, my frustration was, once again, on the verge of erupting. A part of my brain just could not understand why she could not pick right up exactly where she had left off the session before.

Then Jessica finally volunteered how she was feeling, "Something feels real dead and unimportant in me."

The words and the rising emotion in her voice triggered my intuition, and I switched on the recorder.

"When did you first feel dead?" I eagerly asked.

Jessica surprised me with her quick answer. "I've always felt dead. I was thinking about that earlier."

I immediately wanted to cry, "If you were thinking about this earlier, why didn't you say so?" But I did not interrupt and invited her to continue.

"I was trying to think of the first minutes of my life. Maybe because everything was so hectic and everyone was blaming me right away, a part of me must have been screwed up within minutes. Nothing happened the way it should have."

With her last words about the first few minutes of her life, Jessica started explaining, in far greater detail than the partial recall of her birth from eight months ago, how her life had gotten screwed up within minutes. We were sitting across from each other on the floor. She began in a confident, animated tone.

"I remember 'thinking' before I was born all that was going to happen. I was going to be born so somebody could love and touch me, so I could be enough, so I could be a part of a big, working thing, and I could have an effect upon the world.

"All of it was going to be so neat. I was going to be a part of a whole big world. The world was a good place, and I was going to be a part of it! Me! The world was going to be better because I was here...because there was nothing like me.

Nowhere could the world get what it was going to get from me. I was important, as important as anything. Even the tiniest speck!"

What a beautiful way to enter the world! From the effortless way the words were flowing out of Jessica, I did not doubt this was exactly how she had felt. She continued.

"During labor, I felt squeezed. I wasn't frightened. I was going along with the process of being born. I was starting to get out when somebody pushed me back in. Gosh darn it! I was not in charge of my birth anymore. They were pushing my head in, and I couldn't breathe. I was very frightened and confused. I thought I was going to die before I could get out.

"Somebody was jerking me and scaring me. Everything was just jerking and pulling and turning. It hurt everywhere on my body. I didn't know what to do. I was dizzy. I wanted to go back to where it was quiet."

Jessica suddenly switched to talking in the first person, as if she was actually being born again. "Make them stop! Leave me alone! Everyone leave me alone, and I'll be just fine. Let me do it!"

Had she been able to talk, she surely would have uttered these words. Just as quickly, her attention returned from its first-person focus of being back there in time. "The doctor simply plucked me out of my mother and said, 'Here's the little troublemaker. I can tell she's going to be a stubborn one.' My mom hurt, and she hurt physically because of me. There was a lot of confusion. The lights were bright, and the room was noisy. The medical team was in a panic, and everyone was yelling."

"It seemed like the whole world was a mess. Things weren't going right, and it was all because of me—because I was ready to be born and I wasn't doing it right! Everyone was frightened and scared, and they didn't understand.

"Two nurses took me and washed me roughly. They were talking and laughing with each other and were unaware of how they were treating me or how I felt. I remember one of them saying, 'Who do you think you are? You're just another person to take care of.'"

While the nurses did their job, taking care of Jessica's body, they continued ignoring the rest of her.

"I was hungry and screaming and scared. It didn't matter. Nobody wanted to touch me and hold me and smile at me. There was a whole room full of people. I just had to wait! I wasn't any more important than anybody else! Everyone was doing what had to be done, and I had to just behave and stop crying.

"And I'd learn...I'd learn I was a nobody, that I was just like everybody else. It didn't matter what I wanted or expected. I was in the real world, and I'd just have to wait. I was nobody special, and I didn't deserve anything anymore than anybody else. It didn't make any difference who I was. I was just one more person to take care of. It all made me feel like I wasn't what they were looking for, like I was a nobody. Who the hell was I?"

Because no one seemed very concerned about Jessica's basic humanness, what did she think they found more important?

"They weren't concerned about me. They were just concerned with what I had done, with how hard I had made it for everybody. Like I had any control over it! All I had done was be born. And it was no big deal! I came out 'thinking,' 'Ta, ta, I'm here!' and everybody goes, 'Big deal!'"

"Everybody felt like I had to prove myself. It was like everybody thought it was a tough, mean, crummy world. Welcome to it, kid! You're no different than the rest of us. It's all crummy and rotten and look what you're a part of. They must have had a lot of bad attitudes."

Jessica found her last remark quite amusing and had a good laugh. Then she continued. "I felt like going and hiding. What did I do good? I was just born! It didn't matter what I had to offer. Nobody saw any good in me. I was waiting for someone to be so delighted and happy I was here, that I was out, and now the world was a better place because there was one more, good thing. Nobody felt I had contributed something only I could. I thought something unique had just happened and never in the space of time would anything like that happen again because I was different. I was one of a kind, and I could contribute things nobody else could."

"I do feel like I've committed a grave transgression because I was born. Because of me, I added more hurt to this world. I didn't add good things. I wasn't good and special, and one of a kind. I felt so awful, like I didn't have a right to live.

"Everybody thought the world was crummy and a mess and that I added to the awfulness and the crumminess. I felt so disappointed. Yuck! This was what I had waited for?

"After being cleaned up, I went to sleep. When I woke up, I decided to give the world another chance. It was tough being born. It was.

"Do you remember all this stuff? Do you think I'm cuckoo? I know all this happened."

When she finished, she stared at the floor in front of her. She seemed to be silently reflecting on all she had said. It gave me a few minutes to tend to my own feelings.

Jessica's account had taken forty-five minutes. My attention had been riveted on her every word. Her psyche had definitely been on automatic, as if it had been patiently waiting twenty-six years for an opportunity to finally spew out this psychological cancer that had been lodged in some long-forgotten and deeply buried chamber of her mind. She went over a number of parts of the experience several times, filling in details or expanding on her feelings. Often, until the last second before she spoke, there was a puzzled look on her face, as if she knew her mouth was about to open, but she was not sure what might come out.

My silent, attentive presence was all she seemed to need. She never looked at me or asked for reassurance. She sat across from me the whole time. There was no running to another room or yelling at me.

Whatever part of her birth she spoke about, she sounded just like I imagined she must have felt at the time. There was eagerness in her voice over the prospect of being born and what she hoped awaited her. Her most persistent emotion was feeling highly indignant over how she had been treated. At various times, she also felt frightened, sad, and guilty. She shed some tears. She had a good laugh over their bad attitudes. I never doubted for an instant that this was an exact account of how she had felt.

I also believed every word Jessica said about her feelings just before birth, about being a part of a big, working thing. From about six months of age, three months after conception, an unborn child's hearing is fully developed. Even though Jessica could not see the world, she could clearly hear it. Confined to a space barely bigger than her body, a big, working something out there constantly impinged on her senses.

We took a break at about the two-hour mark. We tried taking them as close to the middle of the four hours as possible. Our breaks were now lasting two hours instead of the hour we had taken in the first months of the weekends. With deeper feelings coming up, Jessica needed more time to get her energy back.

After lunch at a nearby restaurant, I stopped a block from her street alongside Hansen's Bay. In warmer weather, I had sat on the boulders and watched the ducks and sea gulls frolicking in the protected environment. It was now early December. The inside of my car was cozy from the midday sun. The wildlife preserve was across the bay. The tranquility of the scene made me realize how peaceful Jessica's birth could have been.

A young father I knew had told me about his daughter's birth. He had been in the delivery room. She was born Cesarean and came out crying. Two members of the medical team attended to her before they gave her to him. She had been crying the entire time. She continued crying while her father took her gently and held her close to his face. In a soft, unhurried voice, he called her by the name he and his wife had chosen. In the same soft voice, he added, "What are you crying about?" He almost lost it when his brand-new daughter abruptly stopped crying and presented him with a big smile.

I mentioned this to Jessica, wondering if the baby had recognized her father's voice from having heard it before birth. Jessica was certain the most important factor was someone talking to her in a quiet, relaxed way.

When we began again, she seemed as alert as when she had finished her account of her birth and we had decided to take a break. She wanted to sit alongside of me while I sat on the floor and leaned against the couch. Getting the healing process going at this midway point was usually easier than at the beginning of the day because feelings were still percolating in her consciousness. She began by reflecting on her birth.

"You know, if a visitor came to this planet, they'd leave and wonder how we got to be human beings. That's exactly what I thought when I first got here. How did everyone survive? It was awful. I could see all the hurt and confusion on everybody. I could see everybody was looking in the wrong places, but I didn't know what to do. I didn't know how I'd survive it all. How I'd adjust to all that was wrong. It was crazy. I knew what I needed and what I needed to do, but there was no way it was going to happen with those people. They were all screwy! I thought the whole world was that way. That's why you look so good! Because you're not as screwy!"

Jessica spoke with conviction, but she was relaxed. It was an unmistakable sign of psychological resolution following a thorough emotional release. The great upsurge of feeling that had started four days ago with her fearing that no one, not even her own mother, could love her had thankfully ended.

The last two days had been recorded. The thought of not having done so was frightening. They were the most startling therapeutic sessions I had ever witnessed or read about. I felt a pang of regret over not having recorded earlier sessions, especially the ones where she ran to the kitchen and screamed, "Do you know who you're talking to?" Fortunately, I had my notes to reference.

We were now in the first week of December. I would not have substituted anything for the past eight months. I had learned more about human psychology and therapy than all my schooling and previous twelve years of experience had taught me. In fact, if anyone had prophesied back then that some future client of mine or any human being anywhere in the world would remember such an event in such dramatic detail, I would have immediately said, "What kind of mushrooms have you been nibbling on?" In my mind's eye, I would be gliding on cross-country skis through a snow-covered forest in a few weeks.

Jessica's next words fully captured my feeling of optimism. She had been quietly staring at the floor in front of us ever since she had offered her opinion about me being not as screwy. She raised her head and peered at me with a look of confidence I had never quite seen on her. She quietly proclaimed, "I now know all that I feel and why!"

I was ecstatic. This was the first time Jessica was agreeing with my silent assessment about her therapy's progress. After nearly nine months of weekends, we were surely now at the end. I held my breath, mentally crossed my fingers, and waited to hear the official words.

The winter sun streamed in through the windows. The living room felt like a tropical paradise against the cold, winter air. Jessica let her body fall forward a little bit, rested her head on my shoulder, and let it lay there for a few minutes. She seemed to be basking in the feeling of finally knowing all that she was feeling and why. Her psyche seemed ready for the final pronouncement.

A voice then invaded the enveloping quiet. Even though the words were coming from Jessica, my immediate reaction was that an alien being had suddenly entered the room. It was the words. They were not human words. They did not have a human meaning. They described a condition I had never imagined as being a human problem. The condition seemed alien to all I knew about human beings and was radically different from all the insights into the infant psyche I had learned ever since we had started the weekends.

Only a brief, few minutes before, Jessica had said, "I now know all that I feel and why." Now, as if continuing the same thought, but in a decidedly different tone of voice, she said, "But I still don't know me or if a me really exists." With panic seeping into her voice, she exclaimed, "I'm trying to find her, and I can't!"

She wrapped her arms tightly around my shoulders and dug her fingertips deep into my back. Her next words came more quickly and with a greater urgency. "I can't get back to what's important because I'm too busy dealing with stuff that shouldn't be there. I can't find me. She's been lost! Are you sure she's there?"

Her fingertips dug deeper into my back. I quietly, confidently said, "Sure."

My attempt at reassurance did not have an effect. The secret terror, the unspeakable terror that had always haunted her and had invaded her mind before she had had words for it, came gushing out.

"I'm not even sure she exists anymore or if she didn't just die or if she didn't just leave somewhere. Oooow! Well, she couldn't have, or I wouldn't be alive.

Right? Will you help me find her? I can't. I can't find her anywhere. Ow! Ow! I can't find her. She's gone! Ow! No! No!"

Jessica buried her face deep in my neck and gripped even tighter what must have felt like her only safe anchor in the world, my body. She had more to say about not being able to find her me.

"My me never had a chance. As soon as I got my hands on it, somebody ripped it away from me!"

Did this mean she once had a me? Before I had a chance to ask, she continued. "It feels like somebody took my human being so I wouldn't die. That part of me that cared about me and the world had to leave. It was being killed. I could feel it pulling away from me." In a terrified whisper, she said, "Just shrinking up!"

Over the next minute, the window to Jessica's unspeakable terror slammed shut as quickly as it had appeared. Her grip on my body gradually loosened. By the time her hands and head were resting lightly on my shoulders, her panic over her missing me seemed to be nothing more than a frightening memory.

It was inconceivable to me that Jessica could have lost her "me". A me was the most basic part of a person's humanness. The equation was simplicity itself. If you were a human being, you had a me. If you had a me, you were a human being. A living, breathing human being with blood coursing through her veins was before me. How could that not be the case?

In her last words, she did not seem to have any doubt that, at one time in her life, however briefly, she had felt her me. Now the problem was she just could not feel her me. But it was there. It had to be. It had to be because that was the only possible way for me to understand, the only way for me to continue to hold out hope for Jessica. If she had indeed lost her me, then who or what was sitting before me?

At the same time, the most frightening questions I could imagine flooded my mind. Had the traumas she had suffered at her birth and in the battle of wills cut deeply enough into her developing humanness so the seed for her me had never taken root? Was her me buried under layers of psychological trauma, patiently waiting all these years to blossom if it could only reach the light of human caring? These were the most fundamental questions about human beings. I was painfully aware that I did not know if answers existed.

There was hope though. If there were answers, I only had to arrange the right conditions and allow the natural healing process to operate. I had not the faintest idea what Jessica had to do to get her me back. I had never worked with anyone who had lost her me. I had never read about anyone doing it either. That did not matter. I only had to know how to operate the healing process, the process that was wiser than my all-too-human brain. I humbly accepted my role as midwife.

I could feel a part of myself shrinking up as well, the part that thought (or at least hoped) I was helping Jessica. Had I been deluding myself? Had I forced her to delve too deeply into her psyche? Had I finally forced her to face a horrible truth about herself? Was she better off not knowing?

When Jessica spoke again, my belief about her lost me being only a symptom of fortuitous events seemed right on target. "They're wrong. Not me. It's not me! Can't they see that? Everybody blamed me and said it was me. And it wasn't. I was good. It's not fair. It's simply not fair! The whole world can't blame me for its problems. I didn't do any of it. All I ever did was be born! They're blaming the wrong person. The world was crummy before I got here. I want to be somewhere where somebody loves me. I want to be enough because I am."

Jessica had not sounded this optimistic the whole weekend, and she had not sounded this hopeful during her whole therapy. Although I had made a promise to myself to never again assume what the next step in her therapy would be, in my mind's eye, the reappearance of her me was just around the corner. How could anyone who sounded so positive about wanting to be enough be that out of touch with her me?

It seemed quite obvious what had to happen next. Jessica's me would come back as soon as she felt real enough. If you felt like a real person, that you were enough, you had to feel your me. It all seemed very logical to me. A few minutes later, my bubble burst into tiny pieces.

In a complete reversal of how she had sounded a few minutes ago, she cried out, "I couldn't have done all this. Could I?"

Once again, temptation proved irresistible. I tried reassuring her that she was in no way responsible for all this. Hadn't she just said so five minutes ago? My well-intentioned efforts were ignored.

"Are you sure? Are you sure?" she pleaded with me. "Ow! That's not what it feels like. I somehow feel responsible for all the trouble in the world. I feel like I did something awful because I'm here and I'm me. When people looked at me, all they could see was bad and no good. They couldn't see I was just scared and wanted them to love me so bad. I'm not awful. I can't be! Can I? I can't be that awful. Can I? No! Please! Oh, good grief! How are we ever going to straighten this out?"

With that, she dove for my body and buried her face in my neck.

20

Searching for Help

When this last surge of emotion diminished, the weekend ended. Despite how panicked Jessica had sounded just a few minutes ago, she gradually returned to her usual alertness over the next several minutes. When I stepped out of her house a short time later and cheerfully said, "See you in a few days," I had not bothered to ask how she was feeling. I had my own feelings to deal with.

Once seated in my car, I gently nudged the recorder under the front seat. All four of the cassettes from the day were already in the inside pocket of my heavy winter coat, which I wore unzipped in the car. As I inserted the key into the ignition, a tiny smirk slowly creased my face over having followed my instincts about recording the sessions. When I came to the road at end of Jessica's street, I carefully double-checked in both directions, even though everyone seemed cautious about the ever-present ducks and observed the twenty-five mile per hour speed limit sign. At the blinking light in town, I assumed none of the other drivers knew what a flashing red light meant and almost came to a dead stop, even though I only had a flashing yellow. In my imagination, I was hauling a highly explosive chemical that could go off at the slightest jarring. On the interstate, I stayed in the slowest lane and kept a safe distance behind the vehicle ahead of me. Every minute, my eyes automatically scanned the rearview mirror to see if a speeding, thundering monster was creeping up behind me.

I negotiated the fifty-five-minute drive home, acutely conscious of every decision I made behind the wheel. My mind was churning with tantalizing, unanswered questions, but I was forced to shove them aside to fully concentrate on my task.

Once inside my apartment, I immediately put the recorder on top of my desk and found a snug place in a drawer for the tapes. Then I threw my coat over a chair, sat down in my favorite armchair, and tried relaxing, but long-suppressed thoughts and feelings exploded in my mind.

Is all this possible? Could all of this have happened in the first minutes of her life? Was it possible just a few minutes after birth to feel responsible for hurting people? To feel no good about whom you are? Was it possible for an infant to feel unreal? To not feel a me?

To gain some control over the turmoil that was threatening to send my brain into an unfamiliar dimension, based on what I knew on what seemed reasonable, I tried understanding how Jessica could have felt all this. It seemed logical that infants did not have to know the word hungry to feel hungry. In the same way, infants did not have to know the word touch to feel they needed to be touched. They knew. These needs were instinctual.

These basic conclusions came quickly. I then continued to a more complicated issue. Could Jessica have felt responsible for so many things going wrong?

I had two thoughts about this. One was to compare Jessica's experience of her life before birth to after. It seemed safe to assume that, before birth, her life was not a mess. How could it have been? The world could not reach her. There was a shield, her mother's body, between her and the world. Before birth, she must have felt in harmony and at peace with the world or her corner of it. Because the outside world could not reach her directly, no behavior by Jessica or movement of her body could provoke a negative response.

So, a major difference in her life before her birth compared to after her birth was no one responding to her in an upsetting way. After her birth, it must have seemed to her that, every time she acted or hoped for something, when she was just being her natural self, she was either hurt or ignored.

All of this led directly to my next major thought. Given a constant barrage of negative feelings and not having them contradicted by a good feeling, it seemed possible for an infant to feel that her actions made others upset. Just as with hunger and touch, an infant could feel what adults called responsible.

These speculations were on the edge of what I knew about human psychology and, particularly, infant psychology, which was precious little. Even so, it all seemed quite plausible. By starting with what I knew and extending that knowledge to a new situation, it seemed to fit. I supposed an infant feeling unreal even seemed possible.

When I considered the issue of a human being, an infant or not, losing her me, I could not find a starting point/frame of reference from which to even begin to understand it. By gaining an understanding of the other, simpler issues, I hoped that this one would not seem as mysterious. That had not worked. I was in unexplored territory. I was lost, without a map or any guidelines about what to do. Psychology had accumulated libraries full of information about human behavior over the past nearly 100 years. Every seemingly conceivable aspect of human behavior had been studied, at least to some degree. However, the possibility of a human being not having a me was not one of them. How could it have been? The very thought of it would have been summarily dismissed as science fiction.

While I was mechanically throwing some leftovers together for dinner, the best I could manage given my present mental state, another unsettling feeling about Jessica's startling revelation began haunting me. Thankfully, this was not unsettling in the way the others were. In its own way, it was just as startling though.

If Jessica had lived for twenty-seven years without operating from her me, how come no one ever noticed it? I had known her for more than three years. How was it possible that I had never noticed it? It was easier for me to understand why other people in her life had missed it. They had not been trained to see this kind of psychological condition, if one could even refer to it as that. I was a highly skilled therapist. Seeing psychological problems the public could not see was my job. As I sat and watched forbidding winter clouds forming on the late afternoon horizon, the world was beginning to feel like a gigantic, spinning top. I was sitting high atop the handle, watching it all whirl around.

For the next few days, I stumbled around. A few wayward parts of my brain had yet to find a landing spot on planet Earth. Every movement, every thought, and occasionally every separate breathe seemed to require a conscious effort. Even my spirit felt blanketed by a persistent feeling that I would wake up from this dream at any moment and discover I was only visiting here and actually belonged in a different universe.

At the same time, a part of my brain clearly recognized that I had been granted a privileged view of a dimension of human life that had been hidden from us for as long as humans have existed, a dimension so fundamental to our psychological well-being. Wherever I went, I kept imagining computer disks in people's heads that held countless examples of how our basic humanness can be shaped so early in life. In my fantasy, I wanted to rip people's heads off and store them away for further research.

Somehow, my body managed to go where it was supposed to go, and my mouth emitted whatever words were called for. At times, concentrating was difficult. The wanderings of my wayward mind sometimes bordered on being dangerous. While driving on the interstate, at times I would suddenly realize I had lost awareness that I was behind the wheel. When I recognized a familiar roadside landmark, with no conscious remembrance of having steered the car or the passage of time, I would silently pray that the car was not careening through one of the few remaining farms alongside the highway.

While driving around town, I probably should have hired a chauffeur. I sailed through a red light one night. Some seconds earlier, I had seen it change to red and had made a mental note that I was going to have to stop when I arrived there. However, by the time I reached it, my mind was a million miles away. Fortunately, it was in an isolated area outside of town, and no one was coming. On the same night, another car honked at me because I had stopped at a green light to look both ways before proceeding. Just the sight of a traffic signal was enough for my subconscious to think, "Stop." The closest call was barely missing another car I should have seen while looking for a space in a mall parking lot.

The next night, when my brain was running on a few more cylinders, I caught myself nearly going through a red light. I consoled myself with the fact that I had at least stopped, quite suddenly actually, at the intersection and had looked to see if any traffic was coming.

The most upsetting effect on my concentration was in my office. When I should have been giving my full attention to a client, phrases from Jessica's last session kept sailing across my mind's eye. A few times, a client would stare quizzically at me. I knew my attention must have wandered. My immediate response was, "Your last words were…" After which, I apologized when the person politely reminded me those were not the last words said. Fortunately, no one felt upset enough to stop coming to see me. They must have given me the benefit of having a bad day now and then.

I somehow managed to stagger through these days without burning down my apartment, plowing into another car, or having a client jump up in disgust in the middle of a session and proclaim I was just too incompetent.

The only way to quiet the maelstrom spinning around in my head was to investigate the latest psychological thinking about infants. I needed a second, if not a third, opinion. I did keep up-to-date on the latest psychological writings, but that had never included infants. In my work as a therapist, there had never been any reason to consider an infant's psychological life. In my seven years at a long-established clinic, there had not been any mention of these issues in the in-service training programs to keep staff abreast of the latest developments in the field. In my education at a first-rate graduate school, more than ten years ago, there had not been any mention of people being able to relive infant experiences or anyone losing her me.

None of the popular books, such as *Sybil*, *Son-Rise*, and the books about Eve, mentioned birth recall. Many other similar stories I had read, none of which had quite the same notoriety, did not mention people remembering events from infancy.

In recent years, mother-infant bonding had become a popular topic. As important as it was to observe and study how a mother and a newborn related to each other, this was a case of adults observing infants. True, such observation was the only means available. Infants could only give clues about what they were feeling through their behavior. Adults did not have a choice; they had to make an educated guess about what the infant was experiencing. As valuable as this research was, I was not interested in conjectures by adults about infants.

Fortunately, I lived only a few miles from one of the major universities in the country, the one where I had done my graduate work. One evening, I went to the university's main library. It felt like an old, trusted friend. Ever since I had graduated, I had been a frequent visitor. Every few months, I would spend the better part of a day or a few evenings reading all the recent information in the latest books and my favorite psychological journals.

When it was not the middle of a frigid Michigan winter, I would park some blocks away and enjoy the walk, a pleasant stroll past historic homes and ivy-covered buildings surrounding the law school quadrangle. I would watch squirrels dart between the trees that dotted the campus. Because this was December, I left just as the five o'clock rush was starting and working folks were leaving the university area. It was also before students who wanted to start studying early found the closest parking spots.

I skipped up the double-tiered, front steps of the library, hollowed out from countless footsteps since it had been built. At the outer doors, with metallic latticework covering the thick plate glass, I grasped the ornate brass handle and slowly opened the heavy door.

Inside, I went up another flight of stairs to the second floor and sat down in front of a computer. I called up a psychological database; entered infant, memory, and birth; and hastily scribbled the call numbers that appeared on the screen. About a dozen caught my attention. I hurried into the stacks to track them down. After a few hours, I had only learned that psychology did not seem to think that remembering infant events was even possible. The current thinking was that the recall of events usually went back to age three or four. There were rare reports of recalls from a late two-year-old.

Because it was not quite nine o'clock, I ran to the medical library where the psychiatry books were housed. Psychiatry studied many of the same types of experiences psychology did, except from a medical perspective. In some ways, it was a more comprehensive approach. I did not follow the psychiatric journals as closely because of the numerous medical terms. Now I did not dare pass up any possibilities.

After skimming through several books, I did not find any mention of infant recalls. I did discover a tantalizing piece of information though. Psychiatry did hold out the possibility that information from infancy might be buried in the adult brain.

The thinking went as follows: Infancy is when we are the most sensitive to what is happening around us. If we are being bombarded by all of this input about how to safely negotiate our way in our immediate environment, why don't people remember it later in life? Psychiatry had a special term for this peculiar inability to remember that far back, infantile amnesia.

Several explanations were offered, but all shared one commonality. If memory traces formed in the infant's brain, it had to happen in a nonverbal way because infants do not think in words. When the child starts using language, it quickly loses the need for remembering events in a nonverbal way. Therefore, the brain just stops remembering things that way or somehow loses its connection with those earlier memories. Either way, the information might still be in the brain. Getting to it was the problem.

The psychiatric texts mentioned standard ways of assisting someone to recall forgotten events. Catharsis, the method I specialized in, was not mentioned. I was not surprised. My understanding of catharsis—and that of some of my colleagues—was radically different from how mainstream psychology and psychiatry understood it.

Ever since Aristotle, mainstream psychological and psychiatric thought has viewed catharsis as nothing more than emotional release. I considered this far too simplistic. I did not understand how just the release of emotion could account for the recovery of a memory. Emotions were one thing; memory was something entirely different. If catharsis caused the remembering of repressed events, it had to be a more complex process than just a release of emotion. More of the brain had to be involved. The concept of catharsis was not being understood correctly.

Because my visit to the two libraries had not produced what I hoped to find, I returned to town the next night, Saturday. This time, I wanted to check on writings that my more traditional-thinking colleagues tolerantly referenced as outside the mainstream. Personally, I felt quite at ease in that area. That is where the most creative work was being done, as well as some of the craziest. One had to be careful in evaluating any of it. I had learned a great amount about how catharsis operates from the person who had been specializing in recovery from traumatic events since the early 1950s. He had been at the start and definitely remained outside the mainstream. His accidental start as a therapist had given him a great advantage. Not having been trained in any particular approach to the study of psychotherapy, he could bring a fresh perspective to this uniquely intimate, human relationship.

The best place to find books outside the mainstream was in bookstores, and a university town had many of them. In the third or fourth one, I found a book with two examples of birth recall. The remembrances were banished to the appendix though, nearly an afterthought. Each report was only a few sentences, and both did not even fill a whole page.

After two exhaustive attempts at investigating what was available, I did not know any more about what mainstream thought had to say about the recall of infant memories than when I had started, except for the interesting tidbit about infantile amnesia.

While that was somewhat reassuring and helped me feel a little more anchored to reality, Jessica's last words continued to reverberate in my mind.

"Oh, good grief! How are we going to straighten this out?"

I accepted the challenge. Once before I had weathered such a crisis. Most of her therapy up to the Sunday afternoon session of our second weekend had been a continual challenge to my vision of what psychotherapy could accomplish. My purely instinctual decision on that Sunday afternoon for Jessica to lay her head in my lap had caused a dramatic breakthrough.

As crucial as that crisis seemed at the time, in retrospect, it was only about overcoming a block, a lifelong, deeply embedded one. It was one that had prevented the healing process from operating. Nonetheless, it was just a block, and that was no longer the problem. Instead of something as simple to understand as a barrier thrown up by her psyche, we were now faced with a challenge that sounded more like science fiction. It was one with unthinkable consequences if it was indeed a real psychological condition.

Whether or not a person could be born without a me or have it stripped away through traumatic experiences, I really did not know. I was not sure if anyone did. However, if my belief that it was merely a symptom was true, then the only way to prove that was forging ahead. The consequences of not trying were unthinkable. If Jessica's lost me was only a symptom, then not trying to help would haunt me for the rest of my life.

In my loneliness, I knew how Columbus felt. His only guide for finding his way was a sextant and the stars. My guide was the natural healing process. If that stopped operating, I was in the same boat, almost quite literally, as Columbus had been when he tried finding his way under a blanket of clouds.

21

"Dead" Babies

For the next few weeks, Jessica did not have any new memories or surprises of any other kind for me. I was immensely grateful because I did not need more excursions into uncharted regions of the human psyche. Time was what I desperately needed to fully digest the impact of her startling revelation about not having a me. I hoped she did as well.

In these next few weeks, Jessica's psyche seemed content to clear up what had already come to light, even though we still had to go through the usually slow beginning phase. With all of the healing that had occurred over the past eight months, she was now able to perceive her past in a new way. She could now see that her reactions as an infant had been perfectly normal, given the circumstances.

She began with a new, freeing understanding about her birth. Now she was very indignant over how she had been treated. She began with the doctor. "That doctor was a joke! He had done his job for the day. No big thing. All he was concerned about was whether I had ten fingers and ten toes. And if I was breathing."

The nurses did not escape Jessica's wrath either. "Those two, old, bitty nurses were treating me like I was a football. They didn't care if the water was too cold or too hot or if they were scrubbing too hard."

She had a few words for the whole group, who had made her grand entrance into the world so difficult. "Do you know nobody smiled at me? Nobody asked me what felt good. Nobody told me he was glad I was here. They were just worried about that stinking mother! They were just worried if I had hurt her! Nobody worried about me. Nobody cared if it hurt me. Nobody cared if it scared me!"

Jessica's final words about her birth clearly showed how far she had come in changing her view about entering the world. "They had to earn their pay that day. They didn't know how lucky they were. They were going to get to take care of me. I was letting them touch me!"

Jessica's vibrant tone of indignation stood in stark contrast to feeling responsible for causing so many problems for everyone and making everyone work so hard. Now she seemed well over that. So much so, her current perception about her birth was the exact opposite of what it had been. Now they had caused problems for her!

Jessica also reached a deeper, more liberating understanding into why she had always been so good. Why had she been a baby who did not cry, need, and want? Why had she been a child who cheerfully and obediently did whatever her mother wanted and never complained about living at her aunt's house and taking care of her grandmother?

Jessica's new insight began with an explanation of what drove her to want to be seen as that kind of a person. "I wanted someone to notice I was important, that I mattered. The only way I figured out how to do that was to do something for somebody."

The person Jessica did the most for, of course, was her mother. As she explained it, "I was determined to show my mom how good I was, how hard I could work, and how much I liked doing for everyone." While that behavior started with her mother, it eventually "became my purpose in life, doing things for other people."

As Jessica was explaining this and going into detail about how she helped her mother, she seemed to lose the feisty attitude that had been so evident just a few minutes before when she had talked about how the medical team had treated her at her birth. When she ended her account of how she tried to do for others with "and I never let what I needed get in the way," I feared she had fallen back into the grip of her old way of thinking. I had nearly interrupted her when she suddenly exclaimed, "Will you listen to this? Will you listen to what's wrong with this human? This is a nightmare. I could kick this couch when I think about that. Look what they've done to me! I don't belong to the human race. All I belong to is hard work!" After a few moments of further reflection, she added, "All my life I've thought of other people first. Nobody will ever get that much from me again. I'm a human being, not a machine. I have to keep thinking of me first. You see what happened when I didn't. I nearly died!"

I was greatly relieved. In this period of retrospection, Jessica also arrived at a deeper understanding of how not feeling loved and wanted had affected her as an infant. Not feeling loved and wanted had penetrated so deeply into her developing psyche that her sense of why she even existed had been profoundly affected.

As an adult, she could now describe the haunting questions that she had only been instinctively aware of at the time. Why was I here if nobody wanted me? Who was I? How did I get to be me and not be enough?

While I could leisurely contemplate these primordial questions and not feel my mind was about to spin out of control, Jessica had to grapple with these life-and-death issues with the meager resources of her infant mind. They intently focused her attention on scrutinizing her mother's behavior, facial expression, and tone of voice for any shred of evidence that she was loved. When, as an infant, she could no longer escape the realization that the person who had given her life did not seem to love her, she had an immediate, instinctive reaction, the only possible kind she could have as an infant.

"I just wanted to pull my hair out! It was driving me crazy. It was like utter senselessness. I could not live in a world I couldn't understand. I have to understand so I can contribute and be a part of it all. That's why people exist."

When Jessica finally realized the exact cause of her experiencing so much agony, her mother not loving her, it was solved in the only way an infant's psyche could. "I blamed me. You know why? Because I couldn't make any other sense out of it. I thought that all that was wrong with the world was me. I didn't know about anything out there. I didn't know about kooky people yet. All I knew about was me. And I had to think the problem was something I was doing, not who I was."

Jessica explained why. "I can change what I'm doing. But there's no hope if she doesn't want me as a person. I can't change who I am."

The result was a baby who did not need, want, and cry—the perfect baby. As with all of her other reevaluations of her infancy during this phase of her therapy, Jessica could see how it had all been forced on her. "It's like I'm just starting to see the sense of all this; how it was all put on me. It wasn't something I did that caused it. The injustice of all of it! I can see how desperate I was to fix all that they had made wrong. How desperately I tried fitting into their nightmare. All this craziness, they expected me to straighten it out! I'm just the keeper of all this mess. It just happened to me. I tried to fix it so I could live. None of it really was my fault. Go pick on them!"

We were in the afternoon session. Jessica was leaning against me. She had been quiet for the past few minutes. Except for the energy I needed to expend in helping to get her sessions going, these past few weeks had been much easier on me. I only had to look attentive and listen to her vent her vibrant indignation over how people had treated her. In the past, I had been wary of these quiet interludes. At this point, I had forgotten the surprises that often followed them.

Four haunting words that flowed out of Jessica's mouth sharply interrupted my fantasy about a cross-country skiing trip to a wilderness area in northern Michigan in a few weeks. Even though those words caused my anxiety to increase, she spoke slowly and calmly, without a hint of anxiety or worry, as if she was making a passing comment about the weather. The words that seared themselves into my brain were, "I see dead babies."

After she uttered them, she stayed snuggled against me. I did not feel her body tensing. Her grip on my shoulders did not change. She did not seem the least bit frightened by what she had just described. I could not understand how Jessica could seem so calm. I nearly jumped up suddenly and declared, "I don't think we should be doing this!" I was greatly relieved that she was sitting quietly because I was trying to stifle very unsettling thoughts that made my mind feel as if it was about to unravel. Thoughts that said, "Uh-oh, now I've done it. I've forced her mind into places it didn't belong." I could only wait and hold my breath.

A minute later, Jessica spoke again. Her voice was a little more animated. "I saw this baby in a nursery once, and the side of its head was very black and blue. It made me sick. It looked like it hurt so bad, and she looked cold. It scared me so much that I couldn't look anymore."

When she stopped talking, I was greatly relieved. This memory had apparently triggered Jessica seeing dead babies. It had a basis in reality. Maybe I had not driven her crazy. I waited.

"I just keep thinking about babies who have died," she continued, in the same, slightly animated voice. "They're cold and alone, and nobody wants them…" She abruptly stopped, but she quickly added, "This doesn't make any sense!"

Most of this was not making any sense to me either. This was not the time to ask Jessica what she really meant, although I was sure she had felt cold, alone, and not wanted as an infant, especially during and after the battle of wills.

She continued, "They just lay there. They just give up. So they leave. They quit!"

All of that seemed very logical to me. If a baby felt cold, all alone, and not wanted, wouldn't it want to give up and leave? Some moments passed without Jessica resuming talking on her own. I wanted her to say more, but I wanted to influence her as little as possible. So, I just repeated her earlier words. "You're thinking about dead babies who felt all alone and gave up."

She sprang to the invitation. "Dead baby girls!" she said emphatically.

I felt greatly relieved. Maybe this would turn from a far-out fantasy to Jessica actually talking about herself.

"Somebody threw them down!"

Aha!

"I'm thinking about a baby girl who died because she was thrown down!"

When Jessica spoke again, she seemed to realize as well that she was really talking about herself. "Don't you see? That was me who died. Wasn't it? Part of me died. No! No! She had to die! No! She's not dead, is she? Nothing died, did it? Oh, I feel like I'm hanging on for dear life! I feel like somebody just offed me." The terrifying words rushed out of her as she wrapped her arms tightly around my shoulders.

Some moments later, she continued, in a questioning tone at first, "I lost something, didn't I? Will I get her back?" She then quickly switched to feeling panicky as she realized the question she had just uttered might be true. "Please! Can I have her back? Somebody give me my me back! Please!"

Despite how frightened Jessica seemed, I was quite pleased. We were back to her lost me. Thinking about dead babies must have been necessary to get here. When the panic lessened, she still was not certain if a part of her had died or not.

"I'm not dead. I didn't die, did I? I'd know? Right?"

The apparent craziness of her question (would she know if she had died) did not worry me. She was talking, even though it seemed she only had one foot grounded in reality. I assumed or at least hoped the healing process was trying to get going. When she remembered the battle of wills, she only talked at the start. The healing release eventually followed.

She continued with a description of the cold, dead, empty space where she feared a part of her had died. "Wherever I am, it's strange in here. Nothing grows here. Nothing moves forward here. There's no purpose, meaning, or direction to my life. It's where everything stops, where everything ends."

This place she was in sounded very barren, desolate, and completely devoid of human life. I was starting to worry again. Was I doing something to her mind I was not aware of?

She continued, "It's just like stone. It's absolutely, stone-cold dead. It feels very cold, very absolutely empty, and perfectly quiet, just nothingness."

She lifted her head off my shoulder and looked at me with a quizzical stare. "This feels stupid! What are you doing to me?"

I had to chuckle. I was not doing anything to her, or I at least hoped I was not. I was just listening and encouraging her to say whatever she was feeling. While what she was saying might seem stupid to her, I was certain she was describing how she had felt, however briefly, after the battle of wills.

Before I had a chance to worry about how a human being, even an infant, could exist in a stone-cold, dead, empty space and what that meant about Jessica's survival as a human being, she gave a more detailed explanation about the psychological space she found herself in. "There's no feeling here. There's no connection between me and what happened. There's no connection between me and being real. There's no connection between me and reality!"

It was just what I imagined an infant would feel while lying in her crib after being yelled at, muffled for shrieking, and suddenly picked up and thrown down. She said, "This is where you go to survive when there's no other choice."

Obviously, Jessica's psyche had put her in this psychological space to save her life. She continued, "This is a very safe place. Nobody can hurt you here because you don't need, and you don't want, and you don't expect." After collecting her thoughts, she added, "You can't die here because you're not real. No one can take your life from you here because you don't have one." With her last words, she squeezed my body and cried, "Oh no! Listen to this. I'm not even a human being anymore!"

When this brief burst of panic diminished, she loosened her grip and continued, "I'm totally lost from myself and any feelings that ever existed for me. It's like I'm two people now. This is weird. It's like my feelings are out there somewhere. They're not here in me."

Undoubtedly, she must have felt like two people immediately following the battle of wills. At that time, her psyche had to pack everything she could not feel into a box and hide it until she was stronger and had more resources. Part of what had been taken from her was her needs and wants. No wonder her feelings felt like they were out there. No wonder the psychological space she was in felt stone-cold dead.

She had more to say, "There's no more me left. It's the world where I died. This is the part that's dead. She just went stone-cold dead, and nobody ever bothered her again. She's never coming out again. I don't have to worry about her. They can't hurt her anymore. She got away!"

She's never coming out again. She got away! I had to remind myself to breathe.

Jessica continued, "I could feel my me just shriveling up and dying, just pulling away from me. It's like somebody gave me a human body, but they left my me out. All that's left is this...Well, I don't know, just this physical thing, this bones and skin. I'm having a hard time understanding. I don't know how a physical self can exist."

I did not know how a physical self could exist either. There was one thing I was certain of though. Jessica had been in this psychological state all of her life, except, perhaps, for the first few weeks of her life. She had survived in it. She smiled, laughed, cried, talked, and responded intelligently to other people. She certainly looked like a human being with a me. Maybe she had been operating from a me all these years but just could not feel she was doing so.

When Jessica stopped talking, the panic she had felt throughout most of this dead baby tale had lessened. She was no longer fighting against the state she found herself in. She then slipped into the retrospective mode she had been in for the past few weeks. "I had to go here. I had to! You can't do anything if you don't live, and this is where I had to go to keep my life. This is what a desperate person would do. But it's not so bad being here."

I wanted to scream, "What do you mean it's not so bad? The place you're in is awful!" But I did not.

She explained why she thought it was not such a bad place. Again, I had overlooked the obvious. "I'm alive! And there's good in the world. There's all kinds of good things if you just look real hard."

She started crying softly. As she started speaking, her voice cracked. I could feel how desperate she must have been. "There's all kinds of good things," she began. As she continued to list all the good things, her voice hesitated and cracked on each one. "The trees are beautiful…and the flowers…and all the rest of it…The animals are nice…and the grass is nice…There's a lot of pretty colors…and things smell nice. I spent a lot of time outside when I was big enough and could get out on my own. That's when I started counting on things like the trees, and the flowers, clouds, grass, birds, and animals. There's lots of nice things in this world. So what if it's not people. So what if people aren't what you expected. You just learn to stay away from them. I've been trying people all of my life, and it doesn't work. I just can't get along with human beings. It's like oil and water."

She mentioned another good reason for being where she was. "For the first time since there's been a me, I've stopped hurting. I know something somewhere really deep is very wrong. But it's okay. It's okay because it's not up here and I'm not fighting it anymore. It's fighting somewhere on a level that I can do what I have to do. It's a little harder to do everything now though. It's kind of hard to even just breathe."

She hesitated a little before adding, "You know all that stuff we've been talking about all this time about who I am and why they did what they did. It's all gone now."

Jessica stopped talking and gave me a penetrating stare. "What are we supposed to do now?"

I gave the answer that immediately popped into my mind, the only answer that made any sense. "Keep crying!"

Jessica looked at me as if I had just uttered the most senseless statement in the world. "Cry about what? There's no me to cry about anymore. There's no me period!"

I did not say anything for one simple reason. I did not know what to say. I did know what to do though. Keep the situation safe. Don't force any feelings before they're ready. Wait.

Some seconds later, she spoke again, "How are we going to get around this? Are you going to have a brainstorm this week?"

I smiled, said nothing, and waited. My brainstorm was very simple. I knew something that Jessica could not see because she was too absorbed in her feelings. She was still reliving defenses her psyche had erected to ensure her survival as an infant. At this point, she felt quite certain that her me had been lost forever. Given the dead baby tale it was easy to understand why she feared that. I was not convinced. She had to work her way to deeper levels of her psyche for us to know the answer. I hoped the natural healing process was not finished. So I waited.

When she spoke again, her tone had softened and reflected the results of internal changes. Deep crying had worked its magic again. "I feel sad. It's a feeling of being sad for me, my human being, the part of me who's been hurt, and all they've done to me. It's sad because there's a part of me missing, my human being, and that's what I feel sad about. It's like some humanness slipped in and said, 'Look what's happened to me.'"

"Something really essential to this human being is missing, all the good, all the happiness about who you are, and all the pride in being a human being. I gave up so much to live. But it's not really living here. This is awful!"

Inwardly, I smiled to myself. Ten minutes before, I wanted to yell the same thing at her. After remaining silent for a few minutes, she continued in this same vein, moving away from the cold, dead, empty space she found herself in. "Part of me is starting to feel it would be okay to be real. It's just happening. I can't stop it. I really don't have any control over this. I don't understand it anymore than you do."

I wanted to grab her by the shoulders and shout, "See, it's the natural healing process."

She quickly halted my hopes. "I'm just starting to think it would be okay to be real. I don't do it!" In a calmer tone, she explained further, "It's not safe to not feel anymore, but it's not safe to change yet. I'm right in the middle, and it's terrible. The old things don't work anymore, and the new scares me too bad. Suddenly, this is starting to really grind me. I don't want to be here. This non-feeling world doesn't feel as necessary. There's no real me here, and now I want it back. But I don't know what to do. I don't know how to get out of it. But I'm willing."

"What keeps you from stepping out?" I asked.

"How can you ask me that?" she quickly replied. "I've always been punished for that!"

I immediately felt a great urge to go into hiding, and she was not finished telling me that my thinking was off. "See what you've done! See, I told you that you were going to screw me up yet!"

I was mystified. I did not have an idea what she meant. "What have I done?" I asked, completely innocent.

"Now I want somebody to like me!"

"So what's the problem?" I still did not understand.

"Because I'm not good enough yet. I used to think I was good enough when I was brand-new. I went around hurting and hurting because nobody else thought it. That's what you've got me back to. You make me into a human being. But for who? I don't mean anything in this world. You'll have to send me to another planet!"

Again, Jessica's sense of humor captivated me.

22

The Earliest Memories

The dead baby tale, for all its frightening moments, ushered a dramatic change in the beginning phase of Jessica's sessions. Although they started as they always had, to my great relief, I only had to ask a few very specific questions before signs of emotional restlessness started appearing, a key sign the healing process was gearing up. My somewhat whimsical sense was that my determined opponent—Jessica's defenses, which often seemed like a real-life demon trying to oppose me at every turn—had finally realized it could not outwait, outthink, out-persist, or out-anything me. So it just decided to give in.

Within a relatively short time after the first signs of anxiety appeared, Jessica was up on her feet and pacing from one side of the living room to the other, a distance she covered quickly in seven or eight hurried steps.

While she tried to keep one step ahead of her anxiety, she talked (or tried to) about incidents since we had last met, usually interactions with her mother. While she did, she interrupted herself with cries of "I can't do this!" and "It's too scary!"

I had absolutely no idea what could possibly be too scary about anything that had happened so recently in her life. Obviously, something else, something that had been submerged in the depths of her psyche and was now threatening to emerge over the psychological horizon, was causing her to pace.

Each incident she talked about took from fifteen to thirty minutes, depending on how much she had to say about it and how long it took her to identify the particular upsetting feeling the event had left her with. When she finished, she would sit for a few minutes, sometimes a little longer, without saying much of anything. Then, just as at the beginning of the session, she would start to become agitated once again. In a few minutes, she would be pacing about, talking about another upsetting encounter while frequently interrupting herself with exclamations of how scary it was.

For three days in a row, sessions followed this pattern. By this time in my work with Jessica, I was beyond being surprised by the twists and turns of her psyche. Undoubtedly, it was working on something, but I had no idea what it was.

On Monday, just as she was into her first bout of pacing and before she had uttered any exclamations about how scary she felt, she suddenly stopped, fixed me with her gaze, and confidently announced, "All this is from before I was born!"

I immediately thought her time frame was minutes before the birth process actually started, as she had described in her birth recall. She sat down across from me in her customary yoga-like position and proceeded to explain. She was quickly into the trancelike state that signaled the emergence into awareness of an unresolved experience. She began her account with the most astounding statement I had ever heard from anyone.

"The first thing I ever, ever thought about was surviving."

Before I had even a moment to wonder how far back before birth she was talking about and why an unborn child would even have to worry about surviving (wasn't growth at this stage automatic), her confident demeanor instantly switched to a mixture of disbelief and fright.

"No, no!" she exclaimed, as she snapped out of the trancelike state. "I'm not doing this! It's not important!"

Within a minute, while I gazed warmly at her, she regained her composure. The healing powers of her psyche then carried her forward. "This is just when my mind started 'thinking,' and I knew I had to do everything to make sure I survived. I wasn't certain if I would. I didn't have any control over it. Those were my first 'thoughts.' doing what I had to do to survive."

Just exactly as it had happened a minute or two before, her confident composure suddenly switched. She exclaimed, "I'm not thinking about this stuff!"

I could only wait and hope that she would once again regain her composure. I had no idea if this recall was too frightening or not, but, purely for my own curiosity I was hoping she would continue.

Jessica continued looking just as agitated. Then she suddenly said, "I must have read this somewhere!"

From her frantic tone, I took these last words as an attempt at finding relief from her struggle in another, much simpler, explanation. When her mind apparently could not produce any such memory, she continued protesting her confusion.

"Listen! I don't want to do this and think about this. No! This was before I had anything for a mind. No! I'm not doing this! It's not true!"

Although she was quite frantic, she continued sitting in her meditative posture, without any further exclamations of how hard or scary all this was or any hint of wanting to run to another room. After a minute or two, the fright lessened enough for her to continue.

"All that was there was nothing. Everything was black and empty. It was like all that was there was my mind. It was before I was a person. And I was 'thinking' about surviving." She quickly interrupted herself again. This time, it was not as dramatic. She lowered her gaze from just over my shoulder. With a pleading look, she said, "I'm not weird, am I? I'm probably wrong. Right? You never heard anybody do this, did you?"

I reassured her that she was not weird. Despite how weird it did sound, whatever was emerging from the depths of her psyche was doing so in the same way all of her other memories had. All of those memories had made sense when we knew all of the facts. Now the facts seemed to be a mind (and nothing else) trying to survive. Just listening to her talk about it, I had to admit it was quite unnerving. But I was certain it would all make sense in the end. That was easier for me to see and feel reassured about though.

She continued, "There was just life, and it didn't have a body yet." She was back to her trancelike mode, where the words flowed from her without any anxiety. "There was just this life trying to survive, and I knew time would take care of it. It's the very spark, or the very second, it all started. It just feels really primitive and really simple. Everything was in the present. There was no past. There was no memory and no meaning. I can actually get to the point where there's no memory. The more my body grew, then it became a past. There was more of me, so there could be a past. There was a time when I wasn't what I was then. There was a time when I was less, and I knew it. Then I was acquiring a past. Then I had a memory. I didn't worry about needs. There wasn't any of that there."

She momentarily interrupted herself, "Don't think I'm strange. None of this may be true." Yet, she did not sound panicked and quickly resumed. "It was all like stages. Every second was important. Every second, something was happening. Every second, something was changing. Every minute, there was more to me. Every minute, I was growing. I can remember first moving. It was all so new. It was all on automatic. I couldn't alter or change any of it. I didn't want to."

Suddenly, she said, "This is crazy!" She then broke off. Just as quickly, she was swept up in the excitement again as she exclaimed, "This is neat!"

She continued, "You know what things you get last before you're born? Your needs. You recognize your needs. You have feelings before then, but you start recognizing your needs and what they are, and you start knowing how you have to get them." She was again momentarily overcome with fear. "Listen to me! This doesn't make any sense!"

She quickly recovered. "The next stage was feelings about me, about my human being. That's when I started wondering who I was and trying to figure out what I was. I stopped just being amazed at how I was growing and settling for that. Something in me knew I had to understand it and figure it out. That must be the first need you get, to figure out who or what you are."

"In order to survive, I knew I had to be born. I knew I needed things, and I became aware that I couldn't get them here. They involved another environment. I had gotten all I could out of that dimension. I knew what I needed to survive, and I knew I had to have more to keep growing. It was time to go on. I was eager, and I was happy. I'm not kidding. All this feels so real. This amazes me. I want to go over this again. I don't want to forget this."

Jessica sounded so excited. I was so pleased she had remembered a good experience, one that made her feel at peace with herself, even though it had not started that way. A few minutes later, there was more to the story, and a definite change in her feeling.

"Do you know though, before I was born, I can remember feeling hesitant, and scared, and not certain about what was out there. I was not certain about how the world would feel about me. A part of me became aware that something was wrong. I was wondering something about my mom and dad—Oh! That shouldn't be there. You're going to think I'm crazy! Let's not do this anymore!"

After a minute, her panic subsided. "Before I was born, things were bad. I can remember my awareness of me and a part of that was the feeling they didn't want me. I knew I was a human being and I needed things. One of the things I needed was somebody to want me. Somehow I knew. Oh, I was scared of them already! I wasn't certain if somewhere somebody didn't want me to survive. Listen! I can't take too much of this! I'm really not kooky, am I?"

I reassured her that she wasn't.

"The feeling they didn't want me, it wasn't all that big of a feeling, but it was there. I knew I was fighting then because they didn't want me. No! No! No! It can't be, can it? It's not possible, is it, for me to know that then? You'd better not let anybody hear this until I get it sorted out. You don't think I'm cuckoo?"

"No, you're not cuckoo," I quickly reassured her.

"That feeling they were giving me. Right there is where things really started going wrong! This is where it got scary. Suddenly, things were in a way I couldn't figure out. I knew it shouldn't be there, and it was affecting how I was reacting to everything. I was not growing the way I should. They had altered how I was to grow."

She suddenly stopped and stared at me. "Listen! I don't think we should be doing this or talking about this stuff. It's starting to freak me out. This is really starting to scare me! I feel like you're tampering with the central essence of me!"

"How could this be tampering with the central essence of her?" I thought to myself. In all of the psychological knowledge I had ever learned from anywhere, I had never heard a word about tampering with a person's central essence. Was I causing that? I certainly hoped not. When all of this was actually happening to her, I did not doubt that her feeling was that her central essence was being tampered with. Maybe it was just that and not something that had actually happened. I could only concentrate on keeping the natural healing process operating.

She resumed talking without any encouragement from me. "Parts of me that were supposed to grow couldn't because of this. Some part of me had to stop growing. Parts of me that were supposed to change couldn't. I was not moving forward the way I should. Some part of me was being altered, and I didn't know how to fix it. I was afraid I wouldn't survive, that I wouldn't get what I needed if my environment changed. No! Nothing's broke, is it? You aren't going to get me this far…" Then she jerked away from me.

"Listen! They didn't miss something putting me together, did they?"

"Nothing's missing," I quickly reassured her, but she was not convinced.

"Are you certain? Are you certain I'm a human being and have everything I need to be happy?"

"Yes, I'm certain you have everything you need to be happy," I said confidently. I smiled at her.

"I'm not."

I smiled and waited.

"I would know if they missed something, wouldn't I?"

"Sure," I quickly reassured her.

"Then I'm okay. This is just what people did to me. Right? Nothing is missing? Right?"

"Right."

"Are you certain with all your heart that everything will be okay?"

"Absolutely."

"Are you sure that, at the time all this happened, it didn't permanently alter anything? It didn't break anything?"

"Right. Nothing's broken."

"Are you certain?"

"I'm certain!"

Actually, I was uncertain about any of these answers. How could I not be? On the other hand, there was not any evidence, despite Jessica's own fears, of any permanent damage to her. I could only encourage her to continue. "What was the part of you that stopped growing?"

"I don't know who or what I am! That's what broke! I was scared for who I was. I started wondering right then if who I was was okay. I knew the feeling of being scared, and it was interfering with my figuring out who or what I was. I didn't know my own worth, my own specialness. What made me different? What made me who I am? How can that be? How can I not be okay? Please don't think I'm strange. This doesn't make sense. Is it making sense?"

"Sure." All of it was making sense, excellent sense, but only if you assumed, as I and Jessica did, that an unborn child was as human as she was saying. Even so, all of this rather stunned me. I was still thinking about how a physical self could exist without a me. Now this!

23

Hiding the "Bad"

Watching the natural healing process operating in Jessica left me feeling like an archaeologist. Instead of an ancient living site buried under centuries of debris, we were slowly excavating layers of the infant psyche. With each new revelation and new discovery, I felt increasingly fortunate that Jessica had enough faith in me to make her courageous proposal for intensive sessions. Not once, but twice!

I was as shocked as she was over her latest revelation about not feeling wanted before anyone had even seen her. In the next session, she continued with the momentum from that one, but, this time, it was from the earliest days of her infancy. It was what happened when her mother came into her room in the morning.

"She'd stand there and shake her head and have this really mean look on her face. She was grumbling and complaining because everything was a mess and I was hungry. She looked all upset because her problem hadn't gone away during the night. She picked me up like a football and dressed me like a rag doll. She flopped me around any old way! She just did what she had to do and put me back down!

"All I had to do was wake up in the morning, and I knew what to expect—the mean, ugly look in the morning and the bitching and grumbling all day. I was always too much for her. My human being was too hard for her to take care of! You see, this has always been the problem. It's my human being she didn't want!"

Did Dorothy actually pick up her newborn like a football and flop her around any old way? Certainly not how we adults would think of it. But, to a newborn, hurried movements repeated mechanically day after day and accompanied by a grumpy countenance had to feel that way.

We were in the living room. Jessica was pacing back and forth, spewing her recollections in sporadic bursts as she moved along, slowing down to speak a few words, and then speeding up. Her path took her from the window just past the doorway that led into the kitchen, past the end table with the phone on it, and then along the front of the piano that was backed along the wall. Two short steps past the piano brought her to the end of the couch I was leaning against, only a step or two from me. She turned around to head back, but she stood in place instead, staring at the window on the other side of the room. Her profile was toward me. The loudest sound was the swinging of the pendulum on the cuckoo clock by the kitchen. Some seconds elapsed. While still staring at the window, she exclaimed, "I've made a real bad wrong in the world!"

With that, she started to pace again, more quickly. When she reached the window she had been staring at, she whirled around and headed back in my direction. I could see how truly frightened she felt and how deep her concentration was. She came to the end of the couch, spun around, quickly covered the distance to the window, spun around again, and started back. When she was a step from the couch, she abruptly stopped. For a moment, her eyes met mine. A flash of terror blanketed her face, followed by anguished words.

"Don't tell anybody, but there's something very bad in me somewhere!" She stayed rooted to her spot. "I have a real, terrible human being in here. I feel her in there. That's what is wrong. It has to be." She peered directly at me, hesitated just a little, and exclaimed, "Listen to me! I'm telling the truth!"

I was ready to spring into the air, fully expecting her to flee into the kitchen. She stayed where she was, near the small space between the piano and the couch.

She then spun partly around and took a step into that space. She stood for a moment or two and suddenly dropped to her knees with one shoulder leaning against the side of the piano. A woeful cry pierced the air. "My whole human being is bad. Did I ever tell you that?"

Jessica had never told me that in those specific words. However, in thinking back on all of the months that had brought us here, it was easy to see that she had been trying to say this. My eyes were starting to water, and my heart was heavy for her struggle. I could only wait and reassure her that the healing process was doing whatever it had to. A minute later, still on her knees, she explained why she had turned away from me.

"I'm sorry you have to look at me! I'm sorry I have to hurt you!"

A sharp image flashed in my mind of Jessica as an infant feeling she was hurting her mother simply because Dorothy had to look at her. Jessica leaned her head against the piano, along with her shoulder, and slid her body forward a bit. The agonized cry then came. "If I'm so bad, why am I here?" With that seemingly, at least in her mind, inescapably logical conclusion, her head and left shoulder slid forward until both were pressed against the wall. Her shoulder tilted toward the darkened space behind the piano.

I immediately thought of the vision she had been born with, that is, she expected to be loved and was adding one more good thing to the world. However, as she suffered more assaults to her developing humanness, she could not understand why she was alive.

I reacted purely from instinct and did not think if what I was about to do was in Jessica's best interest or not. I scooted over to her. She was still on her knees. The side of the piano and the wall held up her limp body. Her feet stuck out behind her. With each of my hands, I reached for a cuff of her jeans and gave a smart tug.

She immediately responded, "What are you trying to do?"

"I'm trying to get you out of there."

"I can't," she cried out.

Just in time, I stopped myself from saying, "Of course you can!" Even though that would have been a perfectly logical thing to say to her in this situation, I would have been telling her what to do. Jessica needed a chance to follow wherever the healing process was taking here. I let go of her pants.

"You see," she began, "my mom doesn't even want to look at me. She just wants me to be quiet and never move. She wants me to stay here and be quiet and not hurt anyone and not make any trouble. She put me in the corner so she didn't have to look at me. She used to get sick when she looked at me! She didn't want to be reminded of what she had done…of what she had made! Listen to me. I'm a human being you can't love. Just ask my mom, she'll tell you."

All of these pronouncements had a definite tone of finality. These were conclusions her psyche had arrived at many years ago. Jessica had quietly suffered with them ever since. Now she was simply reporting what she had always been convinced of. After pausing for a few moments, she simply said, "I'm just going to sit here in the corner. You can come too." In her mind, her infant mind, there was no choice. This was where her mother wanted her.

I immediately replied, "You can't stay in the corner!" I knew it sounded like a command, but I could not help it.

She abruptly responded, "Why? What difference does it make? I've been there all my life."

I was speechless. My exhorting her was not doing any good, so I waited. A minute or two passed. She moved more of her body toward the wall. When she spoke again, it was in an anguished whisper. "I have to hide. I have to hide who I am!"

Having only her face hidden from my eyes was not enough. With that, she slid sideways and tried squeezing her body into the dark, narrow space behind the piano. There was just enough space for her head, an arm, and a shoulder. As she hid as much of her body as she could, she barked, "Don't you see enough bad out there? Do you have to get in here, too? It's worse in here. The worst things in the world are inside."

Pressure was building in my chest, and my eyes were tearing. I felt the way I did six months before when Jessica had cried, "If I was a good baby, I would have died!"

Despite how I was feeling and how Jessica was sounding, I was optimistic. This was exactly how most of her other major breakthroughs had started. An anguished voice then resounded from the space behind the piano and reverberated through the room. "It feels like my life depends on you not doing this. You're looking for bad, and you're going to find it! And when you find it, you're going to throw me down and you're going to blame me. You can't get in there! I'll die before I let you in there. It's just no good. It's my human being in there. All my life, I've been trying to hide this from people."

It was a vivid description of what Jessica had always feared, what she had been struggling with since her first session, perhaps since her first awareness of herself. No wonder she had been so terrified of telling me or anyone else about herself.

Her head, one arm, and shoulder were squeezed behind the piano. Every few seconds, she unsuccessfully tried to squeeze more of her body into the narrow space. A few more tears ran down my cheeks. I was convinced Jessica needed to know I did not want her hiding behind the piano because she did not belong there. I could not force this on her or command her not to do it. I reached for a cuff of her jeans. This time, I tugged very lightly.

A voice boomed from behind the piano. "What are you looking for?"

Her question jarred me into remembering what I had always been looking for. What, despite my frequent scares, I had never stopped looking for.

"The real you," I joyfully proclaimed.

"There isn't one!" she said. "This is it! There's no me in there anymore. There's just this terrible, crummy human being. I'm no good. I've been trying to tell you that. You're going to see things you never knew were here."

This unexpected outburst definitely rattled me. For the past several weeks, the issue of her me and the cold, dead, empty space she was in had returned to the back of my mind. Instead, I had been concentrating on how she could have survived feeling that she wasn't wanted before birth. I suddenly realized she was no longer in the cold, dead, empty space. It wasn't empty. There was something in there. There was life in her, even if it was a bad human being. My ruminations were interrupted.

"There's no me in here. A me couldn't survive all this. We're at the bottom, and there's no me. All my life, I've looked. And I couldn't find her. There's nothing down here, just a terrible, awful, bad human being. We've worked so hard to find my me, and we've been through so much. And now it's over. She's gone. She's not where she's supposed to be!"

Jessica was at a deeper level of her psyche than she had ever been. Even though cold beads of perspiration were forming on my forehead over what she was saying, I remained hopeful. She was crying. The healing process was operating.

Purely out of curiosity, I asked, "What's making you cry?" As soon as I heard her answer, I was sorry I had asked.

"Because I'm trying to find her, and I can't."

In spite of how panicked Jessica sounded, I remained confident. I simply could not accept the idea that she (or we) had been tricked into searching for something that did not exist, her me.

She then scared me to the core. Without any warning, she said, "It feels like someone is just taking it and twisting it and twisting it and twisting it and trying to break it out of me."

"Twist what out of you?" I hurriedly and innocently asked.

"Where my life begins, the beginning of me. Someone is trying to take the center of me—the core of me, the beginnings of me, the most vital part of me—and kill it." After a brief pause, she exclaimed, "You're not going to blame me when all this falls in your face and you see you've screwed up!"

Had I screwed up? My faith in the natural healing process would not let me believe that. But that was hope. Had I held out too much hope for Jessica? Had I finally forced her mind into realms where it did not belong? Despite what she seemed certain of, the most vital part of her basic humanness had been twisted out of her, I had to assume her me was still hanging around somewhere in her psyche. I had to assume that. I had to!

Within minutes after Jessica hurled her latest challenge at me, her psyche shut down for the day. She said she would get out from behind the piano when I left. Because she sounded much more in control of herself, I left.

While I was silently wrestling with the latest barrage from what I sometimes envisioned as the thousand-legged octopus, another experience from her infancy emerged a few sessions later, which initially seemed to be totally unrelated to what she had just experienced.

In this session, Jessica was not feeling anxious in the beginning phase as she usually did. She was not parading around about how scared she was. In a short time, she ran out of things to talk about, none of which had enough emotion to trigger any healing. She seemed listless and without her usual supply of energy. Finally, she grabbed a cushion off the couch and lay down on the floor. With her head resting on the cushion, she closed her eyes. For the next several minutes, her body remained perfectly still. Her breathing then gradually deepened and sounded very deliberate, as if something was making her breathe slowly and deeply. Soon, the rhythmic flow of her breath coursing in and out of her body was the most palpable noise in the room, almost as if it was a separate presence by itself.

After several minutes, she opened her eyes and looked at me with a puzzled expression. "It feels like I have to lie still, and I don't want to. Gosh darn it. Why do I have to lie still?"

As frustrated as she sounded about having to lie still, she was doing just that, as if something invisible was forcing her to do so. She explained why she felt forced to lie perfectly still. "I could feel my face and hands go numb. Then I couldn't feel my skin anymore. Then my whole body felt numb. I kept trying to wake up my body, and I couldn't. I couldn't figure out why my mind was saying move and my body didn't."

After Jessica finished speaking, she continued lying still. Her breathing was very deliberate, and her face was a picture of puzzlement. "You know what?" she said after a minute. "I couldn't breathe on my own. I could hear this breathing in my ears, and I had to keep listening to it and make sure I could hear breathing. I had to listen very hard because I couldn't feel my body anymore. As long as I could hear breathing, I knew I was alive."

Only one experience I knew of fit what Jessica was describing, the effects of the sleeping medication and/or anesthesia given to Dorothy just before Jessica's birth. The doses given to Dorothy were for an adult. Fortunately, not enough had traveled into Jessica's system for her to lose consciousness. However, it was enough for her body to feel completely numb and for her to feel she had no control over her body.

The medications must have started to take full effect after she was taken to the nursery. As she lay in her crib, the nurse undoubtedly thought Jessica had finally calmed down.

While still lying flat on her back and breathing very deliberately, Jessica continued with her description of what she had experienced at the time. "I feel like I'm sleeping with my eyes open. It's like being alive but not being able to feel alive. Tell me! How do you understand that you have no feeling about your physical existence when you look down and see it there? It was like time just suddenly stopped, like I stopped being, but I could see. When you cross into that feeling of just seeing, it's like you're not human anymore. I felt that everything I had known as a human being had left me."

When she was silent for a little while and did not seem to be on the verge of continuing, I said, "What did you think was happening?"

"I didn't know," she quickly replied. "Somewhere, something was in me that shouldn't have been. Something crazy! It was more powerful and stronger than I was. It just did what it wanted. It felt like something was breaking down in me, that something in my human being was going wrong. I didn't understand that it was a drug that was doing that to me. I didn't know that it was happening from the outside, that somebody had done something. I thought I had given up. I thought I had done something wrong."

Feeling very frightened over what was happening to her body was difficult enough for Jessica to handle. The experience had an even more profound effect though. Her ability to make sense of her life was deeply affected. She explained how, "I was afraid I had lost the ability to react, to feel, to think for myself, to understand things. If you can't feel and think and understand, what good are you? What use do you have? What are we here for? Why do you live?"

Jessica had an instinctive need for the world to make sense to her. In this experience, the world seemed very confusing to her, even her own body was not making sense to her. It was perfectly logical for her to wonder (in whatever way an infant's psyche does this) about why she was here if nothing was making sense to her.

Jessica had entered the world with a definite vision about her place in it and an instinctive desire to contribute her share. She was then faced with her birth's ordeal. She had barely recovered from that assault when she was hit with this. After having been in the world for all of fifteen minutes, she was afraid she was giving up.

This experience with the medications emerged right after Jessica had been in a terrible fright over fearing that someone was trying to twist the center of her, her core, out of her and kill it. Was this experience somehow a part of that? Was there another reason why this memory had come up now? I stayed glued to my ringside seat into the excavation of her psyche.

24

Trapped Before Birth

The anesthesia experience had been sitting on top of another one that had made Jessica feel the same way. Something inside of her had taken control and was terrifying her just as the anesthesia experience had. The actual events had taken place many years before.

Bundled in her heaviest winter clothes against the blowing snow and frigid windy gusts from a late winter storm, Dorothy carefully lifted one foot encased in a heavy boot out of six inches of snow and gingerly placed it down in front of her. As if she was testing the thickness of ice on a lake, she slowly shifted her weight onto her front foot before deciding she had secure footing. The howling wind tore at her unwieldy abdomen and threatened to topple her over. In a few weeks, she was due to give birth to her second child.

Henry was late again. Dorothy had fed Ellen and then waited almost an hour before eating herself. When she had finished the dishes, dressed Ellen for the night, and laid her in the playpen, Henry still had not arrived. Not knowing if he had been in an accident or even when he might show up, she once again knew she would have to feed the horses and goats. She continued plodding to the barn behind the house.

When she let herself back in, she was breathing heavily and smoldering with rage. It had been many days since she had received any offer of help from anyone. From where Dorothy stood just inside the back door, she could see through the kitchen and dining room into the living room, where her father and her mother-in-law sat in front of the television. Flickering light from a crackling fire illuminated the darkened room.

She removed her gloves and heavy coat and then slowly maneuvered her body to a chair to remove her boots. Before heading for the stairs, she peered into the living room again. Both of the people comfortably ensconced before the crackling fire turned for a brief, wordless stare. She returned an icy glare, grasped the railing, and pulled herself up the stairs.

After checking on Ellen, who was sleeping soundly in her crib, she made herself a cup of tea. She sank into the soft cushions on the couch, turned on the television, kept the sound low, and waited with her cup in hand.

When she finished nursing her second cup, the sounds of a car struggling to negotiate the snow-covered driveway drifted into the apartment. A few minutes later, she heard the back door opening and closing. Heavy, unsteady footsteps on the stairway followed. She then heard the sound of a key scraping against the lock. When the door finally opened, Henry stumbled in. He swayed in place, just inside the apartment.

"Will you please close the door?"

Henry did as he was commanded. When he turned to face his wife across the table, she issued a single statement, "You've been drinking."

"The roads are bad," Henry pleaded.

"No one else took as long as you to get home." Dorothy's voice was starting to breathe fire. "And you didn't call."

Henry slowly rotated his head and focused on the scene in the kitchen. No food was out. Nothing was on the stove. All the dishes, forks, knives, glasses, pots, and pans were put away.

"Where's my supper?" It was the word my.

"I don't have your supper," she snapped. "I fed your animals again. I did your laundry today. I spent most of the day cleaning your apartment, and all your mother can do is sit down on her backside when I'm downstairs working. Do you know what else is yours? This baby is your idea. This baby is a mistake. Do you hear me? A mistake! An accident! I'm not ready for another kid. When it comes, are you going to hire a babysitter so I can get all of my work done?" She gave Henry an icy stare. "Go get your own supper!"

Dorothy struggled to her feet. She lumbered over to the crib, slowly reached in, and snatched up a crying infant.

◆   ◆   ◆

Two sessions after Jessica's dramatic revelation about fearing her core was being twisted out of her, she started talking entirely on her own about a recent encounter with her mother. Every minute, she interrupted herself and exclaimed her body did not feel comfortable. Immediately following each exclamation of how uncomfortable she felt, she snapped her body into a different position. She sat with one leg under her and then the other. She leaned against the couch with one shoulder and then the other. She extracted herself from me and sat opposite me. After changing her position a dozen times, she suddenly exclaimed, "I can't get comfortable in my body."

Her exclamations about her discomfort only seemed to intensify her agitation, as well as the snap she threw into readjusting her position. After a few more minutes passed, she suddenly jumped up and started pacing about the room. She had taken only a few steps when she abruptly stopped and whirled around to face me. Her eyes were pulsating. Fear was coursing through her veins.

"It feels like something is after me. I can't seem to get away from it."

She stared at me and waited for her fear to abate a little. She seemed undecided about what to do. She then wanted to try leaning against me again. She scooted over to where I was sitting on the floor against the couch and pressed her back solidly into my shoulder. She quickly resumed talking about the recent incident with her mother, but she almost immediately interrupted herself to press another part of her back into my shoulder. She did it several more times over the next minute or two.

She jumped up once again and started pacing around the room. While she paced, she snapped her head around every thirty seconds to look behind her.

"What's happening?" she said fearfully. "I keep feeling like I have to check behind me."

With that, she hurried to the other side of the room next to the small table the telephone was on, sat down, and plastered her back against the wall.

"This feels like the safest place I can find," she announced. "It's even safer than leaning against you!"

I hurried over and sat in front of her. A few minutes passed without a word from her, but all of her attention was obviously on how this position was making her feel. Then her body began shaking. I offered to hold her, but she quickly replied, "No, I still have to lean against the wall." While her body vibrated, she spoke about what she was experiencing.

"This feels like something I talked about the other day, when I first became aware of not feeling wanted before I was born. I'm feeling that again, that something was fighting against me, trying to interfere with my right to survive. Now it feels like it's in my blood. Maybe that's why I feel I can't get away from it."

Although Jessica's body was shaking the entire time, she was talking. She did not seem to be on the verge of freaking out over what was happening to her. She was sitting in place. Even though her body looked as if it had been smeared against the wall, she was coherently describing what she was experiencing. "I can remember my mother yelling when she was pregnant with me," she announced.

These words just flowed from Jessica's mouth, and they did not seem to disconcert her in the littlest bit. I immediately thought, "Now wait just a minute here!" I had barely digested her claim to remember as far back as to when she was nothing but a thought, even though that session was a few weeks back. Now she was asserting she had heard and remembered what people said before she was even born. I barely managed to hold my tongue. Jessica plunged forward. "She and my dad must have fought a lot. She was screaming she didn't want another baby. This was his idea! She..."

I couldn't help myself and blurted, "What did your mom say?"

My mind flashed to something I had learned a few months ago when I was trying to track down information about the kinds of experiences Jessica was reliving. In *The Secret Life of the Unborn Child* by Thomas Verny, MD, I had read that the hearing of an unborn child is nearly fully developed by six months (three months before birth) and that the nervous system of the unborn child is capable of forming memory traces of incoming information from even before that time.

Even so, reading about something was one thing. Actually seeing it was quite another. I was so shocked at seeing living proof of remembering words from before birth that I could not contain my astonishment. I immediately said, "What did your mom say?"

Jessica continued from where I had interrupted her, "This baby wasn't her idea. It was my dad's idea. She hated carrying me around. She hated me growing inside of her because I was a part of him. She didn't want me in there. I was this terrible, awful, disgusting, little creature who had invaded her body. I always wanted to say, 'Mom, it's just me! There's nothing really wrong!'"

With these last anguished words, Jessica buried her face in my neck and cried deeply for a few minutes. She then resumed her harrowing account, "I never knew when they were going to have a fight. I never knew what was going to happen from one minute to the next. I'd wake up and hear them screaming. Whatever was happening to her was happening to me. When she was upset, it scared me. There was never any quiet. I never, ever felt safe. Never! There was nowhere to go to get away from that. Where did she think I was going to go? Get up and walk out?"

Jessica took a few minutes to collect her wits before continuing, "I must have heard her screaming, 'This was all a mistake' or, 'It was all an accident' when she got pregnant with me. Those two words stick in my mind. It all left me with the feeling that it was just an accident that I lived through it all. You see, I feel like I'm really not supposed to be here. I was a mistake! I came into being, and I wasn't supposed to! Oh no! Please! I can't hear no more!"

With that, she lunged for my body. When she regained her composure a few minutes later, she asked if I remembered the first question I ever asked her. My face broke out in a big smile. I indeed often thought about my very first question to her, "What can I help you with?" She had answered, "When my husband works nights, I have to stay at my mother's house."

After I told her that I did indeed remember, she said, "I didn't say why I couldn't stay home. I didn't know why I was having panic attacks. I just had to pace. I just had this feeling, if I sat still, something would get me. I didn't tell you about that because I was afraid I was unexplainably mentally ill, that I had just been made-up that way. Neither you nor anyone else could do anything."

I also learned from Verny's book that intense feelings in a pregnant woman produce chemicals that can pass through the placenta. These chemicals can trigger the same physiological reactions in the unborn child that the adult is having, that is, what we adults call fear and anxiety. When the hormones from Dorothy's body coursed through Jessica's body, it was easy to imagine her sensing that something was coming out of nowhere to try to dislodge her body from the only environment and the only safety she knew.

When we ended for the day, Jessica had another challenge for me. "Now I know there was a reason why I paced the floor at night. But I still don't know that about my lost me."

25

Sending "Her" Away

After we negotiated our way through the slow, opening phase of the next session, Jessica seemed finished with the unexpected detours from the past few sessions. She did not have anymore to say about the effects of medications administered to her mother at her birth, as well as the before-birth experiences of powerful hormones flooding her tiny body whenever Dorothy found herself locked into a shouting match with her Neanderthal-acting husband.

We were sitting on the living room floor, facing each other. Nothing in what she had covered so far seemed to indicate where the session was going. I was acutely aware that she had ended her last session before these detours with the terrifying pronouncement that someone was trying to twist her core out of her and kill it. I could only wait to see if she would return to that.

After a few minutes of staring over my shoulder, seemingly waiting as I was to see what was going to happen, Jessica suddenly exclaimed, "She wanted me to go away."

While I had no idea what these words were referencing, I immediately thought this was not going to be a detour. Some moments later, Jessica spoke again, "I'll go where it doesn't hurt her." She again returned to staring over my shoulder, although her attention remained very much inward.

When she spoke again a few moments later, a very strange thing happened, stranger than anything I had experienced yet in the fourteen-month journey that had started with her original, daring proposal. She started talking to an imaginary person.

While continuing to stare over my shoulder, she issued an urgent command, as if the person was standing just behind me. "You have to go away! They don't love you here. No one wants you. There's no room. Get out of here. Ow! Get out! Can't you see? They're going to kill you." A terribly frightful look came over her, and she frantically urged me to act immediately. "You have to make her go. Make her get out. She's got to leave!"

210

Just as abruptly as she had started her one-sided conversation, Jessica stopped talking. As soon as she stopped, she looked completely dumbfounded, as if she had not understood a word she had just uttered and expressed with such emotion. She looked exactly like I felt. The only time I heard someone talk to an imaginary person was when I worked in a psychiatric hospital, the place to find people who held conversations with someone no one else could see. Jessica was deeply engaged in such an experience. If I had been in another room and overheard her talking like this, I would have been convinced that she was indeed in an animated, though one-sided, conversation with a real person. I consoled myself with the thought, "There must be many things about the human psyche and how it resolves deep, early traumas that we did not know."

Despite how frantic she sounded, her mind was locked into the trancelike state that had become too familiar to me. Two streams of consciousness were operating simultaneously in her. One was experiencing the past; the other was aware of the present and observing the other. All was a sure sign that the natural healing process was operating at its highest efficiency. My task was very simple: Do nothing to disturb this process.

After a brief struggle with her confusion, Jessica exclaimed, "Why am I saying that?" A few seconds later, with even more puzzlement, she added, "It feels like there's two people in me."

She looked quickly at me. I reassured her that she was just reliving what she did not have the resources to feel as an infant. Even though I was as much in the dark as she was about what that experience had been, there was no doubt in my mind that such was the case.

When she spoke again after a minute, she continued with her feeling that two people were in her. "I couldn't help her anymore. So I had to let her go. I didn't want to. I didn't! But something in me knew I had to or she'd die. We'd all die."

The you she initially started with was now a her, a her Jessica was no longer urging to leave and was reluctant to send away. This her that she wanted to help no longer seemed as separate of a person as the you she had been talking to. I was absolutely dying of curiosity about what she meant by "We'd all die." But I didn't dare interrupt.

Jessica continued with having to let her go. "It was like there was something grown up in me that wanted to pick her up, love her, and tell her it wasn't her."

By now, I was so engrossed in Jessica's description that I reacted instinctively. "Why did you want to tell her that it wasn't her?"

"Because she was a good baby, a good human being. I told her that she was a good baby and I loved her, but she would have to die!"

Now the you that was not wanted had become a her that was good, but still had to die. She continued, "Do you hear me? I killed her so she'd never have to be a no one again, to hurt like that again, be so alone again. I promised her."

I found her story so enthralling that I immediately felt I had also been there at the time, intently listening to her every word (assuming she had actually been speaking) and as fully involved, emotionally, as she had been. I was so caught up in the flow or her account that I could not help asking, as I would automatically have done if I had been there at the time, "Why did you think that making that promise was a good thing?"

She immediately responded, as if she had thought about this for years. It was just as real now as it had been at the time. "Because I cared too much about her. Because I loved her and didn't want anyone to hurt her. I promised this little, itty-bitty baby that no one loved or wanted that I'd never let her hurt again. I promised her that she'd never have to feel those feelings again. I believed in her and loved her, but I couldn't do too much for her. I'd send her away though. I could do that!"

At the time, of course, Jessica's psyche had taken over, like some omnipresent spiritual being that was going to do whatever it could to help this little, itty-bitty baby that no one seemed to love or want and, in the process, save Jessica's sanity. When she spoke again, she was still absorbed in her description of her promise to the itty-bitty baby.

"You see," she began, sounding as if she was finally making sense of something that had perplexed her for many years, "I had to give me up. I had to or no one will get through it. This part of me that cared about anything, that loved and needed and wanted, the real human being in me, I had to send 'her' away."

It was all I could do to keep from screaming, "Do you realize what you just said?" I had never known what the oft-heard phrase about hairs standing up on the back of your neck really meant until this very moment. It was the same exact feeling from when I had interviewed Dorothy when I decided to write this book and asked her to tell me what she could remember about Jessica's infancy. Without a moment's hesitation, she exclaimed, "Jessica was such a good baby! She never cried, and she never wanted anything!"

After her last words, Jessica stared at me with her mouth hanging wide open and the most dumbfounded look I had ever seen on her face. "Did you hear what she is?" she finally managed. I did, but Jessica was still uncertain.

Despite saying, "Did you hear what she is?" Jessica was far from grasping the monumental importance of her assertion. After some moments, her mouth slowly closed. She began the task of slowly integrating this new information.

First, she returned to her statement from ten minutes ago of "I feel like there's two people in me now." This time, instead of feeling frightened, she seemed eager to figure it out. She gave me an urgent stare and asked, "Are you understanding this? Are you paying attention?"

I most certainly was. It was all too obvious. When Jessica's psyche had taken control in other life-threatening experiences, it had ensured her survival by making her feel the experience had not happened to her. This was evident when these deeply buried memories from her infancy first came back. Her immediate reaction was intense disbelief.

"No! It wasn't me! I was not the baby who..."

With this experience of not knowing how to stop being the cause of her mother's continuing unhappiness, the instinctive mechanisms in her psyche had to go one step beyond making Jessica feel this experience was not happening to her. The ingenious solution was to make Jessica feel the entire, dreadful experience was happening to someone else, another infant.

I was not going to explain all of this. Jessica would come to it on her own, in a far more profound way that I would ever be able to explain to her. She did not wait for an answer and plunged ahead. "This doesn't make sense. I sent away the baby they hated and didn't love and didn't want. I had to scrape my human being out of me and let her float off."

Jessica abruptly stopped talking. She opened her mouth a few times, but she quickly closed it each time without saying a word. With bewilderment all over her face, she attempted again. "They wanted me to take the bad, but it's me! See," she gestured helplessly, "it doesn't make sense. It's two things."

Despite how confused Jessica sounded over her identity, her description made perfect sense. For her very survival, she could not go on living as an itty-bitty baby, knowing her me and the bad human being were the same thing. So, her psyche took control and made her feel they were two separate identities. From that point in her life, until this session and very minute, her survival depended on her not remembering who she feared she was. Jessica explained why this completely unconscious act of not remembering was so critical for her survival. "This is the only way to keep me alive. It's to not remember who I really am to the world. It all seems like a real, finely worked out plan that had to be executed successfully. It seemed real detailed and important that every single step take place the way it did. My life depended on me doing all that. and it's very hard for me to understand it now. It was all so rigid, and there was no room for mistakes."

Her psyche had saved her life by putting her basic humanness, her me, away for safekeeping. Was it all really necessary? Had the core of her humanness been so threatened that it needed this elaborate protection?

Jessica explained, "I could take a million smacks. I could be thrown down 100 times. But I couldn't take the thought that they didn't love me. I couldn't live with that information. I couldn't take it in and remain the same. I couldn't live and be a human being in the manner I knew."

"My sole reason for being a human being, to be loved and wanted, I couldn't get from people. You can't substitute anything else in the world for that. You can survive without everything else, without people touching you or smiling at you. They can hit you and throw you down and break your bones, but the absolute, most necessary ingredient in a human being is that somebody loves you and wants you.

"This is like chopping you off in your center. This alters the most crucial part of you, the part that just can't be damaged. It's your lifeline. This damages your heart. There's no room for mistakes there, for wrongdoings there. It's a deeper notch in me than just fear or hurt. It's gnawed into a part of me that shouldn't have been gnawed into. A part of me had been gnawed at that should never have been touched. It's the most central part of you, and there's no room for injury there. It simply can't happen! Once you've been wronged there, there's no fixing it. You just can't take that. It means death!"

No wonder Jessica had feared we might be tampering with her central essence. She paused, took a breath, and exclaimed, "Listen to this stuff! I knew it had to be something big. I never realized this was here." After a few moments of silent reflection, she had more to say. "I had to be so careful. They were trying to damage the part of me that can't take it all. They were getting so close to destroying me. That's what I couldn't think about. That's what gave me the feeling of running. When I could see them getting so close, I started running and not 'thinking' about it and not recognizing there was a part of me like that. I (her psyche actually) did all that just to protect me."

"That's a beautiful thing to exist in a human being. Everybody has to be in touch with that part of who they are. But my first thought was that it frightened me. It terrified me to know that that part existed. My defense against them doing that to me was to not recognize that that existed and that they could take it from me because the alternative was death. All of the depths of the real humanness to me I had to give up, to become oblivious to that part of me existing.

"That's the part you'll defend with your life. When that part of you gets injured, there's no way to compensate for it. It's your very center. It can't be tampered with. I had to lose my own reason for being. I had to hide that part of me away from me. I couldn't handle the thought that they were trying to hurt that part of me. So, it just had to cease existing for me. I did not want to die. It was very hard for me to give that up. It left me with the feeling that that part of me was dangerous. I had to stay away from it!"

Once again, I was mesmerized as Jessica described her experience as an infant. In six, simple words, "that part of me was dangerous," she had crystallized the problem that had bedeviled me ever since I had asked, "What can I help you with?"

The significance of her words reverberated throughout the room like a pulsating, gigantic neon sign. She was terrified by the center of her humanness, her psychological essence, the part of her she had to be in touch with to be a human being. She knew it was dangerous territory. The entire time she spoke, I pictured this tiny, vulnerable infant struggling to protect the most critical part of her humanness, her core, from crippling, irreparable injury. When I reflected back on all of my struggles to reach the real Jessica and understand what terrified her so about simply talking to me, I wanted to slap the side of my head and exclaim, "Of course, no wonder I had had such a difficult time!"

I was ecstatic. Jessica had finally (and I did not see how there could be any possible doubt) resolved the fundamental injury to her basic humanness that had plagued her since the earliest days of her life. I was more than ecstatic. I wanted to shout it to the world. I wanted to dash outside and run up and down the street, yelling to all of her neighbors who had seen my car parked in front of her house for several hours a day, several days a week, for more than the past year.

Sitting in smugness, I beamed at Jessica. While I did so, she continued staring over my shoulder. A completely blank look was on her face. I eagerly waited for the same expression to glow from her face that was igniting mine. What could be a more satisfying end to our almost-magical journey than for the two of us to go dancing wildly down the street? I was ready to snatch her up and carry her outside. Jessica continued staring.

26

Not Wanting "Her" Back

She sat silently for a few minutes. Whatever internal processes were happening in her mind completely absorbed her attention. When she finally spoke, what I had felt on one or two occasions over these past months was a knife's edge away from happening finally happened. Her words sent my mind into a dimension it was not familiar with.

"I don't want her back!" Jessica was still sitting yoga-style in the middle of the living room, staring over my shoulder. She continued staring after dropping this bombshell on me. I was very grateful that she was continuing to stare and did not seem to be on the verge of saying more. I would not have been able to pay attention. I would not have been able to comprehend even the simplest sentence.

My mind felt as if it was paralyzed. This was utter nonsense. It was as if I was in a science-fiction movie and had suddenly been transported to a different universe, one operating by a different set of rules. Everything I thought I understood about human beings now seemed the opposite of what it had been. After all she (and we) had been through, my mind screamed for immediate relief.

"Yes, you do!" I screamed at her, or felt like I was. If she did not want her lost me back, I was going to command her to do so.

"No, I don't!" Jessica said and immediately explained why. "She hurts. She hurts because no one loves her and no one wants her." She quickly added, "I don't want to get through this. And you're not talking me into it!"

"But you love her!" I hastened to remind her of what she had so passionately stated just a short while ago. I was not through trying to bully her into taking her me back.

Jessica was as equally insistent about what she was going to do. "No matter what you say, you can't make me. I sent away the baby that everyone hated. Why do I want her back? All that little human being ever did was hurt. You're not giving her back to me! You might as well go home. I'm not fighting for her!"

I was beside myself. While I stared at her and she stared over my shoulder, I could only wait for my mind to regain its senses so I could determine how to get her through this latest and most maddening impasse.

While the pendulum of the clock swung back and forth a few times, I ever so slowly realized the error in my thinking. I had automatically assumed, because it just seemed so logical, that, once Jessica recognized her me and the terrible human being she had sent away were one and the same, she would eagerly welcome her back. What could be more obvious?

After staring over my shoulder for a few minutes, Jessica started explaining why she was not fighting for her. "You see, I killed off the best part of me. Yet, when I looked in my mom's face, I continued to see hurt in her heart and disappointment. And you know what? When I just lay there, she used to get sick when she looked at me. She didn't want to be reminded of what she had done, of what she had made!"

No wonder Jessica did not want her me back! Even after it had been sent away and she had become exactly what she thought her mother wanted, a baby who did not cry, want, and need, she quickly realized that had not solved the basic problem. All Jessica had to do to feel she was the cause of the hurt in her mother's heart was waking up in the morning. The grumbling, complaining, and mean, ugly look never changed. If it did, it was never for long enough to undo the damage that had already been done. Feeling she was being picked up like a football, dressed like a rag doll, and flipped around any old way never changed. Each morning, Jessica desperately hoped to find a more loving mother, a mother who took unabashed delight in her. Each morning, her hopes were dashed.

As this silent struggle for her psychological survival continued in the days following the battle of wills and the loss of her me, the devastating message finally sank into Jessica's infant psyche and seeped deep into her spirit. She could not do a thing to make her mother love her, make her smile, make her stop grumbling and complaining, and make her stop feeling that her problem had not gone away when she saw her new daughter again the next morning. Inexorably, Jessica was forced to conclude that the hurt in her mother's heart was not being put there by anything she was doing because even when she lay perfectly still her mother was upset with her.

When Jessica spoke again, her feelings about the baby she had sent away had softened again. "There's a real human being here, and she's been hurt. I don't want you to leave her with me. I just can't handle all the hurt she feels. That's why I let her go."

She was no longer hissing at me. I felt I could chance a direct question, the only one that made any sense. "What will happen if you take her back?"

Her look of utter disbelief did not leave any doubt that she must have been thinking, "How could you ask such a dumb question!" After catching her breath, she exclaimed, "I'll die! I can't take back somebody who hurts like that."

As I continued to look attentive, her expression and voice softened. She quietly pleaded, "You're not going to let her come back. No one will love me or want me."

Before I had a chance to say anything, she quickly added there was something more frightening than the prospect of no one loving her. "What if I don't like her? Are you sure I won't wish she was dead and I won't hate her anymore? Do you promise me with all your heart?"

"I promise you won't hate her and wish she was dead," I immediately reassured her. How could I not? I was certain that would happen when Jessica's psyche felt ready to take her back. Apparently, this was not the time. I could only wait.

While I kept my eyes open for an obvious sign, that is, a lessening of Jessica's fear about taking her back, something unusual started to happen during sessions. Regardless of where we were (sitting on the floor, leaning against the couch, or just standing), there was more of a physical distance between us. While not as drastic of a distance as the times when she had stayed on the other side of the room and glared at me, it was obvious nonetheless. She made a point of staying about two arm's length away. If I wanted to offer physical reassurance, I could not just lean forward. I had to actually move my whole body. Whenever I offered to hug her, if she seemed on the verge of crying or shaking, which she eagerly accepted in the past, she verbally lashed out at me. "Keep you hands off of me!" She jerked her body away.

This time, she was as perplexed as I was by her behavior. "I don't know why I feel this way," she exclaimed, "but I can't stand the thought of you touching me." Even though she could freely express this insight, she did not have any control at all over this baffling feeling. Even though I took her at her word, there were times when I could not control my instincts to offer comfort. As soon as I moved my hand even the tiniest bit in her direction, she forcefully smacked it away and yelled, "Don't touch me!"

After it was obvious that this unexpected turn in her therapy was not going away, I asked her to explain, as best she could, why she thought it was happening. Maybe talking about it might help. After all, nothing else was. She eagerly accepted my invitation and gave a detailed explanation, as if a part of her mind had been waiting for this opportunity.

"You see, I tried so hard to hang on to my me and then I had to let her go. But that wasn't enough for my mom. She didn't want my body either. Nobody's ever recognized that my body existed and that it needed to be touched and loved, and looked at and held, and just recognized as a part of me. It must have been after I sent my me away that I decided to die."

This all made perfect sense. When Jessica's psyche sent her me away, she hoped the problem of being the wrong in the world had been solved. Unfortunately, it hadn't. Her body (at least in her infant mind) then became the part of her that was putting hurt in her mother's heart. Her psyche, however, could not send her body away as it had her "me." It could only try to make her body disappear, by separating it from the rest of her with a tumor in her throat.

With this seemingly powerful insight from Jessica, I waited to see if it would lead to what seemed inevitable: Jessica crying over all this. I didn't for one second think that she was responsible for hurting her mother as an infant, but she had to cry over the feeling that Dorothy, however unintentionally, had made her feel that way. So I kept a check on my instincts and waited.

I waited in vain. Whenever she talked about her fear of my touching her that was all she did. There was no crying, shaking, or any other emotional release. And she wasn't expressing any deep feelings about anything else. No matter what incident, whether recent or from the past, she talked about, that was all she did, just talk. Her fear about my touching her, like some devilish being, had raised its ugly head and taken complete control, stifling progress on anything.

My only idea for getting through this latest impasse was to persist with touching her, despite her protestations. Without telling Jessica, I promised myself that I was not going to stop touching her, or at least offering to do so, until it either worked or Jessica's or my own thinking convinced me it was the wrong approach.

During our next session, we were sitting on the couch. More or less, we were facing each other about two arm's length away. She had been talking for awhile but fairly emotionless. I could not wait any longer. I slowly lifted my hand and moved it very, very slowly toward her face. While I did so, Jessica kept talking, seemingly oblivious to what I was doing. When my hand was about a foot from her face, she suddenly yelled, "Don't!" She vigorously slapped it away. Her hand went right back to where it had been in her lap. Her gaze went back over my shoulder, and she continued talking. Her reactions were so automatic that I had to remind myself that I was not watching a robot.

A minute later, I raised my hand and very slowly moved it back toward her face. Again, she waited until it was about a foot away before she yelled, "Don't!" She then smacked it away. Her hand fell back into her lap almost as quickly as it had left there. She stared over my shoulder and continued talking.

Without waiting more than a moment or two, my hand was back to within a foot of her face. She yelled, "Don't touch me!" She then whacked it away. Again, without hesitation, no more than a second or two later, my hand was back in that spot. She then completely surprised me. She swiveled her body so she was sitting straight ahead. She arched backward and banged her head, rather smartly, against the wood frame that stuck up above the top of the cushions. At the same moment, she yelled, "I'll make it hurt in a way I can understand!"

With an instinctive urgency, my hand flew between her head and the hard wood it was crashing into. I plastered it in place on the exact spot. I managed to get it there in time for her third try. Her head hit the relative softness of my hand a few times until she stopped and stared straight ahead. Without wasting any time, I very slowly moved my other hand toward her face. I made it past the familiar foot distance to within a few inches of her face. At that point, she slammed her head backward a few more times, banging it into the back of my securely placed hand. The entire time, she cried, "Let me bang my head! I have to make sense of why I hurt!"

The sight of Jessica trying to hurt herself and her anguished cry triggered an instinctive reaction. I completely gave into my feeling of sympathy for her, although this was far from the first time I felt that way. I immediately dropped my free hand, but, just in case, I held the other one firmly against the wood. I hoped she might be able to resolve this in a less agonizing way, for both of us. Maybe at this point, she only needed my encouragement to talk about what she was feeling. Again, she immediately responded to my suggestion, "A human being touching me is the most awful thing I can think of. All it does is remind me of what I didn't have. I have no desire to be near another human being as long as I live. If you stay away from me, I won't have to be anybody that you can't love."

As quickly as she started talking, she stopped and stared blankly over my shoulder. I waited for her to say more, but nothing happened. There was no choice. I had to persist with touching her.

With my hand still on the wood behind her head, I raised my other one and very slowly moved it toward her face. She seemed oblivious until it was about a foot away. She yelled, "Don't!" She whacked it away, slammed her head against my other hand, and screamed, "Let me bang my head. I have to make sense of why I hurt." After she banged her head against my hand a few times, without saying anything, she stopped and stared over my shoulder.

My intuition told me, if I persisted, Jessica would repeat this sequence many times. Her last words about how she felt about being touched were an obvious clue about how to proceed. When I moved my hand toward her face the next time, I snuck it past her raised arm and very lightly ran the tip of one finger across her cheek. Just once.

She instantly grasped the sides of her head with both hands, snapped her body back and forth without trying to hit her head, and cried deeply. After a few minutes, she stopped crying, folded her hands in her lap, and stared past my shoulder. Without waiting, I very lightly brushed my finger, just once, across her cheek. She immediately erupted. This time, while she rocked back and forth and grasped her head, she cried, "Don't! I'm the bad!" She cried deeply for a few minutes.

Over the next twenty minutes, we went though this several more times. Even though I was ecstatic that we were finally making obvious progress, I felt like a bully. I would have said a million prayers in any language for Jessica not to have to do this. I wished human beings had been put together differently and it was not possible for infants to be hurt so easily and so deeply. I was forced to accept that as a reality. My only consolation was knowing that human beings also had the ability to recover. I persisted with touching her.

Jessica had enough energy for only a few more cries. Right after her last one, exhaustion seeped out of every pore in her face. She did not have to say we had done enough for the day. A minute later, she stretched out on the couch and was quickly sound asleep.

Over the next several sessions, we had more episodes of my touching her face. Each was less intense than the last. Even so, I felt like a bully torturing a poor, helpless infant every time. When her last protest about feeling bad was noticeably weaker than the others were, I impulsively said, "Hi, good person!" I did not try touching her. For months, I had been dying to say this to her, but I knew the words would just pass by her until now.

The sound of my voice had not even faded away when she grasped the sides of her head with both hands, rocked back and forth, and cried, "There's nobody good here!" The suddenness and intensity of her response told me that my comment was right on target.

Whenever her crying lessened, I said, "Hi, good person!" One time when I said this, I let my hand slip from the wood, thinking it was not necessary anymore. She immediately banged her head and did it a few times before I could get my hand in place. It was not until her head hit my hand that she started crying.

When I called her "good person" and it ceased to have any effect at all, I returned to what I thought was proof to see if she was finally over all this. I touched her face. Now she had a completely different reaction. She exclaimed, "For the first time in my life, it feels good when someone touches me!"

With that realization, Jessica could explain why she had felt so compelled to fight my touching. Her explanation began with her belief that infants must have a sense of order about their experience. For an infant, this does not happen in words. It is more basic and instinctive. It is as crucial for an infant's well-being as any other need.

Jessica explained how her sense of order had evolved. As an infant, she had a continuous feeling of being unloved and unwanted. Without any good experiences to act as a counter, she had no choice but to feel (a feeling that had the same power as any strongly entrenched belief) that she was, at least in her mother's eyes, the bad in the world. In spite of how desperately she wanted to feel loved and wanted, Jessica needed a reason why such experiences kept happening to her. In thinking of herself in this way, as the bad, how she experienced the world made sense to her.

Jessica then explained why a sense of order is so important for an infant. The opposite of order is disorder, or no sense or no meaning. This psychological state of disorder is so alien to the infant mind that Jessica gave it a special word, chaos. She described it as "just like insanity" and "not understanding is the absolute worse thing in the world" she could imagine. Chaos, or disorder, is a state the infant mind cannot exist in. The infant psyche will do anything not to feel it.

When Jessica's psyche decided that neither her mother nor anyone else was going to love any part of her, the stage was set for her to be threatened with chaos. Anytime someone touched her in a caring way after her psyche had made that decision, the person was saying that Jessica was good and deserved to be loved. That message, however, did not compute in her brain, regardless of how old she was. It threatened her already existing sense of order. It did not matter how desperately she needed to feel loved and wanted. She was too threatened with chaos and having no sense of order to her life. That fear was far more powerful than any other need.

The conclusion that Jessica's psyche had constructed to prevent her mind from plunging into chaos sat like an omnipotent force in the back of her mind for years. When I touched her, and, in doing so, contradicted that conclusion by saying she was good, Jessica was reliving exactly what she had experienced as an infant. Her sense of order was being threatened. She felt her mind was about to be plunged into chaos. That feeling was so threatening that she had to physically stop me from touching her. When that did not work, she had to bang her head to manufacture a reason for her agony instead of feeling the original one (there was not anything lovable about her) from years ago.

Of all of Jessica's sessions, these on chaos were the most difficult ones for the both of us. Jessica's intense resistance to my touching her caused me to fear that I was being a monster. If that was not enough, I was feeling terribly embarrassed over the unprofessional level of behavior I felt I had yielded to.

Originally, I was not going to include these sessions on chaos in any report about Jessica's therapy. Whenever I remembered my persistence in trying to touch Jessica, her forcefully whacking my arm away, her yelling "Don't touch me!" and banging her head, I felt acutely embarrassed. I was terribly afraid that my colleagues, as well as the public, would ridicule me for acting like a bully. Personally, I feared I had resorted to acting like one because I was not smart enough to determine an easier approach. I planned to tell no one about how I had helped Jessica resolve her fear of having her mind in chaos. It would remain a secret known only to the two of us. I believed everything Jessica said about chaos, and I would somehow get that information into the book.

One day, I was in my favorite bookstore in the university town I live near and browsing through the psychology section. A book about autism caught my eye. Actually, the author, a Noble prizewinner in animal behavior and whose name was in large letters on the cover, piqued my curiosity. I immediately thought this renowned scientist, whom I knew to be of advanced years, must have found a startling new perspective to this very puzzling psychological condition. My hunch was right on target.

The book surveyed the best treatment approaches this author had found. One particular approach was deemed far better than any other. This was the work of Dr. Martha Welch, a psychiatrist, who had achieved a startling breakthrough in treating autistic children with a method she described as "mother-child holding." As I read her description of her therapy, what immediately hit me was the striking similarity to Jessica's sessions on chaos.

Dr. Welch theorized that autistic children had suffered a disruption in forming an attachment to their mother as an infant. As an antidote, she devised "mother-child holding." The mother (not the therapist, who supervises) holds her child face-to-face to keep the child from moving away. For extra support, the mother is held by her mother, or her husband, from behind.

Typically, the child sits quietly in the mother's lap for the first few minutes. The child starts getting restless. At this point, it is critical for the mother not to let go. If she persists with holding, the child may cry, scream, rage with terror, and try to bite, spit, and hit to get free. When this intense emotional reaction ends, the child is visibly relaxed, initiates touching of the mother's face, and usually talks, even if only a few words. These are behaviors autistic children do not do.

Dr. Welch reported that most, if not all, autistic children who experienced this holding therapy on a regular basis for a long enough time, usually several years if not longer, have recovered from their condition.

What struck me about this report was that the mothers were doing only one thing, holding their child. All I did was very lightly touch Jessica's face. While Jessica was not autistic, she had experienced a severe disruption in the process of attaching to her mother. In later work, Dr. Welch discovered that even psychologically normal children—that is, children without any serious conditions, such as autism—also reacted in the same basic way to mother-child holding, but they did not react as intensely and for a shorter duration of time.

Reading Dr. Welch's work was a great comfort to me, particularly when she described this therapy as "extraordinarily difficult for mothers." I knew exactly how the mothers felt! More importantly, I no longer felt I had acted like a monster. I was ready to include these sessions with Jessica on chaos, which I believe explains the extreme reaction of the children in Dr. Welch's holding therapy.

27

Resolution

When Jessica felt good when I touched her face, she was finally free of the last obstacle to feeling as she was meant to feel when she had been made-up, as every human being born is meant to feel. For the first time since the battle of wills, nearly thirty years before, she was experiencing herself as a human being with a me. Her unspeakable terror, her fear she had been born or even made-up with a flaw in the basic structure of her humanness, had finally been laid to rest.

Even though Jessica had regained the part of her humanness that she feared had been lost forever, there were not any obvious changes in her behavior. She remained the same responsible, thoughtful person she had always been. The major change was internal. For the first time since she was a newborn, she could base her life and behavior on the answer to a very simple question: What do I want? The most visible change to those who knew her was hearing her express her needs and seeing her less often being the first to volunteer to help out.

No instant of time marked the transition from her feeling no me to feeling like a whole human being. The change was gradual. It had been a year-and-a-half since she had first voiced her unspeakable terror. For most of that time, she had overcome one psychological demon after another that had been blocking the path to her lost me. When she started experiencing feeling good upon being touched, she began having sudden injections of reality, bursts of feeling like a human being. These injections gradually lasted for a longer period.

When Jessica was born and until the battle of wills, she had been in the process of trying to figure out who she was, what she was doing here, what her needs were, how to get them met, and how she fit into the world. That process had been abruptly interrupted and put in cold storage for nearly twenty-six years. Now that she had her me back, she could complete her description of the vision she had been born with.

"I was going to show the world what a good human I was, and I was going to take what I needed. I was ready to be a happy, human being. I was eager to show the world that I was really terrific. I expected somebody to love me. I was ready to love the whole world, and I was so happy to be a human. I wanted so much, and I couldn't wait for every minute.

"It's what everyone can do, and every thing, every leaf and every piece of air and every piece of dirt, and every piece of human. We're all special! We all have it to offer, but nobody has it quite like me, or you, or any other human being. I just wanted somebody to see the real human in me. I wanted someone to recognize my uniqueness, the only thing that I could contribute that nobody else could contribute to the world but me.

"I wanted to be a positive factor in the world. I wanted someone to see I'm good, I'm a human being, and I have as much as anyone else in this world to offer. I wanted to see someone think I added good things just simply because I was born, the world was better because I was here, I had actually added a good something to the world, something okay took place when I got here, and the okay was me.

"I wanted to give me to this world, and I wanted someone to think it's okay and it's good and worthwhile. As a newborn, I wanted that more than anything in the world. I wanted to see my mom smile because of me, just a real basic feeling that, because I was here in this world, there was good, or acceptance, or just an okay-ness."

While I listened to Jessica, in awe as usual, it gave me the opportunity to ask a question that had puzzled me for a long time. If Jessica could not rely on what she really needed—if she did not operate from a me perspective—what had she relied on to guide her behavior?

"What I visualize in my mind," she began before no more than a few moments had passed, "is this broken china cup and it's just lying there scattered. That's what I felt like, like this real delicate thing that got broke before it could be used." After pausing for a few moments, she said, "It's like somebody gave me this being without a set of directions, so I had to act like I had a me even though I knew I didn't." Her act was so good that it fooled everyone who knew her, including me.

Jessica's therapy was not over. We continued meeting, but we went back to three days a week. She and Roger separated and eventually divorced. She had been earning money to support herself and Melissa by cleaning homes three and four days a week, an arrangement that allowed her to leave the other days for sessions. Now they lasted about two to three hours, without a break. Instead of her sessions, including breaks and driving time, taking up eight hours of my day, they now consumed four to five.

There were no more memories from very early in her life. However, there was still some deep crying to be done over the feelings that had penetrated to the core of her psyche, particularly feelings about not feeling wanted. As Jessica so poignantly described it, "My very existence always seemed questionable."

She had a dream about being in an elevator in an incredibly tall building. The elevator began at the bottom and stopped at every floor. On each floor, a sign indicated whom the floor was for. All the signs indicated groups who had suffered from some form of mistreatment or discrimination. This elevator stopped at many floors, but a floor never said "Jessica."

The feeling of having her very existence questioned was the earliest, deepest interference with the development of Jessica's basic humanness. It took the longest to remove altogether. She was still sensitive to other people acting in a way that triggered this feeling. When it happened, she could recognize what she was feeling. A short cry usually restored her equilibrium.

In her relationships with other people, it was very important for Jessica to feel she had something unique to contribute. A smile from such a person meant a great deal to her.

"It's the most meaningful thing in my day if somebody smiles at me, that they just accept me because I'm here…a recognition that I exist and I'm okay, that I've given something that no one else could." When that happened, she felt she had a definite place in that big, working thing.

One day toward the end of a session, Jessica declared, "I want to go to college."

I did not have any particular goals for Jessica when she was finished with her therapy. I was certain she had a vast reservoir of unused potential. Her wanting to attend college did not surprise me. Even though she would be the sole supporter and single parent, she was ready for the challenge of being a full-time college student. She was not sure of her major, but she thought she wanted to get a job where she could help young children develop a sense of who they are.

Epilogue

Five years after entering college, Jessica graduated with honors. During her years in school, we continued having sessions, though not on the same intensive basis. Besides her demanding schedule, which included part-time work as a waitress, she could go for longer periods before a feeling from very early in her life demanded attention. Even then, the effect on her was far less than it had been before her therapy.

During her college years, she formed a number of close, lasting relationships with people of both sexes. When necessary, she could confide with the people she felt closest to and have a good cry if it was necessary. These relationships were very gratifying to her because they were based on her needs. Gradually, I became a less necessary figure in her life.

We have remained in close contact. The very intimate, pioneering journey we traveled together forged a special bond between us. When I told Jessica I intended to write a book, she immediately replied, "This is too important to keep to ourselves."

She offered valuable suggestions for the manuscript. I always deferred to her judgment on my attempts to describe the psychological life of an infant. I sometimes used her as a consultant to check my thinking in my work with other clients. As far as I was concerned, she was the expert on the ill effects of deep psychological assaults to a person's basic humanness, especially during infancy.

In college, Jessica concentrated on the education of very young children. Even before she graduated, experienced teachers and parents quickly noticed she possessed a unique ability to relate to children, particularly children with learning difficulties. Some people even asked her what her secret was. One experienced professional who observed her said, "Your motivation seems to come from somewhere very deep inside of you."

My experience with Jessica has had a lasting effect on my own life. Besides deciding to write this book, I decided to check into the possibility of using my experience with her as a basis for a Ph.D. I wanted to study the method I had used, quite intuitively at times, more rigorously so I could explain it in a way that would not only make it more understandable, but would also invite others to use it. I found a unique school, fully accredited at the national level, which encouraged independent thinking. Students were designated as Learners, in keeping with the school's emphasis on students taking the initiative for their learning. The emphasis on independent thinking was apparent at the beginning. On the application itself, that is, before you were even admitted, you had to describe in detail an idea for a doctoral dissertation. I did not have a doubt about what my dissertation was going to be about. So, at the age of forty-seven, I became a doctoral student.

While I was gathering information on what others had written about recovery from very early assaults to our basic humanness, I discovered a small, but growing, number of therapists, medical doctors, scientists, nurses, health educators, and others who were recognizing the powerful effect that very early experiences can have on our developing humanness. In exploring this exciting new field, these people are true trailblazers because a very large percentage of professionals do not believe it is possible for these very early experiences to register in the infant's nervous system. Therefore, it is not possible for people to be affected by them later. This is unfortunate, though understandable, because these experiences stand so far outside of our knowledge of human behavior. The only way to be convinced of the existence of these experiences is to relive them or watch someone do so. Then they become very real.

One summer, while I was in the midst of hunting for second and third opinions, I attended the first annual meeting of an international association devoted to the study of the psychological life of infants in Toronto. Being with people from throughout the United States, Europe, South America, and Australia was very exciting. All of us shared a strong belief in the crucial importance of these very early experiences. The feeling of mutual support and the joy of having found each other was expressed by Thomas Verny, MD, the organizer. His first words, as he stood before us to officially open the proceedings, were, "I can't believe this is happening!" To which, he received a spontaneous ovation.

People like Jessica and others as well deserve our deep respect for persisting with their pioneering work and for opening a window into an unexplored, so vitally important realm of human experience. They are the true pioneers. They are providing us and future generations with the most important information human beings can have: how to grow a human being from the start.

Acknowledgments

This groundbreaking psychological journey would not have happened without Jessica's unwavering commitment to her own recovery from what she thought of (and was justifiably terrified by) as mysterious ailments. It also could not have happened without the insights into the nature of psychological healing that I learned from Harvey Jackins, a truly pioneering and independent thinker, whom I was fortunate to know personally. It also could not have happened without the insights provided by E. Michael Holden, MD, a neurologist, in his research into the psychophysiological aspects of catharsis, which totally supported what Jackins had discovered as a therapist. As with Jackins, Holden also believed the human body possessed a natural healing mechanism for psychologically hurtful events. I was able to consult with Dr. Holden through the mail for confirmation on certain aspects of how Jessica's psyche (a combination of brain and body) reacted to traumatic events from her infancy. To all three, I am profoundly and eternally grateful.

I also wish to thank all of the therapists and clients who have attempted to discover how effective the process of psychotherapy can be. While you have remained nameless in this section, whatever you wrote was a source of inspiration. There is an excellent chance I might have read your writing because I am a voracious reader. For a therapist, it is impossible to know too much.

For the writing of *Jessica*, which consumed my attention for many more years than I originally anticipated, I wish to thank my longtime friend, Bob Anschuetz, former member of the Eastern Michigan University English faculty. He always had something positive to say about any part of my writing I conned him into reading. He made a critical observation about my role as the narrator when I had nearly given up on trying to find a workable sequence of events.

I also wish to thank all of the agents, too numerous to mention, who offered comments, most of them unsolicited, on the manuscript. I would particularly like to thank Marissa Carter, the only agent to invite me to call. When I did, she freely offered her insights and urged I read *Seven Strategies in Every Best-Seller* by Tam Mossman, the absolute best book on writing, fiction or nonfiction, I have ever read.

My appreciation also goes to the editorial and book design services provided by iUniverse for their commitment to a quality publication.

Bibliography

Chamberlain, David. *Babies Remember Birth*. New York: Ballantine, 1988.

- This title is a misnomer because adults are doing the remembering under hypnosis. Nonetheless, the reports are quite informative.

Gopnik, Alison. *The Scientist in the Crib*, 2001.

- A compilation of what medical science has demonstrated about the capabilities of newborns.

Janov, Arthur and E. Michael Holden. *Primal man: The new consciousness*. New York: Crowell, 1975.

- The chapters are all on separate topics, so one can choose. The writing ranges from quite readable to quite technical, depending on the topic. Even though this book is from 1975, I consider some of the articles as forming the basis for my understanding of catharsis, although the authors eschewed that word in favor of "primal" or "primalling."

Journal of Pre- and Peri-Natal Psychology and Health.

- Started in 1985, this journal is devoted to exploring the psychological life of infants from sometime before birth to just after birth. Although scholarly in content, the language is not. Web site: www.birthpsychology.com/apppah

Journal of Primal Therapy

- Published for several years in the 1970s. See especially articles by Holden in 1976 and 1977. The journal is available only in a small number of university libraries. Copies of articles might be obtainable from Janov's Primal center in California.

Jackins, Harvey. *The Human Side of Human Beings*. Seattle: Rational Island, 1965.

- A small book that presents the basic theory of Re-evaluation Counseling. Available in some public and college libraries. Can also be ordered from www.rc.org. Harvey Jackins was the primary developer of Re-evaluation Counseling and of the Re-evaluation Counseling Communities. The latter, at its most basic, is a rationally thought out set of guidelines for two people to exchange the roles of counselor and client to help each other discharge the ill effects of distressful experiences.

---. *Elementary Counselor's Manual*. Seattle: Rational Island, 1970.

- Basic instruction on how to use the theory of Re-evaluation Counseling. Available only from Rational Island Publishers (www.rc.org). Many other publications on a variety of psychologically-related topics are also available

Janov, Arthur. *Biology of Love*. Amherst, N.Y.: Prometheus Books, 2000.

- Numerous examples of how psychologically injurious events from very early in life create physical symptoms much later in life.

---. *Imprints: The Lifelong Effects of the Birth Experience*. New York: Coward-McCann, 1983.

- Describes how hurtful aspects of the birth experience can affect a person later in life.

Janus, Ludwig. *The enduring effects of prenatal experiences: Echoes from the womb*. Northvale, N.J.: Jason Aronson, 1997.

- A compilation of reports, primarily from therapists, about experiences with clients that involve symptoms later in life from events from before birth. Many of the reports are from the European literature and not found in other books published in this country.

Mossam, Tam. *The Seven Strategies in Every Best-Seller*. 1988.

- The absolute best book on writing, fiction or non-fiction, I have every read. Available at Amazon.com.

Rothschild, Babette. *The body remembers: The Psychophysiology of Trauma and Trauma Treatment.* New York: Norton, 2000.

- A comprehensive review of how psychological trauma affects the body and treatment methods for resolving the trauma.

Solomon, Margaret. F. and Siegel, David. J., eds. *Healing Trauma: Attachment, Mind, Body, and Brain.* New York: Norton, 2003.

- Anthology of information about physiological and psychological effects of trauma as well as methods for resolving trauma.

Verny, Thomas. *Tomorrow's Baby.* New York: Simon and Schuster, 2002.

- Dr. Verny, an internationally acknowledged expert in human development, explains how parents can help actualize their child's full potential, beginning with conception. Includes a wealth of practical suggestions from prenatal communication to enhancing infant's empathic ability, as well as advice for building language acquisition, enhancing intelligence, and developing other social skills. Update of his earlier book, *The Secret Life of the Unborn Child.*

Von Glahn, Jeffrey. "Toward a Psychophysiological Model for Understanding the Effectiveness of Catharsis as a Psychological Change Agent." Diss. The Union Insitute, 1993. DAI 54 (7-B): 3869 (UMI NO. 9332481).

- While necessarily scholarly in nature, the writing is as readable as I could make it. The basis of the psychophysiological model is thinking of catharsis as a sympathetic-parasympathetic autonomic nervous system sequence, as explained by Dr. E. Michael Holden (See above listing for Holden).

Welch, Martha. G. *Holding Time.* New York: Simon & Schuster, 1988.

- A presentation of Dr. Welch's method (the mother physically holding her child) for helping children recover from a disruption in the mother-child bond. Web site: www.marthawelch.com.

978-0-595-36429-9
0-595-36429-2

Printed in the United States
53289LVS00004B/271-318

9 780595 364299